T0301978

Doing Business in India

Elsevier
Asian Studies Series

Series Editor: Professor Chris Rowley,
Centre for Research on Asian Management,
Cass Business School,
City University, UK; HEAD Foundation, Singapore
(email: c.rowley@city.ac.uk)

Elsevier is pleased to publish this major Series of books entitled Asian Studies: Contemporary Issues and Trends. The Series Editor is Professor Chris Rowley, Director, Centre for Research on Asian Management, City University, UK and Director, Research and Publications, HEAD Foundation, Singapore.

Asia has clearly undergone some major transformations in recent years and books in the Series examine this transformation from a number of perspectives: economic, management, social, political and cultural. We seek authors from a broad range of areas and disciplinary interests covering, for example, business/management, political science, social science, history, sociology, gender studies, ethnography, economics and international relations, etc.

Importantly, the Series examines both current developments and possible future trends. The Series is aimed at an international market of academics and professionals working in the area. The books have been specially commissioned from leading authors. The objective is to provide the reader with an authoritative view of current thinking.

New authors: we would be delighted to hear from you if you have an idea for a book. We are interested in both shorter, practically orientated publications (45,000 + words) and longer, theoretical monographs (75,000–100,000 words). Our books can be single, joint or multi-author volumes. If you have an idea for a book, please contact the publishers or Professor Chris Rowley, the Series Editor.

Dr Glyn Jones
Email. g.jones.2@elsevier.com

Professor Chris Rowley
Cass Business School, City University
Email: c.rowley@city.ac.uk
www.cass.city.ac.uk/faculty/c.rowley

Elsevier Asian Studies Series

Doing Business in India

A Framework for Strategic Understanding

C. Lakshman

ELSEVIER

AMSTERDAM • BOSTON • HEIDELBERG • LONDON • NEW YORK • OXFORD
PARIS • SAN DIEGO • SAN FRANCISCO • SINGAPORE • SYDNEY • TOKYO

Elsevier
Radarweg 29, PO Box 211, 1000 AE Amsterdam, Netherlands
The Boulevard, Langford Lane, Kidlington, Oxford OX5 1GB, UK
225 Wyman Street, Waltham, MA 02451, USA

Notices
Knowledge and best practice in this field are constantly changing. As new research and
experience broaden our understanding, changes in research methods, professional practices, or
medical treatment may become necessary.

Practitioners and researchers must always rely on their own experience and knowledge in
evaluating and using any information, methods, compounds, or experiments described herein.
In using such information or methods they should be mindful of their own safety and the safety
of others, including parties for whom they have a professional responsibility.

To the fullest extent of the law, neither the Publisher nor the authors, contributors,
or editors, assume any liability for any injury and/or damage to persons or property
as a matter of products liability, negligence or otherwise, or from any use or operation
of any methods, products, instructions, or ideas contained in the material herein.

ISBN: 978-1-84334-774-3

British Library Cataloguing-in-Publication Data
A catalogue record for this book is available from the British Library

Library of Congress Cataloging-in-Publication Data
A catalog record for this book is available from the Library of Congress

Library of Congress Control Number: 2014955913

For information on all Elsevier Publishing publications
visit our website at http://store.elsevier.com/

Typeset by SPi Global
www.spi-global.com

Printed and bound in the UK and US

Working together
to grow libraries in
developing countries

www.elsevier.com • www.bookaid.org

Contents

List of figures   vii
List of tables   ix
Preface   xi
About the author   xiii
Endorsements   xv

1 **Why India?**   1

    Doing business in India: a strategic framework   7
    Notes   11

2 **The institutional context**   13

    Challenges provided by the institutional context: case example   18
    The role of government in institutions   29
    Implications for MNCs   33
    Notes   34

3 **The macroeconomic context**   37

    Path from mixed economy to liberalized capitalism   40
    Towards a free market economy   41
    Inflation   43
    Fiscal deficit in India   43
    Main sectors of the economy   44
    The informal economy   46
    Notes   48

4 **Political particularities in India**   49

    Parliamentary democracy in India   52
    Federalism in India   53
    Business implications of federalism   58
    Notes   59

5 **Profile of consumers and markets in India**   61

    Contrasting consumer values in India   61
    Notes   74

6 **Strategies adapted to Indian needs**   77

    Industry life cycle and stages   79
    Case example: reliance retail   85

Discussion questions   106
Financial highlights   106
Notes   106

7   Rural India and bottom-of-the-pyramid markets   **109**

India's cultural roots   110
BoP markets in rural India   112
Special challenges in rural markets   114
Case example: ITC and India's BoP markets   117
Conclusion   128
Appendix ITC's triple bottom line achievement   130
Notes   130

8   Competitive advantage of India   **133**

Opportunities for MNCs in this sector   140
Notes   142

9   Leadership of Indian intellectual capital   **145**

Leadership for technological progress in India   147
Leadership for the rights of self-determination   150
Leadership for total revolution   154
Leadership for business and economic development   158
Desirable leadership qualities in India   161
Knowledge leadership for MNC managers in India   162
Notes   163

10 Organization and control systems for India   **165**

Organizational structure to match India strategy   168
Control systems   172
Notes   179

11 Successful HRM for India   **181**

Flexibility for businesses v. problems of contract labor   183
Wages, workers' rights, and union recognition   184
Key HRM challenges in India   185
Best HRM practices in India   186
Compensation and reward systems   189
Integrating an Indian JV partner post acquisition   190
Cultural knowledge-sharing mechanisms   194
Notes   195

References   **197**
Further Reading   **203**
Index   **205**

List of figures

Figure 1.1	Strategic framework for doing business in India	**8**
Figure 2.1	Institutional processes and organizational innovation in India	**23**
Figure 3.1	GDP growth rate in recent years	**38**
Figure 3.2	GDP growth rate since economic liberalization	**38**
Figure 3.3	Inflation rates in recent years	**39**
Figure 3.4	Interest rates in recent years	**39**
Figure 3.5	Fiscal deficit in India (CG = central government; SG = state governments)	**40**
Figure 4.1	Rights and privileges of central v. state governments in India	**55**
Figure 4.2	Public relations campaign material for the creation of Uttrakhand (aka Uttaranchal)	**57**
Figure 6.1	Sales/Profits curves over different stages of the industry life cycle	**104**
Figure 10.1	The control cycle	**173**
Figure 10.2	The big-five dimensions of the BSC at the ITC Maurya Sheraton	**176**

List of tables

Table 2.1	Structure of ICL (five main pillars)	22
Table 5.1	Country of contrasts: consumers of varying colors	62
Table 6.1	Classification of retail formats in India	92
Table 6.2	Lessons from Indian retail failures: top ten mistakes	92
Table 6.3	Seven lessons from A.T. Kearney's 2011 GRDI	93
Table 6.4	Reliance Retail's presence in India	95
Table 6.5	Reliance's retail offerings	97
Table 6.6	Strategic recruitment of key executives	102

Preface

This book is the culmination of many years of teaching and research on India. A few years ago I designed a series of course modules for doing business in India for MBA students at Kedge Business School, Bordeaux, France and taught several of those courses myself. When I started looking around for a book to suggest as a reference to my students, I came up with almost nothing that focused exclusively on India or provided comprehensive coverage of key areas. It was then that I decided to write this book. Not wanting to log too many air miles traveling from my home base in the U.S.A., I had moved to India a few years earlier. This move to India was to engage in more research and learning about a broad array of business practices in India. Having left India for the U.S.A. before the liberalization of the 1990s, it was imperative to spend significant amounts of time in the country. I lived and worked at the Indian Institute of Management in Indore and started working on India-focused research. Later, when I needed to teach my students about India, this research came in handy but still fell short of what students would need to facilitate understanding. During the time I spent in India, my research focused on institutional evolution, competitive advantage, leadership, corporate social responsibility, and human resource management issues. You will see that this book blends all of these research bases into a meaningful India story.

Passionate about the India story, I was interested in providing managers a broad glimpse of what is required to formulate India-specific business strategies and subsequently to execute them. My search for a suitable book was thwarted in that all I could find were those that targeted all emerging markets or a specific group of emerging markets and focused on winning in these markets. I felt that India was very much unlike other emerging markets in many ways and that practitioners would benefit immensely from knowledge of these differences. Thus, I started collecting material, in addition to my own research, on this focal area to prepare for my teaching. The content you see in this book is a strong reflection of what was taught to my students. Each passing year brought more and more students into this series of courses on India. This book is ideal for managers wanting to do business in India as part of their company roles or for entrepreneurs interested in entering the India market. If you are in middle management or above, you will find this book a useful guide for your India adventure. While other books target top management, this book is meant for people at slightly lower levels and those in the middle layers of management. You will benefit from gaining a better understanding which, combined with your own experience on the ground, will make identifying emergent strategies for your company much easier. Thus, the benefits of career advancement for this group of people from using this book are clear. I know MBA students will enjoy this book as a result of my experience of having seen them enjoy my courses structured around the content of this book. One of the unique features of this book is that it presents India as a country of contrasts. This theme prevails throughout the book and provides a perspective that is very different from what you get elsewhere.

I am thankful to a number of people who have directly or indirectly influenced me in writing this book. I need to thank Dean Philip McLaughlin at Kedge Business School, Bordeaux, France for asking me to initiate a new program on doing business in India. It was this that triggered the writing of this book. I am also thankful to Kedge Business School and Tongji University, Shanghai, China for providing me with the intellectual atmosphere and support for this endeavor. I am deeply indebted to all my teachers and guides for encouraging me and serving as an inspiration for my efforts. I thank the publishing team at Elsevier for overseeing the production process through to fruition. I have truly enjoyed working with everyone on this team. Finally, I take this opportunity to thank my family members, particularly my wife and son, for ensuring the right climate at home for me to focus on this work. Thanks are further due to my wife Sangeetha Lakshman for her significant contributions to the Reliance Retail Case in this book. I sincerely hope that readers find this book of use in their efforts to succeed in India's markets and in advancing their personal careers.

About the author

C. Lakshman is currently a Professor of International Management at Tongji University's School of Economics & Management in Shanghai, China. Having obtained a bachelor's degree in Electrical Engineering and gained early industrial experience in industrial marketing, he moved on to the U.S.A. for higher education in the field of business management. He received his Ph.D. in Organization Studies from Southern Illinois University at Carbondale. He has academic and industry experience in three continents with significant stints in India, the U.S.A., and France. He has conducted Management Development Programs and consulted with clients such as NLC India Ltd., ABN Amro, Mahindra Finance, Impetus, Honeywell India, and NTPC India, among others.

He specializes in research that lies at the intersection of global and cross-cultural leadership and knowledge management. He has published his research in distinguished journals such as the *Journal of International Business Studies, Human Resource Management, European Management Review,* and *Journal of Management Studies.* He has also published two books in the areas of Knowledge Leadership and Organizational Innovation, respectively. His multicultural profile and experience have stood him in good stead as a coach and consultant in the above areas as well as entry into India's markets.

Endorsements

"This book delivers a very clear, colorful and convincing description of the reality in India. It discusses relevant information for practitioners and academics as well."

Prof. Diether Gebert, Tongji University, Shanghai, and Technical University of Berlin.

"Business in India is a 'must-read' – full of information to explain, challenge and reassure those wishing to move into India. The eleven chapters cover the questions that any informed businessperson should be asking. More importantly, Lakshman provides stimulating answers and advice to help understand and manage its challenging complexities. The author handles these complexities with passion and clarity and honours his promise to provide a 'strategic framework' that unpacks the Indian 'bundle of contrasts to facilitate a clear and strategic understanding of how to win in India'."

Philip McLaughlin, (Directeur Général Délégué/ Executive Director and Vice Dean), Kedge Business School, Bordeaux, France

"Dr. Lakshman has presented a well paced and researched addition to the world of International Business. His first hand knowledge, coupled with his multi-cultural academic background, has resulted in a primer designed to cover both the comparative and functional aspects of developing business ties and operations in one of the world's largest and fast moving countries. Anyone wanting to establish business operations in, or simply wanting to become better informed about India should start here."

Stephen C. Brokaw, Ph.D, La Crosse WI

"Dr Lakshman´s book is indispensable for anyone interested in India- the largest democracy in the world."

Sten Söderman, Stockholm University

Why India?

1

> *"India isn't a sweatshop for hands; it's a sweatshop for brains."*
> **Anand Mahindra, CEO, Mahindra & Mahindra**

McDonald's opened its first restaurant in India in October 1996 and by November 2004 had opened a total of 58 restaurants, mostly in the northern and western parts of India. It is now reported to be operating more than 250 outlets in the country.[1] Although it opened its first store only in 1996, it spent a full six years, prior to the establishment of the first outlet, studying Indian consumer preferences, developing the local supply chain's ability to deliver consistently high-quality products on time, and creating its overall business approach to the market characterized by a high level of citizenship (Dash, n.d.). Given that a significant majority of the Indian population does not consume beef or pork-based products, it was important for the company to establish a clear strategic plan that would not hurt the religious sentiments of Indian consumers. More importantly, given the political activism and resistance faced earlier by KFC, it was important for McDonald's to avoid political confrontation with either the government or one of a range of activist groups, including but not limited to those against globalization or foreign direct investment (FDI), those against Americanization, and environmental and animal activist groups. Instead the company highlighted the employment opportunities it provided, contributed to green movements, promoted sports events and healthy lifestyles, and got involved in community-related projects, mainly involving children. It transferred technology to the different players it helped develop in the supply chain for fast food, making some of them successful exporters of processed food, in an effort to overcome the poor transport and storage infrastructure in the country. Overall, McDonald's has achieved a great deal of success in this country. This example, however, raises a very important question. Why would a company, whose core competence centers around beef and pork-based products, want to operate in a country where a significant majority of the population does not consume these products? More importantly, why would a company want to go to such great lengths (six years spent in planning activities alone) under such circumstances? This relates to the broader question of why businesses the world over are not only looking at but entering India at the earliest possible opportunity.

The answer, very simply, lies in the fact that, as an emerging market, India represents one of the biggest and fastest growing markets in the world today. Thus, for India to not be part of any company's strategic plans would simply be anathema to business. According to a Goldman Sachs report, over the next 50 years, Brazil, Russia, India, and China (i.e., the BRIC countries) could become a much larger economic force than the G6 (top 6 economies of today) in U.S. dollar terms. Specifically, India is cited in this report as having the potential to become the third largest economy in the world (in

U.S. dollar GDP terms) by 2050, behind only China and the U.S.A. Although this shift in economic terms is likely to be gradual over the course of 50 years, it is likely to be more dramatic in the first 30 years. In the latter part of this 50-year period, although the other three BRIC countries are likely to slow down, only India is likely to grow at a better than 5 percent annual rate over the entire period (Goldman Sachs, 2003). Thus, despite the fact that India is growing at the so-called Hindu rate of growth (Panagiotou and Story, n.d.), this growth is likely to be much more sustained than any of the other emerging markets. The reason India is likely to outperform other BRIC nations and current G6 nations over this time period is that it is the only nation whose population is likely to continue its growth for the next 50 years and the only country where the proportion of working age people will increase for the next 20 years. In addition to real economic growth, the economic force of the BRIC nations, in general, and India, in particular, is likely to be the result of currency appreciation, thereby considerably increasing the purchasing power of consumers in the country by up to 35 times current levels. However, per capita income levels in all the BRIC nations will still be lower than other nations, making life difficult for businesses and their strategy developers. In essence, businesses and their managers the world over will lose out significantly if they continue to ignore India and its markets for too long, notwithstanding the challenges on the road.

The success of McDonald's in India illustrates the change in social values and attitudes of consumers in Indian society. Although the significant liberalization and privatization program begun in the early 1990s has changed the attitude of successive governments, some experts rank India lower on openness than the other BRIC nations. However, the attitudes of consumers and individuals in society are in complete contrast to the cautious optimism of the government. Indian society is moving away from traditional values of non-materialistic spiritualism and is increasingly reflective of materialism and consumerism. This shift in values is accompanied by higher levels of Westernization and the belief that the West represents and symbolizes innovation, productivity, and progress. The U.S.A. is the largest trade partner although trading relationships with EU countries are also relatively higher than most other nations. Compared to the few decades immediately following independence from the British in 1947, the latter part corresponds to growing acceptance of American and Western values, lifestyles, and general influence. India also contains perhaps the largest pool of English-speaking managerial talent anywhere in the world, in addition to an increasing proportion of the population with a similar capability. Consumers in India have always been interested in global brands – there was a huge black market for these products between 1947 and 1991 when the economy was closed – but buy local brands as well. A growing number of Japanese, Korean, American, and European multinationals have an established presence in the country as a consequence of the increased openness and favorable social attitudes that prevail.

Fast food restaurants such as McDonald's, Domino's, Pizza Hut, and KFC have become very popular in the country as a result of their ability to offer consumers products that are not based on beef or pork. Despite the food service industry being the most affected by consumer preferences driven by cultural values and traditions, the potential for success for most multinational businesses in India is great. However, the road is likely to be rough and full of challenges for companies wanting to do business in India. For instance, according to some reports McDonald's made no profit in the first ten years of operations in India, while it took an average of five to seven years for each McDonald's outlet in the country to break even. Although this compares favorably to the average of 12–13 years for the company in any new country (Dash, n.d.), it points up the presence of significant challenges and the need for a clear and strategic framework for understanding Indian markets and its consumers. Among the most important of these challenges is the need to understand the local business ecosystem and players that multinational corporations (MNCs) take for granted in their home environments, which are simply non-existent in India (Khanna et al., 2005). This book is aimed at providing a strategic framework for understanding the more critical factors in India's markets to enable companies to devise effective strategies and to implement them well, given the particularities of Indian business ecosystems.

First, however, one needs to consider the increased levels of openness of the Indian government, its progressive economic policies of privatization and liberalization, and the progressive opening up of different sectors of the economy to global competition. Although India's economy officially opened up to international competition after a wave of economic policy and regime changes in the early 1990s, the seeds for these changes in government and social attitudes were planted well before that time. The Japanese company Suzuki entered a 50:50 joint venture with the Indian government in 1981 to produce automobiles for the Indian market. The company is now entirely in the private sector and holds the largest market share for automobiles, although it has ceded a portion of its territory to other multinationals like Hyundai, General Motors, Ford, Toyota, Renault-Nissan, and Volkswagen, each of which entered the Indian market in succession, following opening up of the economy. These companies now share the spoils with the local emerging giant Tata Motors, which has benefited immensely from global competition. The entry of global giants into emerging markets transforms the local product and service quality landscape, often with far-reaching consequences (Khanna et al., 2005). Growing political resentment, albeit in pockets, and the resulting strengthening of activism by different political groups in some sectors, and growing aggressiveness in international expansion – Tata's acquisition of Land Rover and Jaguar, for instance – are examples of such consequences. At the same time as Suzuki formed a joint venture with the government, Honda, Yamaha, and Kawasaki made their entry into the Indian market for motorcycles, which even today is much bigger than that for automobiles. Although all of these companies entered the market through licensing and/or joint ventures in the early 1980s, many of them now run wholly owned subsidiaries in the country, with some of them competing with their former joint venture partners. These examples from the auto industry highlight the long-term possibility of progressively higher profit potentials in the India market for MNCs, although they may come with higher levels of risk, as is the case anywhere else in the world. More importantly, these examples highlight the growing tendency of successive central governments in India to support and sustain a level of openness to global competition, regardless of their political differences.

Consistent with public perceptions, or perhaps as a consequence of them, the global competitiveness report of the World Economic Forum classifies India as a factor-driven economy and thus in the first stage of economic development. Consequently, all the automobile companies cited earlier are operating in India not only to capture future market potential but also to use the country as a base for low-cost operations, thereby lowering their global cost structures. However, the Indian government expects most multinationals to guarantee a certain level of exports from their bases in India, with the objective of keeping a favorable balance of trade position and making economic progress. The fact that India provides a cost advantage to MNCs operating within its borders cannot be demonstrated by a better example than that of the recently launched Orbiter mission to Mars. While the Indian Space Research Organisation (ISRO) successfully put the Orbiter into its first orbit around the Earth on its way to orbiting Mars at a cost of only $74 million dollars, NASA's Maven satellite which was launched in November 2013 is likely to set NASA back $671 million dollars (Neuman, 2013). Even accounting for purchasing parity differences and specially augmented features and equipment on board, the cost difference is stark. Thus, while India continues to provide a cost advantage (not as much as China, for sure), Orbiter and its launch points up the technological capabilities of the country and the hordes of scientists and engineers it can bring to the table (Kapur and Ramamurti, 2001). The success of Orbiter and its ability to successfully orbit Mars makes one wonder at the bundle of contrasts that India represents and the inherent complexity facing strategic managers in this country of slum dog millionaires. In fact, one theme that will prevail throughout this book is that India is a huge bundle of contrasts. More specifically, this book aims at unpacking this bundle of contrasts to facilitate a clear and strategic understanding of how to win in India.

The political will and ambitious vision of the Indian government, exemplified by its investments in space missions, also transcend domains such as the progressive, though slow opening up of different economic sectors. One such sector is the Indian retail sector, where the government recently managed to obtain approval for majority investment by MNCs in multi-brand retail and 100 percent investment by MNCs in single-brand retail, amid serious activism and potential for political upheaval in the coalition running the government.[2] A.T. Kearney (a global management consulting firm) developed the Retail Development Index and has touted it as the bellwether of future global economic growth.[3] Some experts suggest that there is immense potential for the development of intermediary firms and indigenous business ecosystems (the kind that McDonald's lacked in India) if only the country would open up its doors to FDI in retail, noting China as a case in point where this had already happened (Khanna et al., 2005). In India, the fractious nature of politics and the diversity of the country, which is administratively divided into 29 states, necessitated the framing of the recent (December 2012) Retail FDI bill requiring subsequent approval by respective state governments. Thus, although enacted into law by the federal (central) government, both the single-brand and multi-brand retail sectors in India will receive (accept) investments only after a multilayered legal and approval process. In essence, while some states will allow this investment, others will not. This feature of the Indian political and democratic system is quite different from that of the home nations of many MNCs and is typical of India. Such a system requires more precise awareness and customized strategic plans for India and its constituent states. This book aims at unpacking these challenges for the multinational investor interested in doing business in India.

Despite these challenges, different voices across the Indian political spectrum have time and again regrouped under the increasingly stronger consensus that the country should remain open to global competition and engage in progressive reform. Simultaneous with making the Retail FDI bill law, the government also increased the foreign equity cap in FDI to 49 percent in domestic airlines, 49 percent in power exchanges, and 74 percent in direct-to-home (DTH) broadcasting services, signaling continual efforts to open up the economy.[4] In a recent speech to the U.S. India Business Council (USIBC), M.S. Ahluwalia, deputy chairman of the Indian Planning Commission, reaffirmed India's commitment to such reform, while noting its increasingly difficult nature, and suggested that more serious economic reforms will continue after the impending parliamentary general elections in 2014. The Indian Prime Minister, addressing a recent gathering of the G20 (St. Petersburg), reaffirmed India's commitment to an open economy and promised more tax reforms, reforms in the financial sector, changes in banking regulations, and control of subsidies, all of which are noted by several experts as being serious impediments to doing business in India (Cadieux and Conklin, n.d.). Along with infrastructure deficiencies, these reform areas are key factors in determining the global competitiveness score of nations, and the relatively poorer positioning of India vis-à-vis other BRIC nations. Despite these statements of reaffirmation and commitment, the situation highlights the basic political realities in India and the associated challenges for multinational investors doing business in India. Still, successive federal governments taking up the helm in steering post-liberalization India have taken significant steps forward and none has engaged in regressive policies.

The slow but steady process of economic reform and liberalization has increased GDP growth rates from 3.5 percent in previous decades to around 7 percent or better in more recent decades. According to some estimates GDP per capita increased from 1.29 percent in the 1970s to 4 percent in the 1990s, increasing the disposable incomes of Indian households and consumers. More specifically, real GDP grew at 5.3 percent during the period 2000–05 and at 6.1 percent during the period 2006–10. This growth in real GDP is projected to average well above 5 percent over the next 50 years (Goldman Sachs, 2003). Despite the ongoing debate in terms of how big the Indian middle class is, dubbed by some "the myth of the great Indian middle class" (Saraf, 2013), these real GDP growth rates and projections are hard to ignore. When seen in conjunction with the success of the MNCs mentioned earlier, one must wonder why there is such a huge gap between realized results by MNCs and "objective" estimates of the Indian middle class and income levels. The answer quite simply lies in the existence of a large informal economy and the absence of accurate information from which these statistics are objectively created. Like other emerging economies, the size of the informal economy in India is estimated to sometimes be as big as the formal economy. Without debating the veracity of such estimates, it is sufficient to say at this point that the Indian middle class is significant and possesses serious levels of disposable incomes that would interest most MNCs in doing business in the country. You only have to let your imagination run loose on the estimates provided by the Big Mac index (implied purchasing power parity to the dollar of 11.1). The equivalent of the Big Mac (the Maharaja Mac) sells for approximately $0.75, at which price one can buy up to four times as many Big Macs in India as in the U.S.A. for the same amount of money (Dash, n.d.). Thus, although some estimates suggest that 60 percent of Indians have spending power of only $2 a day (Saraf, 2013), that amount represents a significantly higher purchasing power in India than elsewhere. That still leaves us with 40 percent of the population (representing a huge block of 400 million or more) that has higher spending capacities. One needs to factor in undervaluation of the Indian rupee, purchasing power parity, and the not so insignificant presence of an informal economy when making estimates of the Indian middle class and purchasing power.

That the Indian middle class has become more consumerist is also evident from the increasing penetration of television sets, mobile phones, automobiles (two-wheelers and passenger vehicles), and a whole host of consumer products and durables. The Indian retail market is one of the biggest and fastest growing in the world, with some estimates putting the market size at $450 million a year and growing at approximately 25 percent per year.[5] This gives the reader an indication of the degree to which consumerism has penetrated Indian cultural lifestyle, in stark contrast to earlier decades when people were mostly influenced by non-materialistic spiritualism and curbed consumption. This explosion in consumerism has been fueled by privatization and liberalization of the media resulting in satellite-based TV channels taking off and providing a vibrant advertising medium for the new TV-watching consumer class. In addition, India is one of the fastest growing markets (second only to China in total size of market) for mobile phones and thereby a vibrant medium for m-commerce as in other emerging economies.[6] In most emerging economies, but particularly in India, m-commerce is much bigger than business-to-customer (B2C) e-commerce. India has more Facebook subscribers than most other nations (the top 5 brands providing services being Vodafone, Nokia, Tata-DoCoMo, Samsung, and Fast-Track), despite the mere 10 percent penetration of personal computers in Indian households.[7] Cultural and creative industries such as Bollywood and cricket (a religion - not just a sport in India) thrive here. In sum, the Indian consumer has never before been as consumerist as he or she is today.

Finally, India is fertile ground for MNCs wanting to create a more effective launch pad for their globalization efforts. The country provides a very good mixture of human capital in having a relatively productive workforce and a massive stock of intellectual capital in the form of hordes of science and engineering graduates, among others. One of the world's most respected business leaders, Jack Welch, said that India's real strength lies in its intellectual capital (Kapur and Ramamurti, 2001). A host of MNCs such as General Electric, Intel, Microsoft, and Hewlett-Packard have established R&D centers in India with a view to understanding and capitalizing on the Indian mentality to demand and achieve cost-efficient innovation. The country's convenient location and historically favorable relationships with South and Southeast Asian nations as well as those in Africa also provide India and companies located within its borders relatively easier access to these markets. The experience of Indian firms at operating in bottom-of-the-pyramid marketplaces within the country also gives them the ability to operate in similar markets in these regions. Thus, a successful partnership with Indian firms and/or having a presence in India is a good way for MNCs to gain access to many countries in the region. On the whole, India is an emerging economy that is likely to sustain its growth well into the future. Run by democratically elected governments open to globalization, India possesses a huge middle class that has sufficient levels of disposable income and is increasingly consumerist and at the same time provides easy access to a host of countries in the region. These characteristics are aptly summarized by the conclusion of a recent A.T. Kearney report that suggests that the time to enter India is now.[8]

Doing business in India: a strategic framework

I hope that you, the reader, are by now convinced that entering India and its markets is a must for both you and your business. As you may also have realized, winning in India is not only a challenge but requires a keen ability to understand complex realities. A recurrent theme that Indians are exposed to on a daily basis in one form or another is "unity in diversity". One of the fundamental reasons for the Indian government propagating this theme is that there are 14 official languages in the country, with many more being spoken but not recognized officially. As you move from one Indian state to another, the change in language becomes obvious not only by what people are speaking but through signboards and TV or radio channels diffusing a variety of messages. I present a strategic framework for doing business in India (Figure 1.1) that highlights some of the more critical factors in what follows.

The framework presented in Figure 1.1 indicates four of the more critical factors that need to be considered when making strategic choices in the Indian market: (1) institutional context, (2) macroeconomic context, (3) political particularities, and (4) consumer and market profile. The framework also emphasizes factors critical to implementing the chosen strategy and the need to adapt them to (a) rural v. urban markets in India, (b) successfully leading India's intellectual capital, (c) organizing and controlling your operations in India, and (d) managing people through human resource practices. Each of these issues is discussed in detail in subsequent chapters in this book but they are briefly described here. This framework provides a broad idea of how the different chapters in this book are structured and how the discussion flows from one issue to the next.

Institutional context

Many experts have identified that emerging markets are fundamentally different from the markets in more advanced economies in that they are full of institutional voids. As highlighted in the opening story of McDonald's extensive six years of

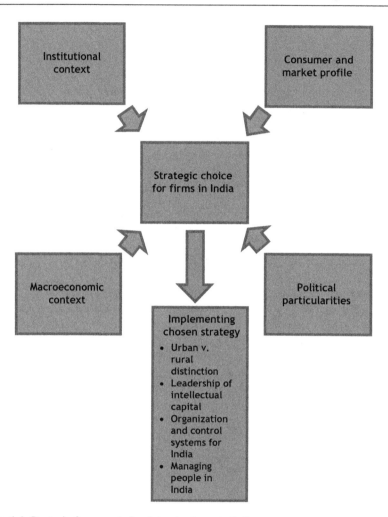

Figure 1.1 Strategic framework for doing business in India

planning before opening its first store in India, there are a number of intermediary firms; legal, financial, and regulatory institutions; and well-developed supply chains in advanced economy markets, which may be non-existent or incomplete in India, subject only to the specifics of the different sectors within which one wants to operate. Under such circumstances, the main task of the multinational firm is to identify and assess the specific nature of the business ecosystem, the degree of sophistication or lack thereof of businesses, the competition from domestic businesses in the sector and its nature, the degree to which these domestic competitors have stepped into the shoes of the government in helping construct the institutional ecosystem (for which they may expect future rents and possess lobbying power), and the degree to which planning is required to fill institutional voids.

Macroeconomic context

The multinational firm also needs to make an assessment of the unique nature of the macroeconomic context of emerging markets, in general, but India, in particular. Although emerging markets share many of these characteristics, the nature of Indian financial markets is very different from all the other BRIC nations in that it is much more developed. Well-developed stock markets regularly monitor and respond to policy and regime changes, in addition to company strategies and earnings reports in the Indian context. Above all, there is a significant level of economic stability in India. However, there is a huge informal economy which needs to be properly accounted for in strategic calculations. We describe these issues in greater depth in Chapter 3.

Political particularities

India is the largest democracy in the world and operates based on a constitutional framework of federalism. This is very different from the home countries of MNCs and their managers. Such MNC managers have to understand that the federalist nature of Indian democracy provides unique rights, privileges, and responsibilities to the central (federal) government and each of the state and local governments in India. Just to note one example, although majority stake FDI in multibrand retail has been made into law by the federal government, the same law notes the need for it to be ratified by each state where the MNC retailer may decide to locate stores. Thus, the MNC manager may be faced with the reality of interacting with multiple governments rather than only one, with the interactions varying in language (medium of communication), duration, and nature of procedures, among others. Although corruption and lack of transparency are relatively higher in India (as is the case in any emerging market) than most other countries, this is not to be confused with multiple layers of governmental bureaucracy on the count of a federalist structure. These aspects are elaborated on in Chapter 4.

Consumer and market profile

MNCs and their managers need to understand the nature of Indian consumers, their cultural traditions, their purchasing behavior, and more generally the nature of markets in India. As with most issues, the range over which consumers vary in their broad purchasing behavior is much more complex and varied than in advanced economies. Perhaps the best way to understand this is the skewed nature of the distribution of income in Indian society and the stark differences between rural and urban areas, each of which is very different from the home nations of MNCs. While, on the one hand, India provides a huge middle class with high disposable incomes, it also possesses many bottom-of-the-pyramid (BoP) markets within its boundaries making the task more challenging.

We focus on each of these more critical factors in detail, in addition to a more in-depth focus on the strategy implementation factors in subsequent chapters. The rest of this book is organized in the following manner. Chapter 2 provides an overview of the

Indian business ecosystem and its so-called institutional voids, which are much the same in many emerging economies. Based on this description of institutional voids and how to recognize them, the way in which firms evolve and compete in the context of institutions going through transformation and discontinuous change is given through a longitudinal case study description of sport business (cricket). The case study highlights successful strategies that are known to overcome the institutional voids an MNC might encounter in India. This chapter focuses on business groups and legal, financial, and regulatory institutions that set the environmental context within which firms run their businesses.

Chapter 3 provides a global view of the macroeconomic context prevailing in India and how this has changed over the years. This should make understanding the competitive behavior of firms in this country easier. In this macroeconomic analysis I focus on stability and growth and the nature of economic policies and the political outlook. More light is shed on the nature and magnitude of the informal economy and what it means for businesses operating in the country. Finally, significant components of the economy and their relative contributions to the country's GDP are highlighted, with a special emphasis on the service sector, which has increasingly become the champion of India's competitive advantage.

In addition to unpacking the bundle of complexities represented by institutional voids and macroeconomic uniqueness, Chapter 4 moves on to demystifying India's political complexity. The federalist nature of the Indian democracy with unique powers granted to the central and state governments, respectively, are quite different from what most MNC managers have seen elsewhere. The diversity among different states coupled with the different languages spoken in different parts of the country complicate issues for most managers. The chapter focuses on the devolution of authority between the central and state governments and the legal framework embedded in India's constitution by specifically linking them to on-the-ground business implications.

Chapter 5 profiles Indian consumers, drawing on notions of culture, traditions, lifestyles, and purchasing tendencies. Further, urban markets are contrasted with those in rural India, highlighting the two faces of India. Consistent with the theme of a country of contrasts, the purchasing power and preferences of urban India are different from the BoP markets commonly found in rural India. This chapter also provides information on how businesses can get their marketing and advertising messages over to Indian consumers.

Based on the preceding analysis and description of the institutional, economic, political, and consumer profile analysis, Chapter 6 provides a discussion of marketing and business strategies specifically focused on Indian markets and consumers. Using the case study of an Indian retail organization, this chapter provides ideas of the conditions necessary for cost or differentiation strategies to work, while also noting the importance of focused v. diversification strategies and their applicability in India. The chapter also addresses the contrasting situations that exist between manufacturing and service strategies, given that India has a significant service sector and enjoys the competitive advantage that brings.

Using the innovative approach of ITC Hotels to capturing rural markets, Chapter 7 addresses unique problems in rural India with special attention to BoP markets.

The complex problem of leveraging resources in such markets and how ITC success-fully leveraged knowledge and IT resources to succeed in rural India is explained. The phenomenon of telecommunications services expanding in BoP markets within India is then described, while drawing important lessons for managers wishing to enter these markets.

Contributions to India's GDP from the service sector, which has a greater global presence than other sectors, are on the increase. Chapter 8 focuses on the root causes of such competitive and "comparative" advantage in services and demonstrates the importance of Indian human and intellectual capital. Significant progress in the business/knowledge process outsourcing (BPO/KPO) and medical tourism sectors are highlighted and point up India's fundamental strength in cost-effective innovation.

Having identified intellectual capital as one of India's fundamental strengths, Chapter 9 focuses on the leadership challenges involved in managing and leading intellectual workers. The chapter also contrasts indigenous models of leadership with more global models of leadership, to identify when and where each of these is likely to work best in India. Providing a special focus on knowledge leadership, this chapter addresses the method and theory of knowledge leadership, drawing implications for MNCs in establishing leadership systems in India.

A wide variety of organizational and control systems uniquely adapted to the Indian context are required for firms to successfully implement their chosen strategies in the Indian market. Chapter 10 turns the reader's attention to the critical aspects of strategy implementation. Such issues as the impact of culture on organization structure and efficacy, performance management approaches, and suitable compensation plans to fit the Indian context are described.

Managing people is one of the most culturally contingent tasks in international business. Chapter 11 describes how traditional Indian family-run businesses (includ-ing business groups of large size) manage their human resources and how their human resource management (HRM) practices have evolved. The large size of the population and significant unemployment, at least up until economic liberalization, are problems that HR managers struggled to handle and still do. Such HR practices as selection are described in this context and light is shed on important labor laws and related industrial relations challenges.

Notes

1. Wikipedia. Available from: http://en.wikipedia.org/wiki/List_of_countries_with_ McDonald's_restaurants [accessed 11 May 2013].
2. *The Economic Times* (20 September 2012). FDI in multi-brand retail comes into effect: way clear for Walmart.
3. The Global Retail Development Index™: lessons learned from a decade of retail expansion. Available from: http://www.atkearney.com/index.php/Publications/grdi-a-10-year-retrospective.html.
4. *The Economic Times* (20 September 2012). FDI in multi-brand retail comes into effect: way clear for Walmart.
5. http://en.wikipedia.org/wiki/Retailing_in_india.

6. Telecom subscription data as of 31 May 2012. Available from: http://www.trai.gov.in/WriteReadData/PressRealease/Document/PR-TSD-May12.pdf.

7. http://articles.timesofindia.indiatimes.com/2013-08-14/social-media/41409040_1_facebook-india-platform-facebook-feature-phones.

8. The Global Retail Development Index™: lessons learned from a decade of retail expansion. Available from: http://www.atkearney.com/index.php/Publications/grdi-a-10-year-retrospective.html.

The institutional context

2

> *"Within ten years we expect India to be one of the top five domestic markets in the World. But the situation on the ground has to change. Today we supply our own private transportation for our employees because we can't depend on public infrastructure. We have our own sources of water and power – because we have to."*
>
> **Tom Schlick, Executive Vice President, American Express, speaking at the Global India Business Meeting in Munich, July 2009**

Tom Schlick refers in the above quote to the well-known infrastructural problem in India, which has contributed to lackluster growth in foreign direct investment (FDI) into the country over the previous decades. In addition to the hard infrastructure, as in the above, any economy also needs a soft infrastructure for its markets to function smoothly. Deficiencies or inadequacies in the soft infrastructure manifest themselves as either a complete absence or a severe inadequacy of various intermediaries and institutions operating in developed markets, which are usually taken for granted by managers of multinational corporations (MNCs) contemplating entry into India or another emerging market. Many experts have pointed out that emerging markets such as India are fundamentally different from the markets in more advanced economies in that they are full of institutional voids. As highlighted in the opening story of McDonald's extensive six years of planning before opening its first store in India, there are a number of intermediary firms; legal, financial, and regulatory institutions; and well-developed supply chains in advanced economies that may be non-existent or at least inadequate in India, subject of course to the different sector the MNC wants to operate in. Under such circumstances, the main task of the MNC is to identify and assess the specific nature of the business ecosystem, the degree of sophistication or lack thereof of businesses, competition from domestic businesses in the sector and their nature, the degree to which these domestic competitors have stepped into the shoes of the government in helping construct the institutional ecosystem (for which they may expect future rents and possess lobbying power), and the degree to which planning is required to fill institutional voids.

Imagine yourself to be the manager of a rent-to-own chain of furniture and consumer durables that wants to establish itself in India. That there is a huge market in India for furniture and consumer durables is beyond doubt, as noted earlier, in light of the increasingly consumerist culture in India. If there are doubts about the disposable incomes and purchasing power of the so-called Indian middle class, that is music to the ears of managers of any rent-to-own chain. The basic purpose of a rent-to-own business is to enable people with poor credit (in a developed market context) or lower disposable incomes to enjoy the lifestyle of those with higher incomes and to be able to afford it. Thus, no one would doubt the value proposition that such a business would bring to consumers in India. But, think about the different questions that would arise in your mind about the viability of the entire business model behind such a business. How would you be able to evaluate the creditworthiness of consumers in India, many of whom may not have a bank account or a credit or debit card to make payments? Are public data on consumer creditworthiness available (for those with bank accounts)? How would you enter into contracts with these consumers? How would you enforce contracts on defaulters? How would you reduce shrinkage or collect on receivables from Indian consumers who do not pay? How would you source furniture and consumer durables and keep your stores well stocked? How would you staff your stores with qualified and/or trained people who can answer all the above questions on a daily basis? If the answers to the above questions involve informal institutions not open to all and consequently heavily dependent on business or interpersonal relationships, these signal the existence of institutional voids. These institutional voids then require intensive local knowledge in either acquiring answers to the above questions or managing in the absence of these answers. Indian sellers of consumer durables, for instance, have been operating in the country for decades in the absence of many of the financial and credit intermediaries in the above questions. However, to argue that MNCs and their managers can do the same would be foolhardy.

To be sure, card payments in India have grown at a compound annual rate of 27 percent or better in the last five years. The number of financial cards in circulation in India reached 456.8 million at the end of 2012, which approximately translates to one card for every three individuals in the population. The value of financial card transactions reached $363 billion in 2012.[1] In keeping with the country of contrasts theme noted earlier, it is interesting to note that approximately 43.8 percent of the Indian population does not have a bank account despite India being the fourth largest country in the world in terms of the number (290,552) of resident high net worth individuals (HNWIs). Thus, in answer to the first question about how to evaluate the creditworthiness of consumers, we must remember we are at the early stages of the development of this type of soft infrastructure in India, which is nowhere near the levels of the advanced economies that most MNC managers are comfortable with, despite the situation rapidly improving. That managing a rent-to-own chain requires special knowledge of how to operate under such circumstances should be obvious.

According to the World Bank, it takes on average 1420 days to enforce a contract in India.[2] Compare this with the world average of 621 days or the 395 days it takes, say, in Australia. Although the common law-based Indian judicial system functions quite well and is familiar to most MNCs, the inordinate delays in justice, as indicated by the above data, indicate inadequacies in the soft infrastructure that are crucial for certain businesses, like the one in question here. This is precisely why special knowledge of operating such a business under these circumstances is primordial. The rent-to-own industry in the United States, for instance, has been subject to numerous attacks from U.S. consumer protection advocates for excessive prices and predatory financing, thereby causing undue hardship to consumers. Such consumer advocacy groups are another example of the institutional intermediaries that facilitate transactions between buyer and seller and help them redress disputes, sometimes as an alternative to an overloaded legal system such as India's.[3] Making an assessment of whether Indian consumer advocate groups will rise up in similar protests and succeed in derailing your efforts to establish in India is also crucial to your efforts and may require months, if not years, of advance planning. The rent-to-own industry's arguments (giving un-privileged people an opportunity to acquire household goods, in a manner amenable to their cash flow, preserving their creditworthiness, allowing them to eventually own goods), which worked in the United States, may fail to work in India, if not handled appropriately. The underlying political dimensions highlight the need to tread softly and in a customized manner to match local conditions.

As noted at the beginning, institutional voids can exist in legal, financial, and regulatory institutions, or in the existence (or lack) of a local ecosystem in the relevant supply chain. It took six long years for McDonald's to plan its operations strategy simply because intermediaries in the supply chain to which the company was used to elsewhere were missing. Instead of the outsourcing strategy McDonald's uses in its home market, for instance, the company had to develop reliable cold chains, cold storage facilities, and logistics partners with these cold chain facilities, in addition to finding and developing vendors of high-quality lettuce, buns, pickles, chicken and vegetable patties, and many other ingredients it uses in its restaurants. The severe inadequacies in India of this sort of supply chain forced the company to open two large distribution centers in New Delhi and Mumbai, thereby limiting the company to open-ing stores within 500 kilometers of these two target cities. The rent-to-own business that you manage may make similar demands on your company resources for Indian operations and needs to be considered carefully.

Now that you have a general idea of what intermediary institutions may be lacking (institutional voids) in India with respect to a specific business, I provide a brief dis-cussion of the legal, financial, retail, capital, and labor market institutions in India, with a view to providing a broad understanding of the institutional context for doing business in India. Based on this description, I tell a story (case study) of how firms evolve and compete at a time institutions are undergoing transformation and discon-tinuous change by providing a longitudinal case study description of sport business (cricket). The case study highlights the successful strategies needed to overcome the institutional voids an MNC might encounter in India. Cricket is not just a sport in India, it is a religion with millions of passionate fans, making it a very critical means of reaching people with marketing messages. Cricket is an intricate part of the fabric of life (culture) in India; it is important for MNC managers to understand this cultural aspect of India. Thus, providing a story of how institutions evolve and how companies manage in this context has more utility to you the reader, over and above the objective of helping you understand local institutions. But, first, let us take a brief look at the different intermediary institutions in India.

Legal institutions

When the British left India in 1947, one of the legacies they left behind was the judicial system, which is based on English common law. In a common law system, law is developed by judges through their decisions, orders, or judgments. These are also referred to as precedents. However, unlike the British legal system, the Indian legal system also incorporates statutory law and regulatory law as laid down by the Constitution of India (established in 1950) and serves as the supreme law in the country. Despite adopting a federal system of government (explained in more detail in Chapter 4) the Constitution of India provides for the setting up of an integrated system of courts to administer both union and state laws, which cover different issues. The Supreme Court is the highest court in the country, followed by High Courts in each of the states, where they are the highest authority. This is followed by various subordinate courts at the district level and lower levels.[4] The Supreme Court and the High Court have the power of judicial review, which is similar to the case in the U.S., and provides for a system of checks and balances. Under the judicial review system, legislative and executive actions are subject to judicial review and can be invalidated if they are found to be in violation of the constitution of the country. The legal system of institutions in India is strong but suffers from overload and a huge backlog of cases, resulting in problems in enforcing contracts, among other things. India has only 12 judges per million people, compared with 50 per million in Britain, and 107 in America.[5] The first mobile court, part of a planned system to bring fast justice to people in remote areas and to prevent their loss of faith in the legal system, was launched in 2007.[6] Despite the system also providing for several quasi-judicial bodies such as tribunals (e.g., Telecom Disputes Settlement Appellate Tribunal, TDSAT) and regulators (Telecom Regulatory Authority of India, TRAI), the overall system still suffers from overload because of the backlog of cases. Thus, court battles can be lengthy and people often joke that their children are likely to inherit the legal disputes initiated by them.

Financial and capital market system

India's financial and capital markets are sophisticated and undergo continuous development, as indicated by the country occupying 19th place in the 2013–14 Global Competitiveness Index (GCI) ranking (Schwab, n.d.), moving up from 33rd place in 2008–09. India ranked in the top 50 in all the different components of the Financial Market Development Pillars of the GCI, and ranked in the top 30 for financing through local equity markets (18th), venture capital availability (27th), regulation of securities exchanges (27th), and the legal rights index (28th). India stands out among the BRIC nations for the soundness and sophistication of its financial markets and the quality of its banking system (49th). There is a general consensus among external observers that the banking system within the country is sound and sustainable. The Securities and Exchange Board of India (SEBI) is one of the financial institutions responsible for the strength of this financial and capital market system in the country.

Retail market

The absence of well-developed retail establishments across the country is an indicator of the presence of institutional voids or the absence of institutional intermediaries. It is important for such retail establishments to have access to all kinds of consumers, urban as well as rural, rich as well as poor, and for this access to be nationwide. The retail industry in India has been historically fragmented, unorganized, and until recently has consisted of millions of mom-and-pop stores, with very few nationwide chains. Now, many of the domestic business groups have either already established country-wide chains of retail establishments or are in the process of doing so. Additionally, the government recently managed to obtain approval (from Parliament) for majority investment by MNCs in multi-brand retail and 100 percent investment by MNCs in single-brand retail, amid serious activism and potential for political upheaval in the coalition running the government.[7] The Retail Development Index developed by A.T. Kearney is intended to be the bellwether of future global economic growth.[8] There is immense potential for the development of intermediary firms and indigenous business ecosystems (the kind that McDonald's lacked) if only India would open up its doors to FDI in retail. The fractious nature of politics in India and the diversity of a country administratively divided into 29 states necessitated the framing of the recent (December 2012) Retail FDI bill, which required subsequent approval by respective state governments. Thus, both the single and multi-brand sectors of retail in India will receive (accept) investments only after a multilayered legal and approval process, despite being made law by the federal (central) government. In essence, while some states will allow this investment, others will not. Global retailers such as Wal-Mart, Carrefour, Tesco, and Metro are in various phases of entering India with different format stores. All this activity is only likely to strengthen the presence of strong insti-tutional intermediaries required by MNCs of all sizes, regardless of whether they bring a big reputation with them, for obtaining success in doing business in the country. This is a rapidly evolving situation, bringing about institutional change for the better. As this situation suggests, institutional voids provide many opportunities for business, especially for MNCs with the right skills and competencies in these areas.

Labor market institutions

For most MNCs a crucial aspect of doing business in a new country is their ability to attract a good supply of talented individuals for positions at various levels in their companies' local operations. India boasts a significant number of people under the age of 45. Not only are they young and have the potential to work long into the future, they are also part of a system that produces the highest number of science and engi-neering graduates in the world. All these graduates are English speaking and fully capable of working in the domestic operations of MNCs. Companies such as Ford, Toyota, Hyundai, Nokia, and Honda have established manufacturing facilities in the country and have been operating there for more than a decade. Despite a few inci-dents of labor unrest and trade union activism, these companies have by and large had few problems drawing on the labor market or complying with labor laws and the reg-ulatory framework. Despite a common negative perception of the nature of labor laws (restrictive) in India, the author is confident that the reality on the ground is very dif-ferent. One only has to look at the Indian experience of the MNCs named here and that of others to understand the strength of the country from this perspective. After all, the proof of the pudding is in its eating. India provides a working environment not just for hands but also for brains. Why would companies like GE, Intel, Microsoft, and Hewlett-Packard establish R&D centers in India, were the previous statement untrue? As far as the labor market is concerned, India provides not only opportunities for cost advantages but also for innovation advantages, as many experts suggest. The labor laws and regulatory frameworks in this regard, contrary to what you might hear in the West, are quite favorable. In fact, the availability of English-speaking managerial talent is higher in India than anywhere else.

Challenges provided by the institutional context: case example

The media are among the institutions that provide the service of being an intermediary in the macro sense. The media in many emerging markets vary in terms of their capabilities, functions, level of freedom, and ultimate impact. The media in India have been very active since market and economic reforms in India began in the early 1990s. Consider the case of the media company, Zee Telefilms Ltd., which tried to expand into the business of creating (and managing) sport content in addition to simply broadcasting the content provided by other players, and the challenges it faced under such circumstances. Managers of MNCs trying to enter India by taking advantage of the opportunities provided by the absence or inadequacies of institutional intermediaries can learn significant lessons from this case example, as will be highlighted at the end. Another case in the retail sector is provided in Chapter 6. As explained above, although emerging economies (e.g., India) are going to be the key drivers of economic growth in the decades to come (Khanna and Palepu, 2010), the fundamental mechanisms that make markets work (i.e., institutions) are either missing or undergoing serious transformations in these economies and the markets operating within them (Chittoor et al., 2009). Correspondingly, in contrast to the cost-based strategies that were key predictors of the global performance of domestic firms in emerging economies, innovation strategies are becoming more important today (Aulakh et al., 2000; Chitoor et al., 2009). Many popular Indian MNCs have their origins in business groups, which normally engage in a diverse set of businesses (e.g., the Tata group of companies). Business groups are common across many emerging markets and normally adopt a diversification strategy to leverage their investments, protect their investments, and share knowledge, especially in terms of the special skills required to operate in the presence of serious institutional voids. Business groups take on the role of making sociocultural investments, which elsewhere would normally be the role of the government. This empowers them to seek future rents for such investments and lobbying power with the government for having played the government's role in many instances. Thus, business groups that spawn emerging economy multinationals (EMNCs) generally have special capabilities to operate in institutional voids. In addition to the capability of EMNCs to operate in institutional voids (Khanna and Palepu, 2010), research has generally emphasized the importance of second-order learning for these firms to prosper globally

(Aulakh, 2009), which in turn necessitates the mobilization of international technological and financial resources. Thus, innovation is simultaneously critical to managing the topsy-turvy nature of institutions at home (and in other emerging economy markets), on the one hand, and to succeeding in developed economies, on the other.

Despite advances, our understanding of emerging economies and their markets is in its infancy. Our knowledge, or lack thereof, of institutions and the micro foundations of institutionally driven change and, hence, the processes through which institutional voids are overcome is a key contributing factor (Lakshman, 2012). In other words, this case will provide the reader with an understanding of how individual actors come together from different institutional intermediary organizations to engage in an act of entrepreneurship (expanding from a media business to a creator of sport content). This type of entrepreneurship, one that brings changes to the nature of the institutional field, has been called institutional entrepreneurship. This case places emphasis on the role of coalitions and politics within and across organizations and the associated role of power and self-interests to subvert attempts to change. Thus, processes surrounding inter and intra-organizational conflicts and how they trigger institutional entrepreneurship are not well understood. Reading through this case study should provide companies with such an understanding and help them make decisions about their impending market entry into India. Such knowledge may be more important in emerging economies than in others, as a result of the transformations and discontinuous change these economies are undergoing. This case examines the microsociological processes in the institutional environment surrounding Twenty20 (T20) cricket in India (with global markets). Recent innovation within the T20 form of cricket in India is beginning to make ripples in other markets such as the U.K., U.S., and even China, thus making it worthy of study not only from our focus on India but also well beyond its boundaries. The primary aim of this case study is to longitudinally examine the birth of the innovative Indian Cricket League (ICL), the subsequent competitive and institutional battles for legitimacy, and the resulting death of the ICL in the face of the newborn Indian Premier League (IPL). The case describes the interplay between internal political processes and external competitive actions in the creation of innovation in sports organizational forms and the subsequent legitimacy struggles through which this organizational field evolves. The case study provides critical lessons about managing in emerging economies by observing patterns in organizational and institutional evolution in such contexts.

MNCs have traditionally developed products and services in developed economies and then targeted developing economies with such offerings. More recently, however, reverse innovation has come to the fore, where MNCs develop offerings for markets in Asia and then take them to more developed markets. Although T20 cricket was first established in England and has been played in other cricketing countries for some time now, (reverse) innovation in business model and organizational form, first in the form of the ICL and eventually the IPL, has gained significant market share in international markets and is all set to spawn more initiatives in this regard in critical markets such as China and the U.S. (Della Penna, 2012). The ICL to IPL evolution is examined as a longitudinal case study to illustrate these issues within the context of professionalizing and globalizing T20 cricket, from a base in emerging economy markets to more advanced economies.

Cricket in India – a national obsession

Cricket in India is a national obsession, almost a religion, and is part of a hegemonic sports culture that dominates the country's emotional attachments (Lakshman, 2008a). Everywhere you look, someone is playing cricket: look out of a bus window, along dusty streets, in tiny villages and big cities, and you'll see a bunch of youngsters playing the game with rudimentary bats and twigs for stumps. For a country that spans a vast and varied terrain and has a diverse culture, it may be difficult to imagine many events or activities that are capable of binding the nation together as one. Cricket is the one thing that unites the whole of India (Lakshman, 2008a). Most marketing professionals point out that should an MNC manager doing business in India want to gamble with his or her marketing expenditures in India cricket provides the best bet.

Cricket in India has been governed by the Board of Control for Cricket in India (BCCI) since its formation in 1928. It is an institutional intermediary in the business of cricket, serves as the main "creator of content", and sells broadcast rights to various media groups. The BCCI runs a number of domestic tournaments, which act as a development ground for young players. It uses these tournaments to assess player performance and for selection purposes to represent the national team. The BCCI comprises 29 state cricket associations that elect BCCI officials through a ballot system. It is also responsible for representing India at the International Cricket Council (ICC), which is the international governing body of cricket.

T20: a new format

When the traditional form of cricket was no longer entertaining, the England and Wales Cricket Board (ECB) started T20 as a club championship in 2003 to get interest back. The first official T20 matches were played between two English counties. The first T20 game to be held at Lord's[9] (Middlesex v. Surrey in July 2004) attracted a crowd of 26,500, the largest attendance for any county cricket game in its class, becoming cricket's newest innovation. The first T20 international match took place on 17 February 2005 between Australia and New Zealand. The ICC adopted this format and held the inaugural T20 World Cup in South Africa in 2007. Despite the presence of T20 cricket in all cricket-playing nations with advanced economies (e.g., Australia, England, New Zealand), the birth of the ICL and then the IPL represent the most successful innovation in business models in T20 cricket.

The development and rapid growth of the IPL is a classic example of innovation management in sport and has completely changed the traditional model of cricket, fueling interest in England for the development of a similar league. During the last 50 years a vast body of research has focused on various aspects of technological innovation. Recently, Birkinshaw et al. (2008) have drawn our attention to the underresearched domain of management innovation which is defined as "the generation and implementation of a management practice, process, structure, or technique that is new to the state of the art and is intended to further organizational goals" (Birkinshaw et al., 2008, p. 829). It is this sort of management innovation that MNCs have special competence in, and is what is required in emerging economy markets such as India. In the context of T20, management innovations like shorter games, auction-based salaries, city franchises, and revenue derived primarily from broadcasting have been adopted by the IPL (Enderwick and Nagar, 2010), none of which have appeared in advanced economy cricket-playing nations. American magazine *FastCompany* ranked IPL 22nd in the world's 50 most innovative companies for 2010. *FastCompany* said that "IPL has transformed cricket, establishing a new model that shows how a nearly 500-year-old game can be revamped, restructured, and tailored to today's short attention spans and entertainment infrastructure – and succeed wildly." Attracting Bollywood royalty (e.g., Shahrukh Khan) and big Indian industrial houses such as Reliance Industries and the UB Group, the IPL was expected to bring in about $2 billion in its first decade, including proceeds from TV rights ($918 million), promotion ($108 million), and franchises ($724 million) (Vilaga, 2012). Consider the following story of institutional evolution from the birth of the innovative ICL to its eventual demise and the birth of the even more innovative IPL.

Innovations that generate tangible benefits, such as the ICL and the IPL here, are contagious and spread readily among populations. The Bangladesh Premier League (BPL) had its inaugural season in 2012, essentially using a business model similar to the IPL. Keith Wyness, CEO of Cricket Holdings America LLC – a partnership between the U.S.A. Cricket Association (USACA) and New Zealand Cricket with responsibility for forming a domestic professional T20 league in the land of opportunity – recently announced that the inaugural season could possibly be launched in 2013 but eventually postponed it to a later date. Additionally, the Chinese authorities have recently made the decision to participate in the 2019 Cricket World Cup (Enderwick and Nagar, 2010). Since its inception, the T20 game has rapidly diffused throughout the cricket world.[10] So T20 cricket readily represents a medium through which hundreds of millions of Indians can be reached, not only within India but within the Indian diaspora as well.

Indian Cricket League (ICL)

The ICL was formed in 2007 by Zee Entertainment Enterprises Ltd., the largest media and entertainment group in India. Its two-year life span (2007–9) included T20 format tournaments between four international teams (The World, India, Pakistan, and Bangladesh) and nine domestic teams located in major Indian cities as well as Lahore, Pakistan. The ICL's mission was to create a pool of highly talented young cricketers. For this purpose, the ICL planned a 3D strategy (discovery, diligence, and display) with the objective of identifying the best talent across the country, providing rigorous training (physical, mental, emotional, and spiritual) by qualified and experienced professionals, and enabling these young players to display their prowess in competition. The ICL was supported by five main pillars: executive board members, talent scouts, coaches, mentors, and players/teams (Table 2.1). Despite favorable commercial factors, the ICL lacked the support of the BCCI, which saw the ICL as a threat to its own legitimacy.

The ICL had sufficient amounts of audience interest (pragmatic legitimacy), but lacked moral legitimacy or the normative approval to be the creator of such cricket content, which would be critical for its survival. To draw a parallel, the rent-to-own

Table 2.1 Structure of ICL (five main pillars)

Executive Board members	• Comprising top names of international cricket (headed by Kapil Dev, former India captain) • Final say in all matters of the league • Responsible for its running (creating, managing, and running)
The talent scouts	• Selecting the best talent to represent the ICL
The coaches	• Important cog in league functioning • Coaches would have access to state-of-the-art video-recording software
The mentors	• Comprising media managers, psychologists and physiotherapists, and dieticians • Players trained under coaches • Desired goal is to excel at cricket
The players and teams	• Initially six teams (to be increased to 16 by third year) in a league format that leads up to semi-finals and finals • Teams would comprise four international, two Indian, and eight budding domestic players • Matches in 20:20 format with all teams playing home and away • Each team would have first and second-division sides so as to maximize talent utilization • Teams to be provided exposure to international cricket for psychological preparation

business will attract consumers for sure, but may face protests from consumer advocacy groups for predatory pricing and financing. Management theory emphasizes the importance of legitimacy (Suchman, 1995), suggesting that organizations must act to enhance or protect their legitimacy in order to survive, and must therefore conform to the rules and belief systems prevailing in the environment. The ICL would be run by a set of professionals with policies benchmarked against the best sports organizations globally. The executive board and other officials in the ICL had a proven track record of managing sport, especially cricket, evidently in an effort to gain dispositional legitimacy (based on the characteristics of individuals) (Suchman, 1995). The five pillars (Table 2.1) provided the ICL with structural legitimacy (based on organizational systems and structures), a critical component of the broader moral legitimacy. Research suggests that new organizations obtain moral legitimacy through evaluations of (i) outputs and consequences, (ii) techniques and procedures, (iii) categories and structures, and sometimes (iv) leaders and representatives. One of the key implications of research involved in the identification and categorization of different types of legitimacy and the identification of legitimacy acquisition v. legitimacy maintenance strategies is that institutional conflicts can result in pragmatic and moral legitimacy dominating over other forms of legitimacy. We now turn our attention to the institutional conflicts in our case, which were mainly driven by the legitimacy maintenance strategies of the BCCI, the institutional defender who had been performing many of the roles that the ICL wanted to perform in this field. Innovations threaten the legitimacy of even the most secure organizations and can become deadly if left unaddressed for long.

Institutional conflict–based processes and organizational innovation

In Figure 2.1 we graphically map the institutional processes through which this innovation evolved in professional cricket, leading to a battle of legitimacy, the death of one organization, and the survival of another. As shown in Figure 2.1, our analysis reveals that the birth of the ICL was a result of the confluence of internal politics within the BCCI and the rejection of Zee TV's bids for broadcast rights for Indian cricket for legitimacy reasons. We describe both of these events in the following sections.

First, Kapil Dev, the Chairman of the National Cricket Academy (NCA), was dissatisfied with the selection procedure for the Indian cricket team and the presence of regional politics in such contexts. Conflict between the different regions (zones in the official BCCI organization) and the politics between them has a long history, with the

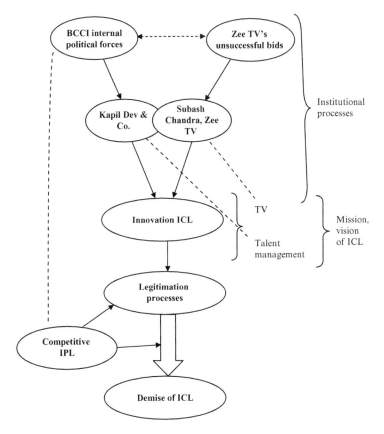

Figure 2.1 Institutional processes and organizational innovation in India

eventual appointment of selectors from each of the zones to the National Selection Committee in the 1990s. Dev, a former India captain, was supported by a number of former cricketers who had been affected by such practices and eventually joined him on the ICL's board.

Next, having had his highest bids for broadcast rights rejected more than once by the BCCI, for (lack of) legitimacy reasons, Subash Chandra, CEO of Zee TV (Essel Group), wanted to create his own cricket content and joined forces with Dev and other dissenters from within the BCCI to form the ICL. Chandra openly criticized the BCCI for what he called selection failures and inability to create a reserve pipeline of players, adding that the ICL would create an ideal pool of players possessing the killer instinct necessary to win matches and that the BCCI was free to draw from this pool. Announcing his $23 million (INR 100 crores; 1 crore = 10 million) investment for the launch of the ICL, Chandra made his views on the BCCI quite clear,

> "We feel that despite cricket being a passion, a religion in this country and despite it having great commercial players, BCCI has only six A-grade players signed up. Therefore, there is need for some united effort to create a talent pool. And this will be done by a three pronged strategy – discovery, diligence and display."
>
> (Cricinfo, 2007a)

The reference to A-grade players above alludes to the three-tier contract system of the BCCI with India's players, with the A grade being the highest. At the same time as the launch of the ICL, Chandra had sent a letter to the BCCI seeking permission to launch a parallel league. In his three-page letter to the then BCCI chief Sharad Pawar, Chandra wrote,

> "The idea is also to develop India, a leading cricketing nation, as the laboratory to innovate new models of cricket so that we set the agenda for innovation for others to follow... we will take a meticulous and out-of-the box approach to the game to raise its standards, which involves creation of international standard infrastructure... In my understanding, their constraints rob the cricket establishments of the flexibility needed to adopt a new vision-cum-action model like the 3-D approach."
>
> (Cricinfo, 2007b)

Thus, both inter and intra-organizational conflict and politics would lead to the birth of an innovative business model in cricket that would eventually lead to a fight for control in what is essentially a multibillion dollar business.

A battle for legitimacy

There were several determining factors contributing to the formation of the ICL. However, the galvanizing factor for formation of the rebel league was clearly summed up by the statement made by Himanshu Mody, the business head of the ICL (and a senior manager at Zee TV), who said "They denied us the cricket content, so we had to create our own." (Singh, 2012). Experts suggest that the pain of rejection could have been a major reason for the formation of the ICL league (Akshobh, 2009). Norms of insitutional legitimacy had prevented the Essel Group from obtaining broadcast rights for Indian cricket, much to their dislike. The rejection of their highest bid for the rights had sown the seeds of discontent, and gave birth to a new organization for professional T20 in India. Cricket in India generates a huge sum (over Rs. 1000 crore) in advertising and subscription revenue alone. A prominent journalist wrote,

> *"It's best to wait and see whether this is a genuine move by Chandra and his vast Essel group or a bargaining ploy by the man who lost out on the BCCI's TV rights three-odd years ago. Will Chandra go the distance or will he be open to adjustments if the right signals are sent out?"*
>
> *(Gupta, 2007)*

Chandra made a bid for the 2000 World Cup and lost. He made the highest bid of $260 million for telecast rights in 2004, was initially selected for the contract, but eventually received a cancellation notice as a result of a court case on a slightly different matter, all of which ended up in an inconclusive court battle (see court decisions in Hegde, 2005; Katju, 2005). In this instance, in response to a case filed by Zee Telefilms Ltd. that the BCCI had arbitrarily canceled its bid for telecast rights, the Supreme Court ruled that the BCCI was not the State and therefore could not be sued for alleged violation of fundamental rights.[11] When the matter moved to the Madras High Court, the case was dismissed with the ruling that Zee did not have a contract and that there was no law requiring that the highest bidder be awarded the contract. He bid for the 2006–10 rights and once again lost (Singh, 2012). These incidents demonstrate the role of the interplay between institutional voids and the diverse sources of legitimacy identified by researchers. First, the role played by institutional voids is evident from the inconclusiveness of the court battles as opposed to the typical case of delayed justice in India. Some of this had to do with the diverse sources of legitimacy and the difference in its interpretation between the BCCI and Zee TV. Being the largest media group, Zee TV argued that it had access to a larger audience base, thereby claiming pragmatic legitimacy. The BCCI turned down the highest bids of this bidder on the basis of their argument that this firm had not demonstrated competence in the broadcast of sport such as cricket, thereby denying moral and structural legitimacy (the acquisition of Ten Sports by Zee TV happened much later in 2010).[12] The presence of institutional voids served to widen the chasm between the two sides. However, the consequent launching of the ICL only served to threaten the legitimacy of the BCCI as the "sole authority" to run India's cricket. This sequence of events turned the focus of legitimacy to more symbolic notions such as organizational identity rather than demonstrated competence, as suggested by experts on institutions. Businesses tend to perform more efficiently if they receive institutional support, which the ICL did not gain, as described in what follows.

In an effort to influence audiences in India, Dev, head of the ICL Executive Board, defended his decision as complementing BCCI's structure rather than opposing it,

> *"Basically we will give more opportunity for players to show their talent and go on to represent the country. We want to improve our domestic cricket as much as we can. We are not looking to create a rival team but helping the Indian board to find more talent and feeding the national team."*
>
> *(Cricinfo, 2007c)*

Although admired by most Indians for his ability and leadership in bringing the cricket World Cup home, Dev apparently lacked influence legitimacy (based on the ability to influence) despite possessing dispositional legitimacy for leadership in cricket. Increasingly, the BCCI felt threatened by the growing popularity of the ICL, termed it a rebel league, and refused to recognize it as an official league, imposing the same view on its counterparts in other countries, with the backing of the ICC. Earlier, it had revoked the pensions of all players who had joined the ICL (Cricinfo, 2007). All the resources, including cricket grounds and other infrastructure, were owned by the BCCI, which refused to release them to the rebel outfit.

By adopting strategies that adhere to institutional prescriptions, organizations gain legitimacy, which secures success and survival by accessing valuable resources, providing a license to operate and innovate, lowering risk, enhancing reputation, and strengthening stakeholder relations (Lakshman, 2012). In its efforts to obtain legitimacy, the ICL hired former international cricketers including Dev himself, Tony Greig, Dean Jones, and Kiran More as board members, which enhanced its dispositional legitimacy. The board positions were paid positions. Dev, captain of the winning Indian cricket team in the 1983 Cricket World Cup, and a former India coach, joined the upstart league (ICL) as chairman of the Executive Board. Kiran More, a former Indian cricketer (1984–93), was once the chairman of the Selection Committee of the BCCI (2001–6). The late Tony Greig was a former England test captain and commentator. His most daring act was when he helped Kerry Packer start World Series Cricket by signing up many of his English colleagues as well as West Indian and Pakistani cricketers, a move which cost him the England captaincy. Greig was glad to be part of the ICL initiative and said,

> *"This will be a platform for players from all corners of India to play with and against some of the stars of international cricket. They can learn from them and gain confidence to excel. I think Indian cricket is ready for a professional cricket league. I'm confident we can make a difference."*

The inclusion of Tony Greig, highly respectable yet controversial for his rebellious (alternatively perceived as innovative) actions, was arguably detrimental to personal and dispositional legitimacy in a collective sense. Dean Jones, a retired Australian cricketer and coach who also worked as a TEN Sports commentator, returned as a commentator for the ICL, broadcast on both TEN Sports and Zee Sports.

The case of the ICL points to how internal politics within the BCCI and the competitive dynamics involved in awarding broadcast rights gave rise to organizational diversity by creating a set of motivational forces for innovation. However, actors within an institutional field do not only exert pressure, they often provide guiding principles, technical assistance, and specialized information that define actions deemed legitimate.

Clash of cricket titans: reaction of institutional actors

The battle for audiences continued as the BCCI thought Chandra was challenging its cricketing monopoly. As described in Figure 1.1, the innovative ICL was launched by Chandra resulting from the unsuccessful bids for TV rights. As a response to the ICL, the BCCI launched the IPL, led by Lalit Modi, IPL Commissioner and then BCCI Vice-President. Since its launch, the IPL has rapidly increased its brand value from about $2.01 billion in 2009 to about $4.13 billion in 2012, indicating the success of this innovative offering. The BCCI launched a number of legitimacy retention strategies that have been identified by experts. First, the BCCI, which has control of all grounds and infrastructure in India, refused to provide these facilities to the ICL. Targeting the moral legitimacy of the ICL, the BCCI opposed the existence of the ICL, terming it a rebel league. The BCCI targeted the personal legitimacy of key board members of the ICL and either criticized them or removed them from executive positions. The BCCI strongly criticized More and Dev for joining the ICL. Dev's association with the ICL was seen as a conflict of interest as he was the chairman of the NCA, a BCCI-owned entity. On 21 August 2007, Dev was sacked from his NCA post. However, Chandra had earlier stated that the ICL would go ahead regardless of the BCCI's stance. The BCCI accused the Zee Group of making large sums of money and offering the same to cricketers to play in the league, thus leading to early retirement from cricket. In order to counter this exodus, the BCCI threatened to impose lifetime bans (from eligibility to play for the country) on players contractually agreeing to play for the league, and even prompted cricket boards of other countries to follow suit. The BCCI therefore co-opted partners such as the boards of other countries and the ICC as part of its counterattack on the influence legitimacy of the ICL, realizing that leaving the threat unaddressed for long could be deadly for its survival.

Taking advantage of the relatively well-established audience interest (i.e., pragmatic and cognitive legitimacy) for T20 cricket, the BCCI started its own T20 league (i.e., the IPL), with the help of the ICC and other affiliate boards. The inaugural season of the IPL was launched in April 2008. The league's business model is a revolutionary one, based on the NFL and Major League Baseball in the U.S.A. It is currently contested by nine teams consisting of players from around the world. In January 2008, the BCCI auctioned eight city franchises for a total of $723.5 million. All subsequent IPL seasons have opened with an auction for players. The addition of a team representing Pune in March 2010 increased the number of franchises from eight to nine.

Earlier in the war between the two leagues, Rajiv Shukla of the BCCI said, "We could allow the foreign players to play in the Indian Premier League if they terminate their contracts with ICL" (Reuters, 2007). On the other hand, Dev said the ICL remained committed to luring the best players,

"We are basically feeding international cricket. . . We are only trying to increase the amount of cricket being played. If anyone is nervous, I'm very sorry. We'll welcome everybody. We want more cricketers from Sri Lanka, Pakistan and Australia. We want the best of the best here."

He further said,

"We don't want to spoil cricket, we don't intend to upset the international calendar . . . The ICC should be happy with what we're trying to do. We aren't trying to offend anyone; we are simply increasing the amount of cricket."[13]

Faced with the threat of young players joining the ICL, the BCCI jacked up prize money for winners, runners-up, and losing semi-finalists across all domestic tournaments. Average domestic cricketers hoped to make around Rs. 35,000 per match day from the season of 2007–8, more than double the Rs. 16,000 they got in 2005–6. To address selection bias issues, the BCCI also planned to do away with honorary selectors. The IPL invited bids from three broadcasters for the broadcast of its matches in April of the next year (i.e., ESPN-Star, Nimbus, and Sony Entertainment Television, SET), whereas the ICL was backed by Zee Telefilms, with Zee Sports broadcasting the matches. Although the Zee broadcasting network was strong and was ICL's biggest advantage, it had highest penetration in the rural and small-town markets of India. SET bagged the IPL T20 championship for a whopping $1.03 billion for ten years. As a result of its weakness in metropolitan cities, at this point it looked like Zee still had a long way to go with the viewers and viewership. The first three ICL matches generated a target rating point (TRP) of only 0.5 on Zee Sports despite aggressive promotions and appearances by film personalities. Even with (aging) cricket stars like Brian Lara, Chris Cairns, and Inzamam-ul-Haq on their side, the poor cable home penetration of the Zee Sports channel translated into poor viewership and advertising for the ICL. The list of sponsors interested in the yet-to-begin IPL at this time were Bharti Airtel (Delhi), United Breweries (Mumbai or Bangalore), and a leading private bank/mobile operator. On the other hand, ICL had Microsoft as a major sponsor. The IPL surpassed media expectations and the ratings were 30–50 percent more than expected (Alchemy, 2008). Viewership for the IPL has been the highest among all programs in India, with an average TRP of 7.[14] According to the Television Audience Measurement (TAM) service in India, the average viewership for the IPL was at 6.28 with the IPL finals achieving a rating of 9.8, the highest rating ever for domestic cricket in India. More broadly, with over 200 million Indian viewers, 10 million international viewers, 4 million live spectators, the IPL has become a sports and entertainment revolution, surpassing all records of viewership. Advertising revenue and ticket sales exceeded all expectations, making the IPL profitable for the organizers, broadcasters, and team owners. Eventually, coaches from the ICL began to desert the league to vie for positions in the attractive IPL and to avoid the wrath of the ICC or other cricket boards which could negatively affect their careers.

Much like business groups that are ubiquitous in emerging economies, the BCCI served to fill institutional voids and strengthen its own position, despite a strong threat to its legitimacy in a rapidly evolving environment, not only on the economic front but also on the professional sports business front. It would serve well to recall that cricket had largely existed as an amateur sport in India, with the BCCI running this as a non-profit entity for most of its history, thus constituting a sociocultural investment v. a business one. Much like members of a business group providing strategic network knowledge to each other, the BCCI, a national board, and an old player had taken advantage of network effects. All other national boards including the ICC refused to accept the ICL, labeling it a rebel league. With the help of the national boards of all ICC member countries, players who signed up for it were banned from all forms of cricket and any other means they had of making a living. In neighboring Pakistan, organizations that employed ICL players had been pressured to terminate their contracts (Samiuddin, 2009). Pakistani players who had signed up for the ICL had been told by their employers not to expect any salaries for the period they participated in the rebel series in India that year. A top official of a bank that employed some players who had signed up for ICL said the decision was based on a directive from the Pakistan Cricket Board (PCB).

> *"For the time being our bank has decided not to pay salaries for the period they appear for ICL. But if the board does not allow these players to play domestic cricket then we will be forced to terminate their employment and get new players."*
>
>   *(senior Pakistan bank official)*

The official said the board had firmly told all its affiliated units not to select players who had signed up for the ICL.[15] The Bangladesh Cricket Board (BCB) banned six players for ten years when they joined the ICL but allowed players to play in the IPL when they were offered to include more players in 2009. Although the BCCI was the only board to benefit financially from the IPL and was also the only board to stand to lose if the IPL failed, some experts have pointed to the network effects and bargaining advantages of cooperating with the BCCI. The ICL collapsed in the face of mounting pressure from the BCCI and other cricket governing bodies under the pressure of the ICC. This is evident from the statement of Ijaz Butt (chairman of the PCB),

> *"We do not want our players to be banned because they have contract with ICL. But unfortunately we cannot do anything unless ICC changes its stance on this issue. The PCB has not banned the players, we have banned under ICC rules."*
>
>   *(Samiuddin, 2009)*

Cricket boards around the world banned players joining the ICL from playing official matches, a move that irked new recruits like New Zealand fast bowler Shane Bond,

> *"We're professional cricketers and we should be able to play anywhere and for anyone... I'm just disappointed that players are getting banned. I just don't think that is fair. All boards want to make money and they have been quick to jump in with the BCCI, basically doing what they told them."[16]*

The South African board imposed bans on players who signed for the ICL. South Africa also removed the accreditation of Daryll Cullinan as a television commentator for Super-Sport because of his involvement as coach of the Kolkata Tigers within the ICL.

The role of government in institutions

Of all the institutions in a society the government is the most important. It can take action to rectify the undersupply of institutions. However, in many emerging markets, business is one of the better functioning institutions and fills institutional voids by making social and infrastructural investments, as the BCCI has done in India. It is well known that former government officials provide valuable non-business perspectives on issues, intimate knowledge of the public policy process, legitimacy, and access to key decision makers still in the government, a phenomenon dubbed the "revolving door". As described above, the government is a key source of uncertainty for firms, so having a government insider on the board can reduce the transaction cost of securing information about political decisions and potentially provide superior access and/or influence with current government officials. The BCCI has always had such a government insider on its board, such as the now former president of both the BCCI and the ICC, who was a minister in the Indian government.

The IPL benefited from the nexus between the BCCI and the Indian government, which the ICL sorely lacked. The then president of the BCCI, Sharad Pawar, was also a central government (India) minister and had the backing of the government. The ICL was deemed an unofficial league for the simple reason that it was a private league promoted by Chandra. Recognition as the official cricket league gave the IPL the moral authority (legitimacy), government backing, and the credibility the ICL lacked.

Additionally, officials of cricket's governing bodies in their respective countries used their connections to influence decision making against the ICL. This can be judged from the statement of a group of Pakistani players who were trying to challenge the ban imposed by the PCB,

> "We tried doing it in 2007 but Nasim Ashraf (PCB chairman) had too many connections in the government of that time."

The player told *Cricinfo*,

> "whenever we did something or tried, it would come up against a dead end because Ashraf would use his friends in power to stop proceedings, so we decided to just wait it out till the government is changed."
>
> *(Samiuddin, 2009)*

Questioning ICL's moral legitimacy

Since the outset a move that was ostensibly meant to harbor domestic talent and a genuine struggle to break away from the monopolistic barriers of the BCCI culminated in the ICL becoming a target of criticism. Allegations of match fixing hit the ICL from the outset. Top sources in the ICL confirmed that Chandigarh Lions players Chris Cairns and Dinesh Mongia, both former international cricketers, were investigated for alleged match fixing. The ICL announced the suspension of Mongia and Cairns[17] who denied all charges and challenged the authorities to prove the allegations that the cricketers termed baseless. A source said,

> "The ICL doesn't want a blot on the League and would go by the international code of conduct while tackling such issues... It is very clear, we cannot tolerate players

taking the ICL for a ride. They think they have got the contracts and the money and can do and get away with anything but we want to tell them that they cannot do this to the game of cricket."

More attacks on ICL's moral legitimacy were mounted by BCCI affiliates. In a letter posted on the Punjab Cricket Association's (a BCCI affiliate) website, Bindra, its president wrote,

"A league conducted among six teams, all picked at random by the organizers, can raise legitimate doubts about the veracity of results what with the SMS [short message service] and multimedia coming into play. There is every danger of the matches panning out to suit vested interests as most matches could turn out to be noora kushtis (stage managed wrestling bouts) with the competitive edge missing."

(Gupta, 2008)

These attacks served to reveal the lack of transparency and led to questions regarding the overall viability of the ICL's business model. According to ICL organizers, its cricket tournaments had obtained good viewership ratings in the overseas markets of Pakistan (5.7 for the first finals) and the U.K. (1.4 among Asians). Within India, the official ratings data released by the two television viewership-monitoring agencies, TAM and aMap,[18] showed that the ICL was a popular sport event, which was evident from the fact that the rebel league registered a television viewership of 2.13 (TAM) and 1.80 (aMap) for its 2008 event: the ICL 20s Indian Championship.[19] However, these ratings are still a far cry from the IPL ratings reported earlier, thus suggesting the efficacy of BCCI's strategies to retain their legitimacy.

The BCCI/ACB contrast and the role of institutional voids

The BCCI's response to its home-grown media baron and business group owner is in stark contrast to the Australian Cricket Board's (ACB) response to a similar attempt in the 1970s. Chandra's ICL could be considered an attempt to emulate late Australian media billionaire Kerry Packer's coup during 1976 against the ACB, which had refused to give him telecast rights for Australian cricket. Packer signed active and leading players from around the world for a series of fast-paced one-day matches and created high-quality cricket entertainment on television called World Series Cricket (WSC). After a failed compromise meeting between Packer and the ICC at Lord's, Packer stormed out reportedly saying,

"Had I got those TV rights I was prepared to withdraw from the scene and leave the running of cricket to the board. I will take no steps now to help anyone. It's every man for himself and the devil take the hindmost."[20]

The enraged ICC and the national cricket boards boycotted the players, but the matches were a huge hit on TV and with the public, although this was not the case for the first of the three years the events unfolded. Despite winning pragmatic legitimacy from audiences, the WSC did not win moral legitimacy and lost the right to use official cricket rules (which were copyright of the Marylebone Cricket Club and the ICC), couldn't call their matches "test matches", and neither could they call their team of Australians "Australia". These were part of the judgment in a court case against the Test and County Cricket Board (former name of the ECB) brought by Greig and others, where they won the freedom to have contracts with anyone they chose. This is in stark contrast to the unresolved court cases in India in the context of the ICL. The success of the WSC made the ACB give in, Packer got the telecast rights for his Channel 9 Network, and the rest is cricketing history.[21] In 1976 the circumstances lined up in favor of Packer: lots of talent, a new technology platform, an exciting new game format and a sports-mad nation starved of entertainment. But 30 years later, the ICL only managed to pull together a set of players who were either former stars, past their prime, or very young players from domestic cricket with little or no big-stage experience. The technological edge of adopting many TV cameras, different angles, and an almost 360-degree view with slow-motion replays used by Packer put viewers at the center of the action, taking the edge from Zee Entertainment.[22] Thus, while Zee TV lacked the technological edge and market penetration of Channel 9, it was also true that the institutional voids that existed in India did not have an Australian parallel. Although the BCCI could afford to attack the ICL's legitimacy and retain its own, in an effort to acquire rents from its years of social investment in Indian cricket, the ACB had to co-opt Channel 9 as a partner. Moreover, although the business group–like behavior of the BCCI was quite effective, the ACB's attempts to influence the other national boards were not always effective. Notable non-cooperators with the ACB were the cricket boards of the West Indies (mainly because they were poor and debt ridden), South Africa (because they were banned from international cricket at the time because of the country's apartheid policy), and Pakistan (for financial reasons). Moreover, unlike the tight control of the regional cricket associations and influence over corresponding state governments exercised by the BCCI, the ACB was unable to prevent the New South Wales government and its premier from making the Sydney Cricket Ground (SCG) accessible to Packer and from installing lights in the stadium for Packer's day–night cricket, an action that was mimicked by the Queensland government in Brisbane. Eventually, local governments in Adelaide and Perth would also offer their grounds, although these would not be accepted by Packer, for reasons of geographical focus. Thus, the business group–like behavior of the BCCI, which was very successful in India in the presence of institutional voids, was not as successful in Australia. The notion that this more recent battle was for pragmatic legitimacy (alternatively, control over cricket audiences) is strengthened by the fact that the ICL kept players' salaries a secret (much like the WSC earlier), unlike the BCCI which organized a publicized auction of leading players for the IPL. Independent analysts had difficulty gauging the financial viability of the ICL due to the lack of transparency of the league's operations. Terms of contracts were rarely known and advertising revenue from match telecasts — considered to be the driver of all revenue — had never been disclosed.

Demise of the ICL

Eventually, all of the above forces (i.e., lack of legitimacy, tough competition from the IPL, the official league, technology related to sports telecasts, resources related to sporting facilities, and the helplessness of the top players) led to the demise of the ICL and the emergence of the IPL as the flag bearer of the T20 innovation in India. The ICL disappeared without any significant announcements or notices about the third season of its matches.

The description and analysis of these events throws light both on the internal political processes within the BCCI and the forces of competition for broadcast rights among global media players including ESPN and Star Sports (a Newscorp subsidiary).

The case analysis clearly portrays the challenge faced by the BCCI both in terms of competing with its cricket and of attempting to establish a parallel league that would govern the T20 form of the sport. The case illustrates the importance of crucial political forces emanating from interpersonal and business relationships in emerging markets with institutional voids. These forces could trigger acts of institutional entrepreneurship, something established players should be aware of. Our analysis supports this by contrasting this case with the Australian case in the 1970s and by showing the different legitimacy retention strategies in each. This case maps the processes surrounding institutional change in a manner that threatens existing intermediaries and substitutes them with new ones. Such a mapping of these processes is crucial for both Indian and international companies trying to understand and operate in such a difficult institutional landscape.

Implications for MNCs

Managers of MNCs thinking of entering the Indian market can learn many important lessons from this story. Learning about Indian business groups and their aggressive and competitive nature is the first of these lessons. Experts on winning in emerging markets often suggest that domestic companies have a number of advantages vis-à-vis competition from MNCs. MNCs and their managers are normally likely to ignore domestic competition, as a result of what they have picked up from other country markets. Thus, MNCs have to unlearn these principles. They also have to analyze and discover whether their entry into India would upset and threaten any local players and size them up to evaluate their strength. This could give them the level of preparedness crucial in such contexts. Managers of domestic companies hunt in packs, so to speak, by virtue of their affiliation to larger business groups. If there is potential in these emerging economies for companies to go global from an Indian base, it is more likely to happen with business group companies. Thus, MNCs and their managers should include such knowledge in their competitive analysis. Perhaps most importantly, if the MNC in question is in the act of filling institutional voids by creating an institutional intermediary, it is more than likely to be exposed to all the challenges Zee TV faced in the above case story. Incidentally, the above case also pointed up the competitive battles that have taken place in the media industry in India involving both multinational and domestic players. Needless to say, the media in India are vibrant and have a very strong voice in bringing about public awareness and potential change in society. Since liberalization in the early 1990s the media in India have experienced explosive growth – from exclusively state-run television in the 1980s to hundreds of satellite TV channels – and transformative change, much as most other industries. We have referred to the retail industry and the recent law passed by the Indian government allowing 100 percent FDI in retail, something many global retailers have been waiting for. The development of nationwide chains of organized retail establishments represents transformative institutional change for Indians from all walks of life who have historically been used to relatively small retail establishments in an unorganized sector. A manager of a global retailer entering India, or someone transacting with such an entity, will find the above story full of lessons to be learned.

The nature of the institutional context and a good understanding of it are very critical to succeeding in markets such as India. The transformative change being experienced by institutions in India can necessitate more advanced and careful planning than in most other markets. Unlike the case in advanced economies, the presence and adequacy of institutional intermediaries or the presence of institutional voids need to be clearly identified before creating a strategy suited to these conditions. This may involve making an assessment of which embedded institutional players may be affected as a result of your entry into this market and how difficult it might be to manage or compete with this affected stakeholder. It may also involve taking advantage of opportunities provided by institutional voids. In many cases, the complexity created by lack of the requisite institutional intermediaries may suggest the need to use local partners in joint venture arrangements or through other means. The Indian economy and markets have shown enough openness and flexibility that many of the MNCs that entered through joint ventures now have wholly owned subsidiary operations, as noted in the first chapter. We now move on to a detailed assessment of the macroeconomic environment and unique features in India.

Notes

1. http://www.rnrmarketresearch.com/indias-cards-and-payments-industry-emerging-opportunities-trends-size-drivers-strategies-products-and-competitive-landscape-market-report.html.
2. http://search.worldbank.org/data?qterm=enforcing%20contract&language=EN.
3. The National Consumer Disputes Redressal Commission does this in India. Available from: http://ncdrc.nic.in/.
4. http://www.silf.org.in/16/Indian-Judicial-System.htm.
5. http://www.telegraph.co.uk/news/worldnews/1561973/Mobile-court-bus-visits-Indias-rural-poor.html.
6. http://www.hindu.com/2007/08/05/stories/2007080560301200.htm.
7. *The Economic Times* (20 September 2012). FDI in multi-brand retail comes into effect; way clear for Walmart.

8. The Global Retail Development Index™: lessons learned from a decade of retail expansion, http://www.atkearney.com/index.php/Publications/grdi-a-10-year-retrospective.html.
9. The Lord's cricket ground is considered the Mecca of cricket.
10. *http://en.wikipedia.org/wiki/Twenty20* [accessed 25 September 2012].
11. Zee Telefilms Ltd. had filed the case against the BCCI arguing that it was a governmental organization subject to provisions of Article 12 of the Indian Constitution (see court judgment in Hegde, 2005).
12. *http://en.wikipedia.org/wiki/TEN_Sports* [accessed 25 September 2012].
13. *http://www.indianpremierleaguevsindiancricketleague.com/2007/12/war-of-words-kapil-dev.html* [accessed 3 December 2010].
14. http://www.studymode.com/essays/Indian-Premier-League-677157.html.
15. *http://sports.indiainfo.com/2008/02/27/0802271443_sport_icl.html* [accessed 17 December 2010].
16. *http://www.sport24.co.za/Cricket/Boards-to-blame-for-ICL-bans-20080905* [accessed 19 December 2010].
17. Cairns eventually won his libel suit against Lalit Modi who had tweeted in 2010 about Cairns being a match-fixer and was awarded damages of £90,000 in addition to costs of £1.5 million (Gardner, 2012).
18. aMap stands for Audience Measurement & Analytics Ltd., an overnight TV audience measurements system providing data on television in India.
19. http://www.business-standard.com/india/news/rebel-icl-improves-viewership-score/341030.
20. *http://en.wikipedia.org/wiki/World_Series_Cricket* [accessed 25 September 2012].
21. *http://en.wikipedia.org/wiki/World_Series_Cricket* [accessed 25 September 2012].
22. *http://en.wikipedia.org/wiki/World_Series_Cricket* [accessed 25 September 2012].

The macroeconomic context

"The outlook for the economy has improved, with export growth regaining momentum, but growth is still weak. The challenges of containing inflationary pressures limit what the monetary policy can do ... To maintain the momentum ... it is imperative that long-delayed legislative reforms are pushed through, stalled infrastructure project clearances continue and fiscal consolidation remains on track."

Dr. Raghuram Rajan, Governor, Reserve Bank of India, December 2013

India's economy has been going through a slump as a result of the recent global financial and economic crisis, and has experienced successive years of sub-5 percent growth, for the first time in the post-liberalization era and since an earlier such occurrence in the period between 1984 and 1988.[1] Raghuram Rajan, the new governor of India's central bank – the Reserve Bank of India (RBI) – who took office in September 2013, has been fighting the challenging battle of maintaining growth while curtailing inflation, and keeping the Indian rupee from losing value rapidly.[2] He has succeeded in making the Indian rupee stronger despite the turbulence created by the U.S. Federal Reserve's decision to cut bond purchases, which triggered tumbling currencies in other emerging markets, but not in India. However, that did not stop him from complaining at a recent G20 gathering, of which India is a part, about the breakdown in international monetary cooperation and the need for Western central banks to keep emerging economies in mind when making such decisions.[3] His skills and activism are critical during this phase of political transition, with the country having elected a new central government in April 2014. In this context of uncertainty, it is important to remain positive about India's economic future, what with uncertainty arising from several different sources. Rajan has highlighted the importance of political stability in the post-election period for this positivity to become reality, especially in the face of trends suggesting a hung parliament. Comfort can be taken in the knowledge that India has experienced increased political stability since the economic reforms and liberalization policies of the early 1990s. Despite its inefficiencies, the Indian democratic juggernaut has run effectively and there is no reason to expect it to be any different this time around.

The economy of India is the tenth largest in the world by nominal GDP and the third largest by purchasing power parity (PPP), according to the International Monetary Fund (IMF). The per capita income situation, however, is not so glowing, with India ranked at 141st by nominal GDP and 130th by GDP in PPP terms. The rate of GDP growth for the year 2013–14 was a measly 4.9 percent, following the previous year's GDP growth of 5.0 percent. Two successive years of sub-5 percent growth has not happened since the reforms of the early 1990s and one has to go back to the 1984–8 period to see such an occurrence. That India's economic growth is going through a tough phase, as elsewhere, is therefore not exactly unexpected. However, economists at the World Bank, among others, express confidence in the fundamental strengths in the Indian economy. Thus, as stated earlier (Chapter 1), the long-term prospects for India are very bright. Figures 3.1–3.5 provide basic information on the country's recent and historic rates of GDP growth, inflation, and interest rates.

In a series of reports, Goldman Sachs has cited India as having the potential to become one of the largest economies in the world by 2050. Additionally, although the other BRIC countries are likely to slow down in the latter part of the period leading up to 2050, India alone is likely to grow at better than 5 percent over the entire period. India's demographic factors, relative to the other BRIC nations, with continued population expected to grow for 50 years and continued increase in the proportion of

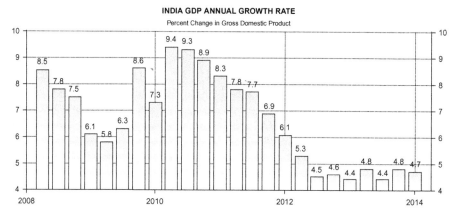

Figure 3.1 GDP growth rate in recent years
Source: http://www.tradingeconomics.com/india/gdp-growth-annual

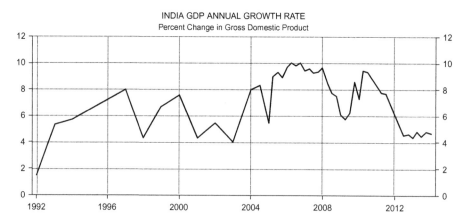

Figure 3.2 GDP growth rate since economic liberalization
Source: http://www.tradingeconomics.com/india/gdp-growth-annual

Figure 3.3 Inflation rates in recent years
Source: http://www.tradingeconomics.com/india/gdp-growth-annual

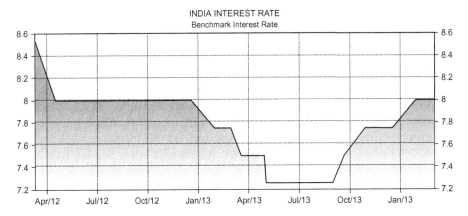

Figure 3.4 Interest rates in recent years

working age people, are likely to be the main underlying reasons. Some of the factors that have contributed to India's growth in recent years, according to leading economists, are (1) its increased level of openness as a result of liberalization, (2) better resource allocation as a result of growth in the financial sector, (3) success of India's information technology (IT) and information technology–enabled services (ITES) industries, (4) significant improvements in physical infrastructure such as the Golden Quadrilateral project, and (5) rapid urbanization (Goldman Sachs, 2007).

Still, to achieve the full potential growth rate, which these economists[4] rate to be very high for India, the need for governance overhaul as one among many imperatives is underlined. Whether or not this will happen with a new government in place in 2014 is anybody's guess. The Indian political atmosphere is stable and consensus oriented and at the same time cacophonous and fractious (country of contrasts). The political

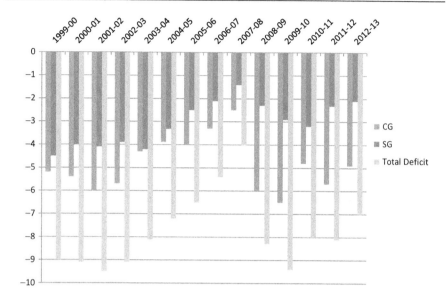

Figure 3.5 Fiscal deficit in India (CG = central government; SG = state governments)
Source: Based on data from the Planning Commission of India.

will of the new government to push ahead with more serious reforms will determine the extent to which India is able to achieve its full potential. One of the more basic requirements that many economists highlight as vital is development of the physical infrastructure in the country. Although the Golden Quadrilateral project connected the four corners of India, bringing together the four largest metropolitan areas, this is but the beginning for a country with a dismal infrastructure. Services (56.9 percent) contribute more to India's GDP than from either manufacturing (25.8 percent) or agriculture (17.4 percent). In the minds of some experts, the country and its policies have bypassed its manufacturing potential, leaving it unrealized. Just as the country's intellectual capital strength has been achieved with disproportionate investment in higher education v. basic literacy programs, there has been disproportionate encouragement of the service (read IT and ITES) sector at the expense of the manufacturing sector. This needs to be addressed fairly quickly for the country to achieve its full growth potential. Thus, addressing basic literacy and education issues along with pushing the reform process to its logical end, while addressing inflation and currency strength issues, will ensure India is well on its way to achieving its potential. But, looking back over the last six to seven decades since independence from Britain, India has made remarkable progress.

Path from mixed economy to liberalized capitalism

For much of its history since independence, India has remained a secluded and closed economy, with an overbearing presence of the state in economic activity. The mixed economy was based on a combination of capitalism and socialism, but with heavy emphasis on import substitution and self-dependence. Many state-run public sector organizations, the largest employers in the country, were involved in the manufacture and sale of products such as aircraft (Hindustan Aeronautics Ltd., HAL), earth-moving equipment (Bharat Earth Movers Ltd., BEML), heavy electrical goods (e.g., Bharat Heavy Electricals Ltd., BHEL), and electronics (e.g., Bharat Electronics Ltd., BEL), to name a few. In addition, the production and distribution of electricity (e.g., National Thermal Power Corporation Ltd., NTPC) and oil and gas (e.g., Oil and Natural Gas Corporation of India, ONGC) were entirely dominated by the public sector. Even in transportation and services, Indian Railways, Air India, and Indian Airlines exerted monopolistic power. The airwaves were also dominated by the government with state-run television and radio broadcasting. The dominance of the public sector was so large that the typical Indian, at this time, was either a farmer or was employed by the government in one form or another. The size of the private sector was small and insignificant during much of this period, in addition to being heavily regulated. All this was to change drastically with the onset of liberalization and privatization that began in the early 1990s. The current growth and activism of the private sector is one of the factors that fuel economic reports highlighting India's amazing potential. However, between 1947 and 1991, economic growth rates in India were so low that economists referred to it derisively as the Hindu rate of growth. Many of these policies were fueled by the socialist inspiration of the Soviet Union and the negative exposure (perceived exploitation) to British policies before independence. With the collapse of the Soviet Union in 1989, India's then largest trading partner was lost. Turbulence in the oil market[5] caused a serious balance-of-payments crisis in India, which eventually led to the initiation of liberalization and privatization, as required by the IMF in return for a bailout package.

Towards a free market economy

India is one of the fastest growing economies in the world. This is mainly as a result of the initiation of deregulation in the economy through a series of initiatives to liberalize and privatize the economy. Deregulation of the economy served first to dismantle the Licence Raj, a system of strict governmental controls on setting up new industries, and removed import substitution policies, thereby allowing FDI in many sectors and opening the economy up to MNCs. These reforms, which touched all major sectors of the economy, gradually removed many restrictions and controls. Although many political forces still continue to slow this process of allowing FDI in certain sectors of the economy (e.g., financial services), the latest example, albeit contentious, of removing restrictions on FDI came in the single and multi-brand retail sector, as reported earlier. The government also gave statutory powers to the Securities and Exchange Board of India (SEBI), which was set up in 1988 to monitor and regulate the activities of the stock exchanges and accounts of registered companies. In the financial services sector, private banks were allowed to operate for the first time alongside nationalized banks such as the State Bank of India (SBI). Banks in India had been nationalized in the

1970s and served as an instrument of the government, but today continue to serve the entire country, regardless of market size considerations that would normally prevent private players from entering certain geographies. Another thing that happened in the 1970s, which has been reversed with the onset of these reforms, was the exit of many MNCs from India such as IBM and Coca-Cola. These and many other MNCs are back in India today as a result of the reform process that started in the 1990s and continues to move forward today. These reforms also led to a continual decrease in trade barriers and tariffs, in addition to a more active engagement with the World Trade Organization (WTO).

A major component of the economic reforms was the privatization of public sector firms and the dismantling of poorly performing public sector businesses. The airline industry, for example, has been completely deregulated and a number of private companies now operate in this booming sector, which compensates to a certain extent for the otherwise poor infrastructure. Today, people are even calling for the public carrier Air India to be privatized. Relaxing FDI restrictions further in the airline sector continues to be debated in parliament and many external observers are calling for this to be accelerated.[6] In 2012 the government already approved up to 49 percent ownership for foreign airlines in Indian carriers. As a part of these reforms, private companies, domestic or foreign, have been encouraged to invest in many sectors that were traditionally reserved for the public sector. Among other consequences, this resulted in the media industry dramatically expanding, with hundreds of TV channel and radio station operators entering the market, and today constitutes a very competitive and vibrant market. All of a sudden, people who were stuck with one or two TV channels and only a few radio stations were now able to watch and listen to literally thousands of programming options, which provided a significant boost to consumer markets and marketing. The media explosion also resulted in the growth of regional language newspapers and print media, which suffered previously from numerous import restrictions for machinery and technology. Thus, people from all walks of life have become included in the consumer boom as a result of these economic reforms.

Benefits of the reforms

These reforms resulted in higher average GDP growth rates than before, as can be seen in Figure 3.2. Although these relatively large-scale reforms were initiated in the early 1990s, several piecemeal reform measures were launched even earlier. For example, the Japanese company Suzuki entered into a 50:50 joint venture with the Indian government in 1981 to produce automobiles for the Indian market. This company has now been completely privatized after the gradual rollout of large-scale reforms. Another example of MNC involvement in India in the 1980s was the entry of Japanese motorcycle manufacturers such as Honda, Kawasaki, Yamaha, and Suzuki in the form of strategic alliances. All these players now have wholly owned subsidiaries in the country. Thus, the overall economic reform process has been very gradually rolled out over a long period of time, with the general support of different political parties or coalition governments that have been in power the past 30 years or so. This underlines stability in the political arena associated with the reform process, without which it would have been impossible.

India has made considerable progress towards a free market economy as a result of continuing reforms and has brought about substantial reduction in state control of the economy. These reforms and the accompanying financial liberalization have also produced increases in life expectancy, literacy rate, poverty levels, and food security, although these benefits have accrued more in urban than rural populations. India's credit rating (by Moody's and S&P) has been at the investment level since the economic reforms, despite being at its lowest grade in the most recent evaluation.[7] Public opinion in India has been strongly in favor of initial reforms and their continuation as reflected by voting patterns in parliamentary elections following reforms.

Inflation

Although India has not been subject to dramatic increases in inflation rates over the years, many of those who predict a very high potential for India's growth also note that it is important for India to control inflation in an effort to achieve higher levels of macroeconomic stability. Figure 3.3 shows that inflation has ranged from 9 to 11 percent in recent times and has shown a decrease since the measures initiated by Rajan. The appointment of Rajan came in the wake of discord between the Ministry of Finance and the previous governor of the RBI over this precise issue (i.e., priority of growth over inflation-curtailing measures). Goldman Sachs, among others, would like to see more independence for India's Central Bank in this domain. Leading economists also argue that India can only realize its amazing potential when it is able to master the art of getting inflation down to single digits and even then within the 5 percent threshold. Officially, India has traditionally used the Wholesale Price Index for measuring inflation, while the rest of the world uses the Consumer Price Index (CPI), which in India is not credible as a result of the poor information technology framework that exists. Another problem in targeting inflation is the large number of food products that constitute a typical CPI, but many of these prices are administered by the government. The obvious recommendation of free market economists is to do away with the mechanism of administering prices, which would be politically complicated, although not impossible, in India. For instance, while petrol prices had been freed from government control in June 2010, the Petroleum Ministry recently announced that diesel prices would also be deregulated in six months and allowed to move in tandem with open market prices.[8] It is important to note, however, that prices of essential (to the people) fuels like kerosene and liquid petroleum gas (LPG) are still subsidized by the government and all such deregulation would fall into disfavor with the voting public. The magnitude of these and other subsidies also poses a problem for India in terms of its fiscal deficit, which we turn to now.

Fiscal deficit in India

In the most recent union budget, India's Finance Minister announced spending cuts that would reduce the country's fiscal deficit to its lowest level in seven years, reducing it to 4.1 percent of GDP for 2014–15 from its current level of 4.6 percent. Although this demonstrates a commitment to reducing the fiscal deficit and to satisfying world investors, some warn that this may also curtail GDP growth.[9] Rating agencies and leading economists have been calling for a credible fiscal policy from India's government for quite some time and have highlighted the need for a strategic approach. Figure 3.5 shows that India's fiscal deficit over the years has been much higher than acceptable relative to other BRIC nations and even to the average of a larger sample of emerging markets (around 2 percent) (Goldman Sachs, 2008). India's central government subsidy on food, oil, and fertilizer is equivalent to the entire collection of income tax, the biggest factor contributing to fiscal deficits. Misdirected but populist expenditure measures by successive governments, focusing on wages and subsidies, rather than on growth-enhancing domains such as health, education, and infrastructure are at the root of this seemingly endless problem in India. Discipline by politicians combined with a fundamental and strategic approach to growth, inflation, and deficits are what India's future governments require. Thus, according to many experts, reducing agricultural subsidies should be the focus of the next major wave of reforms, without which the country's path to achieving full potential regarding growth will not be possible. A positive thing for India is the passing of the Fiscal Responsibility and Budget Management Act of India (FRBMA 2003) and its efforts to institutionalize financial discipline in an effort to improve macroeconomic stability. Although this legislation worked for a while, the IMF and many economists suggest the need for more legislation as a follow-up to this good work to create a more permanent institutional structure at both the central and state government levels.[10] These observations point to the importance of accounting for both budgeted and non-budgeted items in the projection and calculation of fiscal deficits. Several states in the country have already legislated fiscal responsibility acts (Karnataka, Kerala, Punjab, Maharashtra, Tamil Nadu, and Uttar Pradesh). The extension of such practices to the remaining state governments is also crucial for India to grow in a stable way. In Chapter 4 we provide more details on the peculiarities of the Indian political system by describing the devolution of authority from the central to state governments.

Main sectors of the economy

Much of the surge in FDI flowing into India can be attributed to the country's strengths in telecommunications, IT, auto components, chemicals, apparel, pharmaceuticals, and jewellery. Among the other main industries are steel, food processing, transportation equipment, cement, mining, and petroleum refining. Manufacturing accounts for about 26 percent of the nation's GDP and employs about 22 percent of the workforce in the country. Although manufacturing potential is high in the country, according to leading economists at the World Bank the priorities of previous national governments have been aimed at growth of the IT services industry, the result of which has been failure to reach this potential. Many global auto majors have manufacturing operations in India, as previously noted, both in the four-wheeler and two-wheeler segments. The market for two-wheelers is still much bigger than that for four-wheelers in the country. Several landmark acquisitions in international markets by the Tata Group of companies also highlight the strong manufacturing presence and potential of this sector within India. Additionally, textile manufacturing is the second largest employer after agriculture in India and accounts for more than 20 percent of manufacturing output in the country.

Agriculture accounts for about 17 percent of the nation's GDP but employs more than 50 percent of the workforce, thereby having a much larger sociocultural than socioeconomic significance. The increasing rapidity of urbanization and the migration of people to the manufacturing and service sectors has not kept pace with required levels for overall balance in labor productivity vis-à-vis the economic contribution of different sectors in the economy. Labor in India is four times more productive in industry and six times more productive in services than in agriculture. However, farm output in India ranks second in the world, and the significant green revolution that took place in the 1980s followed by the white revolution[11] have drastically improved both the economic and social fabric of life among people in these occupations. India is the largest producer of milk in the world and also leads in jute and pulses. India is also the world's second largest producer of rice, wheat, sugarcane, cotton, groundnuts, cattle, and silk. Although enormous progress has been made in the agricultural sector, much more is still possible to improve the lives of farmers and rural populations, which will only serve to enhance the long-term growth prospects of the country. More details on rural markets and consumers and their role in the country's economy are given in Chapter 5.

The rapidly growing services sector contributes about 57 percent of the nation's GDP but employs only 27 percent of the country's workforce. Information technology and business process outsourcing constitute a significant part of the service sector and increasingly provide India with a unique source of competitive advantage. An increasing proportion of the country's exports comes from the IT service sector. The availability of a low-cost, high-skilled, English-speaking workforce is one of the main drivers of service sector competitiveness. Moreover, seven Indian companies are listed in the world's top 15 companies for IT outsourcing.[12] Additionally, the availability of low-cost, good (international) quality medical facilities and English-speaking doctors and service staff contribute to a rapidly growing (30 percent) medical tourism industry.[13] The most popular treatments medical tourists seek in India pertain to advanced medicine such as cardiac bypass, bone marrow transplants, and eye surgery in addition to alternative medicine in the form of traditional Indian medicines.[14]

The country boasts a strong banking and financial services system and ranks within the world top 30 according to several global competitiveness indices, as mentioned earlier. When Indira Gandhi was Prime Minister of the country, she nationalized around 20 banks and mandated them to take on social developmental goals such as providing credit to agriculture, small business, retail trade, and small-scale industry. This helped growth in the number of bank branches in the country from 8260 in 1969 to around 72,170 in 2007, providing many small towns and villages with banking facilities. Rural branches alone increased from 1860 in 1969 to 30,590 in 2007. However, only 32,270 of 500,000 villages have a branch of one of these nationalized banks, leading to the incredible number of people without bank accounts mentioned earlier

(43.8 percent of the population). Significant reforms in public sector banks have been in the form of privatization, encouragement of mergers, reduced government intervention in their operations, and an increased profitability and competitiveness focus. Banking reforms have also allowed the entry of private banks and foreign banks, thereby allowing the sector to revitalize itself and reach global standards. Many voices are calling for further easing of restrictions in the form of a cap on FDI in the insurance and (non-banking) financial services sector, which currently stands at 26 percent.[15]

The informal economy

There is wide consensus that India's informal economy may be the largest in the world and the most difficult to estimate. Whereas informal economies exist in all countries and may range from 0.8 percent of GDP in the U.S.A. to more than 50 percent in sub-Saharan Africa, India's informal economy is half of the whole economy and could lead to severe underestimation of the country's GDP. Some analysts call this "India's better half".[16] Although it is well known that the size of the informal economy is quite high in emerging markets, India's informal economy is higher than that of most emerging markets. Given India's size, it has to be the largest in the world. This is a serious structural problem in that informal economic activity does not pay taxes, does not have access to credit, the workers in this sector lack the protection of labor laws, there is little respect for intellectual property, and there is disincentive for the formal sector to innovate. However, it is also true that GDP estimates are significantly underestimated as a result of this, which when fully accounted for may well improve India's economic health assessments. Several indicators such as the level of current account deficits (CADs) and fiscal deficit as a proportion of GDP begin to look much more favorable once the informal economy is accounted for. Additionally, the size and nature of this informal economy also serves to provide India with more economic stability than normally perceived and lower quarterly variations in GDP than most countries. However, many experts suggest that India's economy is like no other and that estimating the size and impact of the informal economy is a complex and difficult task. Techniques that serve reasonably well in other economies – measuring demand for electricity consumption or measuring demand for currency – are non-starters in India as a result of low electrification and the incredible number of people without a bank account.

Economic activity by unincorporated enterprises is called informal and includes examples such as the neighborhood barber, pushcart vendors of fruit and vegetables, service providers such as plumbers and electricians, domestic help, and numerous retail establishments such as stores, restaurants, etc. Most MNC managers from the West think of illegal activities when one mentions "informal or black economy", thinking of bootlegging, drugs, etc. However, as a result of having no choice in whether or not to incorporate one's business, most activity in the informal economy of India is a result of the lack of reach of governmental services. This is precisely why this is a structural problem of serious magnitude. The growth of organized retail is likely to alleviate this problem to a certain extent. This provides plenty of opportunity for MNCs to develop business proposals that would convert informal economic activity and its workers to the formal sector. This would have appeal to the Indian government and would thus make it easy for approval, as long as the MNC in question can provide a "chaining" or "franchising" solution to any service business of choice. The rent-to-own business discussed earlier, a chain of restaurants, or even a chain of automobile services, etc. would help pool together local talent (workers) and provide real business opportunities that are simultaneously likely to help formalization. The number of different opportunity options are almost limitless. Large businesses engaging in these efforts would be able to satisfy the governmental need for tax collections, provide better (credible) balance sheets for raising capital and credit, provide labor law protection for workers, and by virtue of economies of scale create disincentives for not respecting intellectual property. As noted by a study conducted by analysts (Credit Suisse, 2013), governmental programs to bring basic services such as electric power to villages, power to individual households in these villages, building roads and improving connectivity to small towns and villages, increasing provision of LPG and small appliances, and increasing mobile telephone connectivity would all have virtuous cyclical effects on the economies in many parts of the country. These can serve the basic infrastructural needs of businesses engaged in creating a value proposition out of formalizing the economy.

Although the Indian economy has been getting less informal, largely as a result of the job switch from agriculture to services, the enormity of the problem makes it difficult to overcome in a short period of time. However, the presence of the informal economy as indicated by its size, extent of participation, numbers and types of transactions, numbers and types of workers, etc. is a good marker of the basic strength and stability of the overall economy. Increased taxes that would result from formalization of the informal economy would likely lower the higher-than-average tax rate in the formal sector, thereby providing a significant boost to further investment. As in any other economy, GDP in India is an estimate, based on hard data, added to which are estimates. However, the size of the informal economy, nearly as large as the formal one, is what makes the estimation task in India very difficult. It is for these reasons that this large informal economy is often overlooked in calculations of disposable income and purchasing power, much of which is hidden by people hoarding black money,[17] the total amount of which varies in estimates from several billion dollars to trillions of dollars. As noted earlier, the demand for currency, at a more basic level, is also difficult to estimate as a result of the lack of bank penetration. However, the estimated size of the informal economy indicates that the purchasing power of people, on average, is nearly twice as much as public estimates indicate. This should provide more confidence on the part of MNCs and their managers to take the plunge, enter Indian markets, and ride its rapids.

Overall, therefore, it can be concluded that actual GDP and income in India are significantly more than officially reported, thereby providing a good base for MNCs pondering market entry. Additionally, the long-term growth prospects and the potential to reach levels unimaginable elsewhere are very bright in India. The reform machine that was set in motion in the early 1990s continues to run its course, albeit slower than most would wish. These reforms continue to penetrate sectors that have been untouched previously, creating numerous business opportunities. Successive governments have not only shown commitment to maintain the course of reforms but also to take measures to maintain economic stability by aiming for growth while curtailing inflation, and keeping interest rates and deficits in check. Despite the problems posed by the informal economy for the government,[18] it provides plenty of reassurance and opportunities to businesses. The country's intellectual capital and high-quality, English-speaking labor force has served as a driver of the services revolution and provides India with competitive advantage. This also facilitates MNCs operating in the country to engage seamlessly in the challenging task of winning in the country's markets.

Notes

1. http://economictimes.indiatimes.com/opinion/mythili-bhusnurmath/whither-green-shoots-dismal-q3-gdp-numbers-have-scotched-hope-of-quick-recovery/articleshow/31306335.cms.
2. http://economictimes.indiatimes.com/markets/analysis/raghuram-rajan-wins-in-sydney-but-indian-markets-dont-care/articleshow/30965893.cms.
3. http://economictimes.indiatimes.com/markets/analysis/raghuram-rajan-wins-in-sydney-but-indian-markets-dont-care/articleshow/30965893.cms.
4. http://www.goldmansachs.com/our-thinking/archive/archive-pdfs/ten-things-india.pdf; and Goldman Sachs. Global Economics Paper No: 99, Dreaming with BRICs: The path to 2050, October 2003. http://www.gs.com/insight/research/reports/report6.html
5. India imports over 90 percent of its oil needs.
6. http://www.firstbiz.com/corporate/fdi-in-aviation-why-not-allow-foreign-airlines-to-fully-own-indian-carriers-44587.html.
7. http://www.livemint.com/Politics/DWjsj3xElRTNzyiyMYxL3N/Moodys-says-Indias-fiscal-deficit-target-may-hurt-GDP-grow.html.
8. http://www.thehindu.com/news/national/diesel-prices-to-be-deregulated-in-six-months-moily/article5371396.ece.
9. http://www.livemint.com/Politics/DWjsj3xElRTNzyiyMYxL3N/Moodys-says-Indias-fiscal-deficit-target-may-hurt-GDP-grow.html.
10. http://zeenews.india.com/home/india-s-fiscal-responsibility-legislation-should-be-reformed-imf_555740.html.
11. The white revolution turned India from a milk-deficient country into the world's largest producer of milk, even surpassing the U.S.
12. http://online.wsj.com/news/articles/SB124344190542659025?mg=reno64-wsj&url=http%3A%2F%2Fonline.wsj.com%2Farticle%2FSB124344190542659025.html#project%3DOUTSOURCING09%26articleTabs%3Dinteractive.
13. http://en.wikipedia.org/wiki/Medical_tourism_in_India.
14. http://timesofindia.indiatimes.com/city/chennai/-Chennai-High-City-gets-most-foreign-tourists-/articleshow/6442393.cms?referral=PM.
15. http://articles.economictimes.indiatimes.com/2013-08-06/news/41131984_1_fdi-inflows-foreign-direct-investment-insurance-sector.
16. http://www.credit-suisse.com/newsletter/doc/apac/aic2013/20130712_indiamkt.pdf.
17. http://en.wikipedia.org/wiki/Indian_black_money.
18. http://www.thehindubusinessline.com/opinion/columns/c-p-chandrasekhar/india-still-a-vast-informal-economy/article5282078.ece.

Political particularities in India

4

Having received permission from the Foreign Investment Promotion Board (FIPB) of India in April 2013, followed by a no objection certificate (NOC) in September 2013, AirAsia was making big plans for its low-cost entry into the Indian aviation market.[1] They were given a sudden jolt when, in an unprecedented move, the Directorate General of Civil Aviation (DGCA) made the waters murky by seeking fresh objections to the granting of an air operator permit (AOP) to AirAsia, if any existed, from the public on 20 January 2014.[2] Whereas AirAsia, a joint venture between the Malaysian company (49 percent owner) of the same name, Tata Sons (30 percent), and another investor from India (21 percent),[3] was planning to launch operations in February 2014, this move by the DGCA put a spanner in the works of such intentions, delaying any such launch. The Civil Aviation Ministry announced that it wanted to be more careful in such procedures, as the government was under heightened scrutiny from various quarters and sought strict observance of the rules. However, it is seen as unprecedented because the company had gone through a two-month waiting period for the same purpose the previous year before obtaining an NOC from the ministry. Although the DGCA eventually dismissed all the objections on 26 February 2014[4] and cleared the way for an AOP to be granted to AirAsia, it must have been a heart-stopping roller coaster ride for the protagonists investing $50 million in the sector. A top official at the Civil Aviation Ministry said: "No one wants competition, so there is this opposition from other airlines." In addition to objections from competitors, in the form of the Federation of Indian Airlines (FIA), a senior opposition leader from the Bharatiya Janata Party (BJP) had also objected to the granting of a license to AirAsia.[5] The grounds for this objection were that the government had cleared FDI in the aviation sector for multinational corporations (MNCs) to invest in existing Indian air carriers and not for a greenfield venture such as AirAsia India. The BJP leader had also filed a lawsuit in the Delhi High Court questioning the approval of FDI for this company. The competitors (FIA), much as happens anywhere else, were engaging in all manner of tactics to derail or delay a new player from entering the market. One can only imagine the behind-the-scenes political tactics and maneuvers involved in this struggle for a share of the airline market in India.

In an interesting twist to the story, one of the existing rules in the sector has been labeled as "nonsensical" by AirAsia's CEO Tony Fernandes.[6] He says,

> "These are bizarre rules . . . that you can't fly abroad before five years and (have at least a) 20 aircraft (fleet). That rule makes no sense. It is a negative for the Indian airlines. I, as a one-plane airline in Malaysia, can fly to India. India is the only country which has such a rule."

This pertains to rules that had limited the operational freedom of other Indian carriers in the past. This is especially important in an industry that has been struggling.

Doing Business in India.

The combined losses of Indian carriers amounted to $500 million a year as of September 2013.[7] This gloomy picture of the industry players explains some of the competitive objections raised by them.[8] The competitive scenario gets even more complicated when the decision of Tata Sons to sign a memorandum of understanding (MOU) with Singapore Airlines for the launch of a full service domestic airline is considered. One of the Indian joint venture partners of AirAsia claimed it was unethical and made without their knowledge.[9] Tony Fernandes, the CEO of AirAsia Group, however, reportedly had no problems with Tata Sons launching another airline in collaboration with Singapore Airlines, as he considered that to be a fundamentally different business model from his (ultra) low-cost airline.[10] Meanwhile, the FIA has decided to oppose the Tata–Singapore Airlines venture as well. "We are starved of capital. Banks are not lending to us. All odds are stacked against us. Obviously, the principles on which we opposed AirAsia India apply to Tata–SIA, too."[11] AirAsia has finally managed to clear the last hurdle and, as fully expected, launched its operations in May 2014.[12] The decision by the DGCA to dismiss all objections came after the Delhi High Court's decision to dismiss the senior BJP leader's petition. So, AirAsia India's actual operations may finally get off the ground, a full year and a half after Tata Sons announced their joint venture. In this time frame, Etihad Airways picked up a 24 percent stake in Jet Airways (India's leading carrier), Tata Sons announced a joint venture with Singapore Airlines, and Singapore's Tiger Airways announced its entry into this exciting market.[13] The political and competitive games are not quite over in this case and only time will tell what face the consolidated industry shows to the external world. However, what is clear is that winning in India's markets is tough and likely to be challenging both politically and competitively. Fortunately, AirAsia's case represents the challenges companies face when dealing with one government. In many other cases, MNCs entering India will face not only the central (federal) government, but also the governments of all the states in which they want to have operations.

Consider the case of Metro AG, which took advantage of the opportunity to enter the Indian market as a result of FDI restrictions in the wholesale (cash and carry) sector being relaxed. Metro AG is a Düsseldorf-based holding company formed through the 1996 merger of four giant German retailing groups. The company operates 2250 stores in 25 countries and employs almost a quarter of a million people. Metro concentrates on four core businesses: cash-and-carry wholesale outlets, retail food markets, consumer electronic stores and home improvement centers, and department stores. With strong price competition in the German marketplace, the company has aggressively pursued growth in foreign markets. The cash-and carry business accounts for 75 percent of foreign sales and is the company's most profitable division overall. India has potential for a large number of wholesale stores as the country has an estimated 12 million mom-and-pop outlets whose needs modern wholesalers can meet.[14] Metro was one of the first international retailers to open a wholesale (cash-and-carry) outlet in India in 2003. The central government subsequently (December 2012) made it possible for majority ownership by MNCs in multi-brand retail, but with some caveats. Under normal constitutional rules regarding the decentralization of authority, which we will see in more detail in what follows in this chapter, agriculture is subject to state level regulations rather than those at the federal (central) level. However, the central government made an exception in 2003 amending the Agricultural Produce Marketing Committee Act (APMC) to allow deregulation of trade in fruits and vegetables in the country, but left it up to the individual states for subsequent approval in their domain. Thus, although enacted into law by the federal (central) government, both the single-brand and multi-brand retail sectors in India will receive (accept) investments only after a multilayered legal and approval process. Only 16 of the states had amended their APMC act following the model bill provided by the central government.[15] In essence, while some (16) states will allow this investment, others will not. In Metro's case, they were prevented from buying fruit and vegetables directly from farmers in their first store in Bangalore (Karnataka) in 2013, as a result of the original (unamended) APMC act being in place. Although the state government of Karnataka had promised to amend the act to allow them the freedom to buy directly from farmers (a key piece of their business model), it was not forthcoming for various political reasons and local opposition from stakeholders. Under the original APMC, each of the state governments was tasked with establishing a local body to administer and control the market for fruit and vegetables, as well as establishing authorized agents as appropriate to engage in these transactions. Farmers were only allowed to sell their produce within this APMC mechanism, and thus Metro AG was not able to engage in an activity that was crucial for its business model to work. The model bill approved by the central government (in parliament) provides for freedom in this regard and deregulates these activities. However, it is the privilege of the states to rule on this subject, according to the system set up by India's constitution. In a nutshell, companies engaging in this business need to deal with each of the state governments separately in trying to seek approval for their efforts. Thus, although the first step is to seek clearance for FDI from the central government, that is only the beginning. Metro learned this lesson the hard way.

According to some reports, Metro has revamped its strategy and its business model in the country as a result of regulatory hurdles and other challenges. The company has been dragged into court in several regions for violation of the APMC act.[16] Most of the company's legal and regulatory problems in Karnataka and other states have been sorted out either through exemptions granted by the court on payment of a cess[17] or designating their stores as designated agents (*mandis*) in accordance with the APMC act. Only one of their stores in the Yeshwantpur area of Bangalore is still under dispute in court, with all other stores in the country cleared of these problems. According to one Metro spokesperson, "Over the last 10 years, a lot has changed. There is a lot more acceptability now, even from farmers. The government and people have come to realize that a company like Metro cannot pose a threat of a monopoly with the scale of business we have."[18] Handling other challenges has been a learning curve for the company, however. To create a more India-focused strategy, Metro Cash & Carry India Pvt. Ltd. (MCCIPL) has decided to tailor its offerings in India to what it calls "multi-specialization", a focus on fewer sectors, especially the fruit and vegetable sector. According to Eckhard Cordes, Metro AG's CEO,

"In the initial years, we merely transferred learning from other countries into the country, but later realized that we lacked local market understanding, which was very

India specific. Over the years we learnt about choices specific to this market and started to design a new store concept for the potential wholesale buyers. We also took to basic marketing initiatives to identify target customers and their buying behavior. The company has now narrowed down its customer segmentation and is setting up leaner stores. The new stores are two-thirds the size of existing ones and sell 9,000 items across food and non-food segments, just half of what the large stores sell."[19]

In essence, the company is moving from a generalist wholesaler to a multispecialist wholesaler, with fewer categories of stock-keeping units (SKUs – a number identifying a specific unit of item in stock), thereby precisely targeting specific customer needs.[20] Armed with this new customized-to-India strategy, the company planned to open another 50 stores in five years, on par with its growth plans in China. Although Wal-Mart has an India sourcing strategy worth about $1.5 billion and plans store openings on a competitive level, Metro only sources products worth about €65 million for its global operations. India's potential for both retail and wholesale segments is quite clear, what with other players such as Carrefour S.A. of France and the U.K.'s Tesco also in the fray. All of these businesses, however, have to deal with the federalist administration in the country, with its decentralized authority structure. The constitution clearly specifies the subjects (domains) that are under the control of the central government and those that are under the control of the state governments.

We now turn our attention to a description of these specificities in India, which are very different from most other countries in the world. It is very important for companies to have an understanding of the political and administrative setup of the country to be better prepared for what entry into India entails.

Parliamentary democracy in India

India is a parliamentary democracy, with the Prime Minister of the country as the head of the government. The President of the country is the official head of state but only has ceremonial powers in this system of parliamentary democracy. Whereas the Prime Minister is an elected member of the parliament, the President is not. The Prime Minister and the Council of Ministers run the central (national) government, while the Chief Minister and his or her Council of Ministers run the state governments. The President of India is elected indirectly, not by ordinary citizens, but by members of parliament (MPs) who are elected directly by the people of the country. Although the President mainly has ceremonial powers and only executes them through the Prime Minister and others on the Council of Ministers, it is the President who formally appoints the Prime Minister of the country. Under normal circumstances, when a party obtains a clear majority in the *Lok Sabha*,[21] presidential discretion is not called into use. However, as has often been the case in recent years, no single party or coalition of parties attains this required majority in the lower house. In such cases, the President uses his or her discretion and invites the head of the largest party to form the government, sometimes accompanied by the required demonstration of support through a subsequent vote of confidence in parliament. When this confidence vote fails, the President has the power to dissolve the government.

The Prime Minister and his or her Council of Ministers have to be MPs and should have the support of the majority in the *Lok Sabha*. As head of the Council of Ministers, the Prime Minister becomes the most important functionary of the government in the country. Typically, the party that has obtained the majority of seats in parliamentary elections chooses (elects) a person to become the leader of the party in parliament and hence as Prime Minister. Typically, this person is politically the most powerful within the party that has obtained the majority vote. It is the Prime Minister who forms the Cabinet of Ministers, following party traditions. At the state level, the Chief Minister and his or her Council of Ministers are elected members of the legislative assembly (MLAs) and are required to have majority support in the assembly. The Governor of the state has the powers to appoint the Chief Minister, sometimes based on use of discretionary powers, as the situation demands. The Governor of a state is appointed by the President based on the advice of the Council of Ministers. Recent years in India have seen the growth in popularity of regional parties at the expense of national parties, resulting in the dominance of coalition politics. Coalitions of parties obtain majority support under these circumstances, instead of a single party, and thus the voices of a multitude of interest groups (regional, ideological, linguistic, cultural, etc.) have gained prominence.

In addition to the central government's *Lok Sabha*, there is also the *Rajya Sabha* (Council of States), the upper house of parliament. The upper house consists of 12 representatives who are nominated by the President and typically includes people who have distinguished themselves in the service of the country in their chosen profession. Cricket star Sachin Tendulkar, who has the respect of the entire country, is an example of one such individual nominated to this upper house of parliament. The rest of the 250-strong house are elected by the state and territorial legislatures. The two houses of parliament have combined responsibility for the legislative functions of the country.

Federalism in India

The two houses of the Indian parliament recently approved the creation of the 29th state by dividing the state of Andhra Pradesh into Telengana and Seemandhra. These states officially came into existence on 2 June 2014. The practice of redrawing state boundaries is not new and has precedence in the last 60 years or more. India epitomizes the concept of unity in diversity, a value it instills in its young people right from a very young age. Despite the failure of many similar multilingual federations, such as the U.S.S.R., Czechoslovakia, and Yugoslavia, the federation of Indian states has successfully worked and lived together for a long time and will continue to do so. One of the reasons for this success is the concept of federalism embedded in the Indian constitution and guaranteed by it. India and the people in the country are committed to values of democracy and regional autonomy. Regional autonomy is essential in a country where more than 20 major languages are spoken in addition to several hundred minor ones. India is often referred to as a subcontinent by virtue of the immense regional, religious, and linguistic diversity it possesses. Millions of indigenous people occupy different parts of the country and it is the home and breeding ground for several major religions of the world. Despite all this diversity, people are united in that they fought a common war against the British for independence and desire to remain united as a result of a vast shared history. At the time of independence from the British in 1947, India was not only divided into provinces created by the British, but there were also 500 princely states that were only indirectly ruled by the British, all of which needed to be integrated into a single whole.

The creators of the Indian constitution were aware of the importance of the necessity to divide powers between the provinces and central government. They were also aware of the need to formally recognize the regional and linguistic diversity that exists in the country. The overriding principle was that people in different regions, speaking different languages, had to share powers and work together in a spirit of cooperation, within the system of self-governance (regional autonomy) to be established. Federalism in India is an institutional mechanism to provide for the existence of two polities – one at the state level and another at the national level. Unlike some other federal systems, India does not have a system of dual citizenship – all people are Indians, regardless of the state in which they were born. However, every Indian has two identities, one pertaining to the state in which they were born and the other of being an Indian national. For example, the author considers himself an Indian and a Tamilian (from the state of Tamilnadu). Which of the two identities is more important for any one individual, however, has often been an issue in the past in several instances, especially with the presence of a critical mass of people with similar priorities in identities. There have been several rebellious movements in India, where people have called for a separate nation state (Khalistan in Punjab is an example from the 1980s) based on the predominance of views that influence people in a region. The Khalistan movement resulted in the assassination of the then Prime Minister Indira Gandhi. Several other such movements still exist today in India, with varying degrees of activism. One solution to this problem is to provide for a redrawing of state boundaries, as appropriate, based on a study of local concerns in different parts of the country. Parliamentary approval for the new state of Telengana, alluded to earlier, is in fact quite consistent with the report of a commission charged with studying the issue in the 1950s. This commission stopped short of dividing the state of Andhra Pradesh into two at that time to give the various local bodies a chance to try their hand at cooperation. Given serious levels of ongoing dissidence, recent efforts to divide the state into two have been presented as parliamentary bills and subsequently approved, although not without opposition.

The constitution of India spells out the distinct powers and responsibilities of each level of polity (i.e., center and state) and its system of government. Some issues such as defense or currency, which concern the whole country, are the responsibility of the Union or central government. Other issues such as public health or agriculture are the responsibility of the respective state governments. Figure 4.1 provides a summary description of the rights and privileges of the central v. state governments in the country.

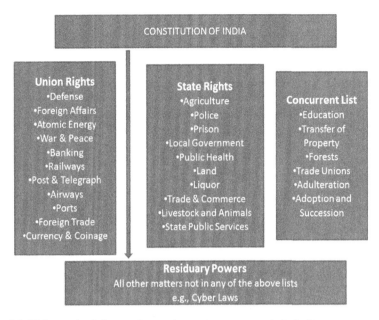

Figure 4.1 Rights and privileges of central v. state governments in India

As shown in Figure 4.1, economic and financial powers are responsibilities of the central government. Although the states have immense responsibilities, they have meager revenue resources. The constitution was framed this way to ensure a strong central government that would accommodate diversity, stem disintegration, and facilitate social and political change. The states are mainly dependent on the center for grants and financial assistance. The very existence of a state is in the hands of parliament at the central government. Parliament has the power to form a new state by separating the territory of a state or by uniting two or more states. At the center of parliament are the two houses containing representatives from all the states and union territories in the country, ensuring that decisions are made with inputs and votes from all concerned. Remember that all such decisions are subject to judicial review as noted earlier, to ensure that they do not violate the basic principles set out in the constitution. The executive powers of the center are superior to the executive powers of the state and the center may at times legislate on matters on the state list. But the constitution lays down specific procedures to be followed for this to be carried out by the central government. Amendment of the APMC act, alluded to earlier, is an example of something on the state list that was legislated by the center, which resulted in instructions being given to the states to carry them out as appropriate within their territory. In extreme cases, the constitution provides for emergency provisions to the central government. Once an emergency is declared, the central government can become a highly centralized power and the sole source of authority in India. During an emergency, power becomes lawfully centralized and the center assumes the power to make laws on subjects that are normally within the jurisdiction of the states. Such an occurrence happened in June 1975 when the central government invoked article 352 of the constitution (severe threat of internal disturbance) to declare an emergency, which lasted until January 1977. Under a state of emergency, the central government has the power to curtail or restrict any or all of the fundamental rights granted by the constitution, including restricting freedom of speech and making arrests without having to show cause. This bitter experience, which lasted 18 months, subsequently led to the removal of ambiguities in the interpretation of the original constitution. Now, an emergency can only be declared for internal disturbance reasons in the case of an armed rebellion, which was not the case in 1975. Two important conclusions can be drawn from this experience. First, the constitution provides for superior power at the center than at the state. Second, the constitution is a living document that is amended from time to time to address current concerns that could not have been foreseen at the time it was initially drafted.

At the time of independence, having decided that India should have a federal system of government, the consensus among leaders was that states should be created on the basis of linguistic and cultural identity. The States Reorganization Commission (SRC) was set up in 1954, which conducted in-depth studies into the needs and demands of various regions of the country. The SRC's eventual recommendation of creating states along linguistic lines reflected public consensus. Some states were reorganized in 1956, which began a process that is still continuing, with the most recent instance being the creation of the state of Telengana. Gujarat and Maharashtra were created in 1960 as a result of Gujarati and Marathi, respectively, being the major languages in these two states. Punjab (Punjabi) and Haryana (Haryanvi) were separated from each other in 1966. The northeast region was later reorganized to create the states of Meghalaya, Arunachal Pradesh, and Mizoram. In the 1990s, the reorganization of states moved away from linguistic lines and focused more on administrative efficiency and responses to local needs concerning development. Thus, Bihar, Uttar Pradesh, and Madhya Pradesh were divided to create three new states in Jharkhand, Uttaranchal (see the public relations campaign image in Figure 4.2), and Chattisgarh. It is illustrative to briefly study the case of the creation of Telengana[22] to understand how political, cultural, ideological, and historical forces play a role in creating the trust and mutual respect necessary to ensure smooth and cooperative relations between the center and the states. For businesses, especially MNCs and their managers, this will help provide an understanding of the unique political scenario in India. Such an understanding can also help foresee problems that are brewing in different regions and could ultimately impact the smooth operation of businesses. However, the hope is that readers will ultimately come away with a feeling that these processes, however flawed,[23] are fundamentally stable and based on sound democratic principles.

Despite the 1954 recommendation of the SRC to separate the two regions of Telangana and Seemandhra from each other, the central government led by Jawaharlal Nehru decided to keep these two regions together. According to the SRC report, "One of the principal causes of opposition of Vishalandhra (combined state of Andhra Pradesh) also seems to be the apprehension felt by the educationally backward people of Telangana that they may be swamped and exploited by the more advanced people of the coastal areas." To address these concerns, Nehru brokered a gentleman's

Figure 4.2 Public relations campaign material for the creation of Uttrakhand (aka Uttaranchal)

agreement between the leaders of the two sides. The agreement provided safeguards with the purpose of preventing discrimination against Telangana by the government of Andhra Pradesh. Alleged violations of this agreement are cited as one of the reasons for demands of separate statehood for Telangana.[24] Twelve years after the formation of Andhra Pradesh, there were complaints and the people of Telengana region expressed dissatisfaction over how the gentleman's agreement had been implemented.[25] Despite the best efforts of all political parties to reach an accord, several times over the course of four years, the movement became violent and the army had to be called in to control the situation.[26] Finally, in 1973, a political settlement was reached between the leaders of the two sides and the government of India, creating a six-point formula to address the sources of dissatisfaction. This was a dispute that was not fueled by linguistic differences but by political ones. Despite this six-point formula being legally sanctified by suitably amending the constitution, serious differences and problems continued to exist over the years leading to continued attempts by various groups to restate their claims for an independent state. Throughout this whole process, meanwhile, there have been continued attempts to appease the population of this region under the banner of a unified state.[27] On the other hand, however, dissidents from the Telangana region seem to have grown stronger over the years (in hindsight) with one of their publicity campaign messages summarizing the issues as follows:

"Telangana region is part of Andhra Pradesh state in southern India. It constitutes Hyderabad, Adilabad, Karimnagar, Khammam, Mahaboobnagar, Medak, Nalgonda, Nizamabad, Rangareddy and Warangal districts. Telangana region is one of the least

developed regions in India. Rampant poverty, illiteracy, malnourished children, child labor, farmer suicides, unemployment, water scarcity and electricity shortage are some of the problems of this region. There are millions of people who are not fortunate enough to send their children to schools or feed their children three times a day, or provide safe drinking water to their families in this area." [28]

After a very long battle, in February 2014 the two houses of parliament finally approved the creation of the new state of Telangana, separating it from coastal Andhra Pradesh. Despite it being unclear whether this is going to solve the on-the-ground issues faced by the millions of people in these regions, the new state officially came into existence on 2 June 2014. This decision has had a mixed reception with one side resorting to massive demonstrations and protests in one part of the unified state, while the other side was engaging in vociferous celebrations, highlighting the divisiveness of the issue. From a business standpoint, one consultant report noted, "the lack of political will that had kept the Telangana issue festering has rendered the business environment uncertain enough to deter fresh investments from corporates."[29] Whether or not this newborn clarity (removal of uncertainty by making the new state real and official) on the Telangana issue will lead to a change in the investment scenario remains to be seen. The city of Hyderabad, which is now the capital of both states, created by the division of the larger one, has been the center of an IT revolution in recent decades with massive investments coming in from the likes of Microsoft and Google. If the problems noted by the Telangana movement are as serious as they have noted, the new leaders will probably try to attract new investment in basic infrastructure to bring about more even growth.

Business implications of federalism

One of the biggest implications of the federalist system of government in India for businesses is that states are free to attract investment, often in competition with one another, from foreign or domestic firms. Competing states often develop and create investment packages with tax and other benefits to woo investors. MNCs attracted by such efforts will have to deal with both the state and the central governments to facilitate their entry into India and then the state in question. Although companies like AirAsia deal mainly with the central government in the management of their operations, there are others like Metro AG (its Indian subsidiary) who are better placed to deal with multiple state governments, simply because they happen to operate in a sector that is the prerogative of state governments. If you are the manager of a liquor[30] business such as SAB Miller, you will be dealing with a highly fragmented market because of the diversity of rules and regulations in the different states and the existence of different companies across the country. Some states in India are dry states and enforce prohibition even today. Additionally, MNCs need to be equipped with the skills necessary to work through multiple layers of bureaucracy and approval processes not only at the center but also in each of the states in which they plan to have locations, as appropriate. The question of appropriateness depends only on the list of subjects/domains shown in Figure 4.1 vis-à-vis the nature of the business the MNC brings in to the country. As adequately demonstrated in the case examples, it should be evident that MNCs also need to equip themselves with the necessary skills to collaboratively manage the needs and issues of the multiple stakeholders involved in such instances. Language issues should also not be forgotten. Most states were created on language lines. Although English is the official language of the central government and all the state governments in India, knowledge of the local language can always help. Additionally, although knowledge of Hindi (the *national* language) can help in some cases, there are likely to be many states in the country where it is not necessarily considered a local language. This adds a particular nuance to relationships where the deft use of language skills is a must. With the recent rise in power of the states (via regional political parties) at the center, India is perhaps becoming more decentralized than before. For MNCs not to acknowledge this diversity would be a critical mistake.

India has been a victim of negative public perception from outsiders for a long time, especially from those who lack knowledge of the country and its functioning. As noted earlier, despite technological advances and the resulting progress made on this front, it is still seen as a factor-driven economy. Similarly, corruption indices developed by different global organizations are also subject to these perceptual biases. One big contributor to this perception is the lack of understanding of the federalist system of government in the country. Thus, when an MNC is made to jump through several hoops as a result of this system of administration, it is very easy to perceive this as a devise for demanding bribes. Although, no one would deny that corruption is a serious problem in the country, it should be remembered that this problem is blown up out of all proportion in some cases. Nevertheless, an understanding of the federalist system of government should facilitate the smooth flow of the various required regulatory processes for MNCs and their managers. Furthermore, India is truly the epitome of unity in diversity, thereby representing a range of voices so different from one another that it can be overwhelming to the uninformed observer. Hopefully this chapter has enabled you to demystify some of these complexities.

Notes

1. http://indianexpress.com/article/business/companies/airasia-offers-half-a-million-free-tickets-on-select-routes/.
2. http://archive.indianexpress.com/news/dgca-seeks-fresh-public-objections-after-clearing-airasia-for-takeoff/1218442.
3. http://indianexpress.com/article/business/business-others/airasia-indias-tony-fernandes-softens-tata-sons-singapore-airlines-deal-stand/.
4. http://www.business-standard.com/article/companies/airasia-set-for-takeoff-114022100637_1.html.
5. http://timesofindia.indiatimes.com/business/india-business/Swamy-opposes-licence-to-Tata-AirAsia-LCC/articleshow/30072774.cms.
6. http://indianexpress.com/article/news-archive/web/airasia-chief-tony-fernandes-india-has-bizarre-rules/.

7. http://www.thehindu.com/news/cities/chennai/air-asia-to-begin-country-ops-in-may/
   article5754275.ece.
8. http://www.financialexpress.com/news/fia-writes-to-pm-manmohan-singh-to-hold-
   permit-for-airasia-india-launch/1232002.
9. http://www.financialexpress.com/news/singapore-airlines-deal-airasia-india-director-
   accuses-tata-group-of-being-unethical/1172249.
10. http://indianexpress.com/article/business/business-others/airasia-indias-tony-fernandes-
    softens-tata-sons-singapore-airlines-deal-stand/.
11. http://www.business-standard.com/article/companies/airasia-set-for-takeoff-
    114022100637_1.html.
12. http://timesofindia.indiatimes.com/business/india-business/DGCA-examining-AirAsia-
    Indias-application-for-flying-permit/articleshow/31055453.cms.
13. http://archive.indianexpress.com/news/after-airasia-tiger-airways-eyes-tieup-with-indian-
    carrier/1084034/.
14. http://www.fashionunited.in/news/apparel/metro-ag-to-open-50-stores-280220111736.
15. http://timesofindia.indiatimes.com/city/delhi/Amendment-to-APMC-Act-holds-key-to-
    taming-veggie-prices/articleshow/28256717.cms.
16. http://www.business-standard.com/article/companies/metro-cash-carry-revamps-india-
    strategy-113102400942_1.html.
17. A cess is a tax for some special administrative expense.
18. http://www.livemint.com/Companies/eoYH6bOHHolVTM04FleVfN/Metro-to-open-50-
    wholesale-stores-in-next-five-years-in-Indi.html.
19. http://articles.economictimes.indiatimes.com/2011–02–14/news/28540283_1_stores-
    business-model-india.
20. http://www.business-standard.com/article/companies/metro-cash-carry-revamps-india-
    strategy-113102400942_1.html.
21. The *Lok Sabha* (House of the People) is the lower house of the Parliament of India.
22. http://www.hindustantimes.com/india-news/telanganathetroubledstate/parliament-
    adjourned-till-noon-over-telangana-issue/article1-1185194.aspx.
23. http://www.thehindu.com/opinion/lead/small-states-big-problems/article5774395.ece?
    homepage=true.
24. http://www.livemint.com/Opinion/90RgTMq51N5NEh1X2jJJZL/The-politics-of-
    Telangana.html.
25. http://en.wikipedia.org/wiki/Telangana_movement.
26. http://en.wikipedia.org/wiki/Telangana.
27. http://www.newindianexpress.com/states/andhra_pradesh/Jagan-Promises-to-Tour-
    Telangana-to-Campaign-for-AP/2014/02/03/article2034788.ece#.UxplLPldW7g.
28. http://www.telangana.com/.
29. http://www.deccanchronicle.com/node/105560.
30. In India the term liquor includes beer.

Profile of consumers and markets in India

> *"We are now easily confusing the things with what we need and what we want – It's true, if we work hard, we deserve nice things. But stuffing plenty of nice things which we really do not need deprive the other consumers from the things they require for their survival. Keeping four cars for four persons in the family is ultimately going to affect others and also more consumption of nation's resources like petrol etc. Our sense of entitlement can muddy the waters when it comes to what you want and what you really need. The sizes of our houses are expanding as per our income and resources irrespective of the fact what we had in olden days. People were having more kids but still living in houses far smaller than we're willing to settle for today. Now, we want a room for every child, plus a living room, family room, media room, and kids' playroom. And if we have to share a television, we are very uncomfortable with the idea . . ."*
>
> **Consumer blog statement[1]**

Contrasting consumer values in India

The statements made in the consumer blog shown above reflect the changing cultural scenario in India and highlight the contrasts in cultural value involved in being part of the modern economy. As is evident, this particular consumer is struggling between the traditional Indian values of spiritualism and leading simple lives with modern values of materialism and consumerism. Incidentally, this is also reflective of a whole range of people in India who vary in their own values starting at the spiritual end and moving to the materialistic end of the spectrum. Thus, this is a market where multinational corporations (MNCs) are likely to find extremely spiritualistic individuals and households as well as those who are strongly materialistic. Instead of being just two types of individuals, this and all other contrasts shown in Table 5.1 should be considered as two ends of a large continuum. Thus, fine variations exist between one point and another on this value dimension among consumers in India. Approximately in the middle of the spectrum you will find those who are representative of the constant struggle between separating needs from wants and tending to think about broader philosophical implications v. those that do not engage in these thoughts. Table 5.1 shows a comprehensive set of dimensions that contrast Indian consumers as they vary from one end of the spectrum to the other.

Table 5.1 **Country of contrasts: consumers of varying colors**

Theme	Low end of spectrum	High end of spectrum
Philosophy of life	Spiritual	Consumerist/Materialistic
Family	Extended (joint) family	Nuclear family
Spending habits	Spendthrifts	Lavish spenders
Driver of purchasing behavior	Necessities	Desires/Shopping is fun
Technology	Low tech or no tech	High tech
Wealth/Income	Very poor	Very rich
Education	Illiterate	Highly educated and sophisticated
Role of women	Very traditional – homemakers	Very modern – key breadwinners
Location	Very rural	Metropolitan
Telephone connectivity	One mobile phone per household	One fixed phone and several mobile phones
Internet connectivity	None, even on mobile phone	Mostly through mobile devices
TV access	Only free state-run television channels	Complete range of satellite TV
Individual–group relations	Collectivists	Individualists

Before any description of the individual dimensions shown in Table 5.1, it should be noted that, although some of these dimensions could be interrelated, they are by and large independent of each other and the two columns shown in the table are not representative of any two specific customer segments in India. In other words, the focus here is on different dimensions and how consumers in India vary on each from one end of the spectrum to the other, with the range of variation being a very significant aspect for the marketer. This range of variation is consistent with the country-of-contrasts theme referred to repeatedly in this book. Although these dimensions could cluster together in different ways to form different segments, that is not the focus of any of the statements made here. Such clustering of dimensions into meaningful segments needs research and analysis, data on which are not available at the time of writing. The interested reader should consult the psychographic segmentation[2] reports of Indian consumers for this purpose.

Spiritualism v. materialism

For thousands of years, Indian culture has been dominated by spiritualistic values focusing on the overall well-being of individuals leading wholesome lives in the company of family members. Consumption is not a core value in this group, with any existing consumption serving the *needs* of the family as a collective unit rather than the individuals within. Today, for example, this could translate into the same motorcycle or car being used by anyone in the family at different points in time, with very little individual ownership attached to goods. This is essentially a focus on satisfying *needs* rather than on satisfying *wants*, presenting a space for the enterprising marketer to convert wants into needs. To present a simple example, the Indian government, and consequently most Indians, considered having a telephone or a television at home a luxury rather than a necessity for decades after independence from the British. Such a thought process also translated into a system of meaning and interpretation pertaining to a range of consumer durables and branded fast-moving consumer goods (FMCG) products. For instance, consumers and households at the spiritualistic end of the spectrum prided themselves on making various food products for domestic consumption at home rather than buying it from any vendors. These consumers also depended on low-tech and traditional options for the refrigeration, heating, and cooling needs of homes. As a result of economic reforms, however, the country has been going through rapid economic and social change, resulting in many spiritualists converting into materialists who value consumption for its own sake and value the possession of personal objects. At the very extreme, there are individuals who develop a unique sense of personal identity as a result of their consumption patterns and consider each of these items of consumption as an extension of their personality. Thus, owning a particular brand of motorcycle or a special brand of mobile phone is a unique part of individual identity among consumers in this materialistic group. For instance, today women go out with each other, spend time at clubs or with friends, pamper themselves at salons, try out experimental surgery, or enroll in fitness centers – a trend that was not previously seen. They are also much more into indulgence and satisfying their emotional selves.[3] Overall, then, there are people who fit into many different points on this broad continuum.

From "two faces of India" to many

The next and perhaps most important contrasting feature of the Indian consumer, and one that is used by many[4] to divide the Indian consumer market into two broad categories, is whether the consumer is rural or urban. This rural–urban distinction provides a two-sided description of Indian markets precisely because they are very different from one another. Unlike advanced economies, rural and urban areas in emerging economies are very different from one another. At one extreme, it is almost as if rural markets in emerging economies are isolated from the rest of the world by virtue of a lack of technological connectivity. In India, in particular, there is very low penetration of banks and financial services, very low levels (relatively speaking) of electrification of villages and households, very low levels of Internet/telephone/ utilities penetration, and very low penetration of mechanized farming or the use of technology. A city dweller could wake up in the morning and (1) watch the weather forecast on TV or through a mobile device to decide what to wear before stepping out, (2) use teleconnectivity to check on the traffic and decide what route to take to work or school, (3) stop at his or her preferred ATM to pick up some cash, (4) stop at a restaurant for breakfast, and (5) end the day (after work) by going to a sporting event or other choice of entertainment. These options are not available to a rural individual to help decide when to buy seeds, when to plant crops, when to irrigate, etc., let alone do things that are important to having a good work–life balance. These aspects of rural v. urban life are so distinct from each other that they create completely distinct consumption habits. Although recent reports suggest that this rural–urban distinction is blurring rapidly as a result of urbanization and as a result of bringing banks, electricity, Internet, phones, cooking gas, technology, road connectivity, and a host of other facilities that hitherto were the sole privilege of city dwellers, this is still a strong distinction by virtue of the structure of households and the importance of family in the lives of people in these two categories. In fact, instead of just two faces, what this rapid urbanization and connectivity-enhancing development in rural areas are bringing to India is growth in the number of more precisely defined segments of consumers on this dimension of very rural to very urban. The growth in tier 2 and tier 3 cities and towns has been very rapid in the last two decades, according to many reports. Thus, the "two faces of India" is no longer an apt description for the range of submarkets that exist in the country.

Extended v. nuclear families

As neatly captured in the consumer blog at the beginning of the chapter, traditional India differs very much from modern India with respect to the nature of the family. The technological and economic development of the last few decades has changed people's preferences from traditional extended families to increasingly nuclear families. In traditional India it is common for up to three generations of a family to live together under the same roof. The sense of collective is much higher in traditional India in this system of extended families. Individuals within such a system are open to sharing the owning of objects of consumption regardless of their monetary value or significance. The idea of "get your own bag" (from an advert for a famous brand of potato chips) would be anathema to people living in such a system. Thus, the prototypical traditional Indian (as noted in the consumer blog) would be more willing to share space in a smaller living arrangement and would not think twice about sharing a television or other consumer durable with others in the household. There are still many of these people around in India. Although they could be cast more in the rural mold than the urban, that would be stereotyping and inaccurate. Many families in urban areas live in these types of arrangements as long as they are not physically constrained by the size of their family vis-à-vis living space. Many others replace their original houses with ones having multiple, individual (semi-independent) units with different sons of the head of the family living in each of these units with their own nuclear families. This arrangement therefore creates an alternative to the extended v. nuclear family arrangements by creating a third (extended and nuclear) option. Others choose options such as locating close to other members of a previously extended family to maintain close ties while guaranteeing some level of independence. Thus, there is a range of options on this dimension of extended family to nuclear family, while conserving the basic Indian value of the family to varying degrees. There are also an increasing number of people in nuclear families compared with previous decades. The type of family has an obvious impact on consumption volumes and patterns as there is a shift from household to individual in some cases and a shift from a larger household to smaller ones in others.

Spending habits

The average Indian consumer is more price conscious than anywhere else in the world. Still, the range of consumers is wide – from spendthrifts to lavish spenders. Most consumer products are offered to Indian consumers at a wide range of retail price points as a result of the diversity of price segments in the Indian market. This diversity and hence range of price points is much wider than most MNC managers are used to in their home markets. One of the factors driving this type of competition among players is the price consciousness of people across the entire spectrum from the low end to the high. For instance, in the $35 billion a year apparel market in 2011, only $5.5 billion was sold in the organized sector. Branding, a key tool for marketers, is an imperative in the organized sector but non-existent in the unorganized sector. There is a marked difference in the range of price points offered in the organized v. unorganized sectors, mainly as a result of high levels of price consciousness among consumers. In the INR20 billion market for jeans, for instance, almost all global denim retail brands are attempting to ladder down the price pyramid in a bid to stay competitive and attract people away from the low-priced unbranded category. Levi Strauss, Lee, Pepe Jeans, and Wrangler are among the top brands that are discounting prices despite their premium positioning. This is also driven by tough competition from many lower priced local brands such as Reliance, Max, Big Bazaar, Flying Machine, Cambridge, Newport, and Buffalo. After a lukewarm response to its efforts at launching the Denizen brand for the mass market, Levi Strauss decided to focus once again on its premium and core brands rather than the mass market (Thakkar, 2013). Thus, even though most product markets can be segmented into three or four price segments, there is a similar range of price points, albeit at drastically lower levels, in the unorganized sector within the same product market in India. So MNCs and their marketers need to chart out a very clear strategy for their positioning right from the beginning to avoid loss of brand image and confusion among core customers. The reality is that the range of price points and hence the number of price-based segments in India is much larger than anywhere else in the world.

Driver of purchasing behavior

The overwhelming driver of purchasing behavior among Indians is the fulfillment of needs rather than wants. Still, there are those who flaunt their wealth and show off their material possessions, consuming mainly to fulfill desires and to enjoy the simple pleasures of shopping and purchasing. Consider for a moment the fact that the market for motorcycles is still much larger than the one for automobiles. The overall market for automobiles is dominated by two-wheelers (77 percent), followed by passenger vehicles (15 percent), commercial vehicles (4 percent), and three-wheelers (3 percent).[5] Automobiles are considered by many, although not all, a luxury good and not entirely necessary. Even among two-wheelers, the growth in the lower priced moped segment is significantly higher than in others. All of these are used as basic means of transport rather than as personal possessions by many, although there are an increasing number of people who create their sense of personal identity by what they drive. Daimler-Benz, for example, has a thriving business in India, a network of 31 dealerships, and 41 service stations across 31 cities in India, and experienced sales growth of 80 percent in 2010 over the previous year.[6] Almost 70 percent of the rapidly growing and large market for mobile phones is in the feature-phone segment rather than in the smartphone segment.[7] However, the smartphone segment is itself a huge $500 million market with upwards of 60 million users and rapidly growing.[8] Once again, this demonstrates the great range of purchasing behaviors and their drivers in India, relative to other markets. Marketers are increasingly succeeding at converting wants into needs, especially among the young in the population (pegged at around 600 million). Overall, there is room for a wide variety of companies in different consumer product markets for a large range of price–quality positioning points.

Technology preferences

Consumers in India vary greatly in terms of their technology preferences for the products they consume. Whereas the vast majority of people prefer no-technology or low-technology products to satisfy their daily needs, there are others that increasingly prefer higher levels of technology in their products and services. The size of the feature-phone market v. the smartphone market is also illustrative here to show the difference in preferences for technology. Although the world at large has moved on to 4G technology in mobile phones and devices, the largest market for mobile phones in India is still in 2G phones. However, 3G phones have been growing at record rates, nearly doubling in number sold each year in recent years. The rates of Internet penetration are also illustrative in this regard, suggesting that people take their time to think about using more technology in their lives. Turning to a different product market, that of washing machines, there are more indications of this pattern of technology preferences. The overall market for washing machines was about 4.7 million units in 2011. The size of the market in monetary terms was about INR5000 crores in 2013.[9] These numbers indicate the very low penetration of washing machines in a country of more than a billion people, not all of whom lack purchasing power. According to a 2013 research report only 8.8 percent of Indian households have a washing machine.[10] Instead, it is their attitude towards technology and their preferences in this regard, combined with the availability of labor in plenty, that determines the no-technology or low-technology choice. However, the market for home appliances, in general, and that for washing machines, in particular, is clearly large enough to attract all the major global players in this business such as Whirlpool, LG, Samsung, Haier, and TCL. Thus, there is a growing segment of the population that is wooed by increasingly higher levels of technology in one product class after another. Although fully automated front-loading washing machines are the biggest chunk (about 70 percent) of the market in developed countries, it occupies only 10 percent of the market in India.[11] Examples from different product classes and categories are almost limitless. The overall lesson to be drawn from these examples is that getting Indians to adopt new technologies by breaking traditional habits is going to be time consuming. This would be true for the vast majority of the people but not all. Thus, there is a sizable chunk of the population that is increasingly open to higher and higher levels of technology choices in different product categories. There is significant variance and thus a huge range in this issue of attitudes toward technology and related preferences. To succeed in this challenging market, MNC managers therefore have to conceive of different options for products with a suitable blend of key default features and a larger set of other features that can be added on as options by the consumer. This will provide the company an easy means of targeting people from a large number of segments. In the washing machine segment, for example, LG has a higher number of options (32 stock-keeping units, SKUs, in four broad model types) than Whirlpool (only two models)[12] and consequently has a much higher market share (31 percent) than Whirlpool (13 percent).[13] Most MNCs have to dig back in their catalogues to fish out products that have been phased out in home markets because of the obsolescence of those technologies. Such products may work wonders in India, while not ruling out a market for state-of-the-art technology. Thus, to the extent feasible, product proliferation that straddles the whole consumer pyramid is a really strategic option in India.[14] Regardless of the specific level of technology preferences, all segments are growing in India and provide reassurance to the MNC manager intending to enter the country.

Wealth/Income

Most people are well aware of the poverty situation in India. According to the World Bank, India has the highest concentration of poor people in the world.[15]

Although the percentage of people living below the poverty line has declined from 56 percent of the population in the 1970s to about 35 percent in the 1990s and even dropped to 22 percent in 2014, more than 300 million people live below the poverty line.[16] In a report titled, "From Poverty to Empowerment", McKinsey & Co. suggested that 56 percent of the population are not able to meet their essential needs.[17] However, as stated earlier, India is the fourth largest country in the world in terms of the number of high-net-worth individuals (290,552). Additionally, India is home to the fifth largest group of billionaires in the world, with 70 billionaires in the list – 17 more than 2013.[18] The number of ultra-high-net-worth individuals in India is expected to double in the next ten years, and only three countries will have more billionaires than India in 2023.[19] According to this Knight Frank report, wealth creation in the country is likely to double in the next decade, reflecting the long-term positive outlook for the third largest economy in the world. Between these two extreme levels of wealth and poverty, however, there is a wide range of wealth and income levels in the country, making for a very diverse set of consumption patterns. McKinsey & Co.'s report of the Indian consumer market in 2007 segments the market into five different income groups between these two extreme levels of wealth.[20] Thus, much like the other dimensions used to classify consumers here, there is a huge range of wealth and income levels among Indian consumers. Thus, MNCs and their marketers are spoilt for choice in terms of which segments to target in the country for their products and services.

Education

Most media researchers and brand managers use the traditional Securities and Exchange Commission (SEC) classification developed in 1988 and ratified by the Market Research Society of India (MRSI). This classification uses occupation and education as the two main criteria to segment the population into multiple groups to understand consumer behavior within these segments. This classification uses seven different categories of education from illiterate at one end to people with graduate/postgraduate degrees at the other.[21] The basic assumption, although not always true in India, is that higher levels of education lead to higher income levels and therefore broader levels of consumption. India's literacy rate at 74 percent is well below the world average rate at 84 percent. Although the current level of literacy is a significant development from the 12 percent level seen in 1947 at the time of independence,[22] most people are dissatisfied with the progress made on this front. Additionally, more concerning is the wide disparity in literacy rates between men (82 percent) and women (65 percent). Traditional gender role stereotypes that dictate what men and women should do features among the list of factors that contribute to the low levels of literacy. Other factors such as poverty, lack of physical (school) infrastructure, lack of teaching staff, and caste-based discrimination contribute to the low levels of literacy in the country. Like gender role stereotypes, caste-based stereotypes dictate what people in different castes ought to be doing. As will be explained in Chapter 7, India's centuries-old caste system was basically created along occupational lines, with people in different occupations given different labels, which eventually evolved into a rigid caste system. These two sources of discrimination contribute to the very high number of dropouts in schools reaching upwards of 50 percent among those who enroll in Class I but do not reach Class VII.[23]

While the literacy situation in India may not be all that favorable to economic growth, India's competitive advantage in services has been driven by highly educated people, in stark contrast to the illiteracy levels. A recent Ernst & Young study noted that India outperforms the U.S., Europe, and Japan in the number of mathematics and science graduates it produces.[24] The study also shows that India is home to the second largest number of scientists and engineers, and the second largest pool of trained doctors in the world. With a very strong university and college system, India produces nearly 2 million mathematics, science, and engineering graduates each year, and has succeeded in keeping enrollment levels consistently high over the years.[25] Although many of these graduates leave the country to go abroad for higher education and settle down there, this brain drain is increasingly reversing with many choosing to return to the country. Thus, while India needs to mobilize efforts to beef up its primary education system, it tertiary education system is a source of worldwide admiration. As with the other dimensions, between these two extremes lies a huge range of education levels, making for significant diversity in this dimension. By opening up the economy through liberalization and privatization these graduates are increasingly able to find jobs and earn more money than ever before. The basic assumption that higher education leads to higher income is therefore increasingly holding true in India. Higher income among these young graduates eventually leads to higher levels of consumption, representing a large pool of potential for MNCs to tap. In addition to the potential for consumption, the large number of English-speaking graduates produced in the country is fertile ground for MNCs to recruit employees for their business operations at considerably lower costs than would be the case in their home markets. In fact, many MNCs train their pool of India-recruited managers in readiness for various worldwide assignments.

Role of women in India

What this dimension desires to capture is the variation in consumption patterns across households as a result of variation in the roles women play in these households. There is a great deal of variance in this dimension, ranging from the extremely traditional gender role stereotype of women as homemakers to the modern notion of women as key breadwinners for the family. Whereas girls in rural India do not get the same opportunity to get an education as boys, urban India presents a different picture with almost equal opportunities in this regard. This is reflected in the different female literacy rates in rural v. urban India and is primarily a result of prevailing traditional gender role stereotypes. However, women in rural India participate in much larger numbers (89.5 percent) in the workforce compared with women in the cities.[26] Although India has reportedly the lowest participation of women in the workforce among the BRIC (i.e., Brazil, Russia, India, and China) nations at 29 percent,[27] other estimates put it even lower at 22.5 percent.[28] However, many data collection agencies accept the statistics seriously understate the rate at which women participate in the workforce.[29] Many believe that this is because of their extensive participation in the informal economy, where data sufficiency is a serious issue. Thus, there is reason to believe that women contribute much more to the workforce than is commonly believed. Moreover, women in India have held such positions as President, Prime Minister, Chief Minister, Speaker of the *Lok Sabha*, and Leader of the Opposition in parliament. In the private sector, one research study reported that 11 percent of companies in their sample had women CEOs who wielded a fair degree of global power.[30] Even in the technology sector, there are five women CEOs in India heading the Indian arms of such companies as IBM, Intel, Capgemini, Facebook, and Hewlett-Packard.[31] The top 10 most powerful women CEOs of 2012 included many from the banking and financial services sector.[32] In March 2010 the upper house of India's parliament approved a bill reserving 33 percent of seats in the lower house of parliament and in all state legislative assemblies for women.[33] This bill is waiting for approval from the lower house of parliament. Overall, at one end of the spectrum there are instances of traditional gender role stereotypes, at the other end such stereotypes completely disappear, and in between there is a wide range of variation.

In terms of consumer behavior, it is common knowledge that it is the women in India who define the environment at home and "silently" influence all purchasing decisions for the family. Many MNCs and domestic firms have increasingly targeted women with their products and services across such sectors as mobile phones, computers, apparel, jewellery, automobiles, and financial services.[34] Many women engage in shopping sprees – especially during festive seasons, of which India has many – buying products like household necessities, consumer durables, clothes, and jewellery. A further symbol of female freedom and liberty are the number of women driving two-wheelers and cars around India's towns and cities. The market for products targeted primarily at women is still very young but offers huge potential for MNCs and other companies interested in this market.

Rural v. urban markets

The SEC classification used to segment India's consumers provides two different versions: one for urban markets and the other for rural markets.[35] Although rapid urbanization is taking place, India is still predominantly a rural country with approximately 69 percent of its population living there, according to the most recent census.[36] Not only do more people live in rural India, they also consume at increasingly higher rates than urban India. According to one recent report, the monthly per capita expenditure growth in rural India between 2009 and 2012 was 19.2 percent, a full two percentage points higher than urban India.[37] It is rural India that holds the key to future economic growth and many more opportunities for businesses than urban India. Efficiency in selling and distribution and the logistics cost of serving rural markets are highlighted by most executives as the most important challenges in rural markets. According to a study by Credit Suisse, there is a huge economic (productivity and wage gap) difference between rural areas that are connected by roads, are electrified, have supplies of gas and water, and have access to mobile phones than those that do not benefit from these. Before the government's rural roads construction program, these areas were economically deprived and people had to travel significant distances to do business. The Credit Suisse team discovered that in the connected villages they visited there were textile shops, packaged consumer food products, and stores selling a range of consumer electronics and white goods. These stores were absent in unconnected villages. Other factors that have pushed up consumption in these rural areas are clear land titles enabling people to pursue economic activities such as poultry farming, and higher levels of awareness, availability, and use of *Kisan*[38] credit cards. Other categories of rural consumption growth that have closed the erstwhile rural–urban consumption gap are in such areas as light commercial vehicles (LCVs), cigarettes, personal care products, housing and housing loans, and satellite television subscriptions. With global auto brands looking to rural markets for sales growth in these tough times, villagers will finally have a bigger choice than simply choosing the color of their Maruti 800,[39] hitherto the only choice available to them. Domestic makes of vehicles dominate rural markets because of extensive distribution and service networks, which is the primary challenge in rural markets.[40] But for connectivity – both physical and digital – there is little difference between rural and urban consumers in terms of spending power. Many experts suggest that spending potential is much higher in rural India than in the urban part of the country and only remains to be tapped by skilled marketers.

Digital connectivity and m-commerce

Today, India is home to the second largest telecommunications network and has the second largest number of mobile phone users in the world, behind China.[41] While mobile telephony was launched in the country in 1995, it acquired only 0.1 million users in the first five years. The number of users has grown rapidly since then, reaching 10.5 million in 2002, 26.5 million in 2003, 48.5 million in 2004, 80.5 million in 2005, and 123.4 million in 2006. The latest figures indicate that India now has more than 900 million mobile phone users, with a teledensity[42] of 77.04,[43] a number that continues to grow at the highest rate in the world.[44] This dizzying growth in mobile phone connections in the last decade augurs well for a similar growth in Internet connections, which now stands at 164.81 million, putting India third in the number of Internet users in the world.[45] Despite being the third largest in this category, Internet penetration in the country is much lower than many other countries in the world. India, like many other emerging markets, has more people connected to the Internet (seven out of every eight individuals) through mobile devices than through regular Internet service providers (ISPs). The sales of tablet PCs in this market are on the increase, making it easier for people to access the Internet.[46] Mobile number portability within zones has been permitted[47] for some time now and efforts are being made to provide interzone number portability in the near future.[48] Unlike developed economies where e-commerce in both B2B (business-to-business) and B2C (business-to-consumer) markets is the rage, m-commerce is much bigger in India. This is more the result of the much larger penetration of mobile phones in the country than Internet penetration. For instance, the popular instant messaging platform WhatsApp (which was acquired recently by Facebook) has signed agreements with several mobile phone service providers in India, whereby the service provider gives unlimited access to WhatsApp for a small monthly fee. Users can subscribe to this feature simply by dialing a coded number and registering with the provider.[49] WhatsApp, which has 30 million users in India and 450 million users worldwide, is all set to add voice calls to its service after being acquired by Facebook.[50]

In addition to the commercial side of mobile telephony, there is a social and economic developmental value to high teledensity, which eventually is likely to fuel higher consumption levels. The Indian Health Minister, in a recent speech, outlined a number of initiatives that would help bring better health to the masses.[51] In the speech the minister highlighted the recent steps taken by the government of India to enable health-related IT systems such as the Mother and Child Tracking System (MCTS), and a range of mobile-based information dissemination programs. These services will provide information and help on a range of prenatal, intranatal, and postnatal care, including vaccinations, thereby targeting mortality rates for infants and mothers. The major policy objective is to reposition the mobile phone from an instrument of communication to one of empowerment by providing a range of m-health services. The success of these initiatives is likely to breed healthy consumption levels on an ongoing basis, guaranteeing growth in rural and remote areas of the country. As noted above, m-commerce is the best means of reaching Indians with advertising and promotional messages, in addition to enabling commercial transactions such as buying and selling.

An increasing number of Indians now have access to a television (TV) set than ever before. Although not as impressive as the penetration of mobile phones, more than half of Indian households have a TV, with 33 percent of rural households and 75 percent of urban households owning one.[52] Much like mobile phones, there is variation across rural and urban areas as well as variation across regions of the country.[53] TV is a huge industry in India with thousands of programming options in many different languages. The government runs a number of free terrestrial distribution–based TV channels that are received across the entire country and represent an economic way for the marketer to reach the masses. In addition, there are more than 1000 satellite channels provided by private operators that are likely to be useful to marketers for more specialized targeting of customers.[54] Digitization of TV signals by providing a conditional access system[55] requiring a set-top box (STB; receiver) is progressing in different parts of the country amid resistance from several stakeholder groups in each location. This would require the consumer to buy an STB and then pay extra money for special pay channels. Newer advances such as Internet protocol television and real time audience metrics[56] are slowly trying to establish themselves in this complex market. There is healthy competition in the audience metrics side of the industry with key global players involved in providing reasonably reliable measurements of viewership.[57]

Collectivists to individualists

Experts on cultural issues have identified India as a country with both collectivist and individualist traits.[58] Based on his first study in the late 1970s, social psychologist Geert Hofstede reached the conclusion that both individualist and collectivist traits are present in India, unlike many other countries in Asia. The traditional extended family in India has fostered the collectivist side of Indians for a long time with the dominant Hindu religion fostering the individualist side by highlighting individual responsibility for life outcomes. The basic difference between individualists and collectivists is in their self-image, with the former defining themselves in terms of the "I" where the latter define themselves in terms of the "we". Whereas Western cultures are highly individualist and Eastern cultures (e.g., Japan or China) are highly collectivist, India is home to both these traits. However, as a result of increased economic liberalization, rapid urbanization, and growing participation of women in the workforce, there has been a breakdown of the extended family arrangement in most households in recent years, as explained earlier in this chapter. For the purpose of understanding consumption behavior, suffice it to say there is increasing emphasis on the individualist side of human beings rather the collectivist. As illustrated in the opening blog, people are more reluctant to share material objects of consumption than was the case in earlier times. The dominant cultural trait highlighted in popular Bollywood (or other regional) movies is also consistent with such social and demographic shifts toward higher levels of individualism. Nevertheless, there are many families and households in the country who cling to their traditional mixture of collectivist and individualist traits. All in all, there are people across the whole range in this dimension. Rural markets could be distinguished as being more collectivist and urban markets more individualist, but this would reflect inaccurate stereotyping. Thus, marketers need to understand this aspect of life and how it affects consumption behaviors in order to target people with appropriate products and services and to reach them with customized messages.

Reaching consumers in India

Despite the huge variance among Indians in the dimensions considered, it is clear that there are a wide variety of ways in which Indian consumers can be reached. This spans the entire spectrum from conventional print media, radio and TV commercials, Internet advertising, e-commerce to very likely the most far-reaching tool, m-commerce. Unlike many other markets around the world, print media are growing at a strong rate of 10 percent per annum and are all set to become the sixth largest newspaper market in the world by 2017.[59] Much of this growth is driven by increasing literacy rates and the rising popularity of regional language newspapers and magazines. The explosive growth in recent years in this segment of the print media is a source of much excitement for both marketers and media managers. Every officially recognized language in the country has at least one newspaper and several magazines with significant reach in local and regional markets. In some language categories the competition between multiple newspapers and dozens of thriving magazines provides unique opportunities for the marketer to understand different segments of the population and target those that specifically interest them. The growth in print media, especially in the regional language category, is so high that the Indian Newspaper Society (INS) is actively lobbying the government to increase the ceiling on foreign direct investment (FDI) in this sector.[60] Despite growth in the print media, advertisers are increasingly targeting electronic media. Although this is likely to be more rewarding in the country's urban markets, rural markets with much higher growth potential would need targeting using more conventional media forms.

The best option is likely to be the m-commerce route, not only as a medium for conveying messages but also for carrying out actual transactions. The m-commerce market in India has been reported to have grown tenfold in the last few years,[61] with forecasts of 76 percent annual growth in the next few years.[62] As the number of mobile subscriptions grow, India has seen increasing regulatory support from the government enabling more companies to enter this sector. For instance, eBay India, which gets 23 percent of its orders through mobile devices, has launched new mobile-only initiatives for selling products in different categories such as perfume, watches, audio accessories, auto accessories and video games.[63] Some analysts predict that m-commerce will overtake e-commerce in India within the next three years, especially now that even small and medium-sized enterprises (SMEs) are increasingly using this route for their transactions.[64] Seizing the opportunity presented by consumer preferences turning toward m-commerce, many vendors have obtained licenses from the Reserve Bank of India (RBI) to provide a prepaid wallet service to the vendors' customers. The prepaid wallet service enables an amount of currency to be charged to a mobile phone. In general, m-commerce provides the ability to conduct commerce on the move using a mobile device. With m-commerce the user can complete any type of transaction, including buying and selling products, availing services, transferring ownership or rights, transacting and transferring money by accessing wireless Internet services on a mobile handset. For m-commerce to work high levels of collaboration between service providers and banking institutions are required. This is already happening in many parts of the world, but only more so in India.[65] Mobile phones are increasingly affecting purchase decisions as they serve as crucial windows to the world for individuals who possess them, replacing conventional media tools. As the number of mobile subscriptions grow, Indians are beginning to trust them more and rely on them as they get on with their lives. With a majority of the Indian population in the youth segment, there is unprecedented opportunity for m-commerce as a direct consequence of the relative ease and comfort young people have with technology. These are exciting times for marketers to be in India and technology is making it easy for companies to reach even the remotest of consumers.

Notes

1. http://blogs.consumerawakening.com/consumerism-in-india-and-its-effects/.
2. Psychographic segmentation divides the market into groups based on social class, lifestyle, and personality characteristics.
3. http://content.spencerstuart.com/sswebsite/pdf/lib/India_ConsumerRoundtable_web.pdf.
4. http://www.ibef.org/industry/consumer-markets-snapshot.
5. http://118.67.250.203//scripts/market-share.aspx.
6. http://en.wikipedia.org/wiki/Mercedes-Benz_India; http://www.carwale.com/news/5470-mercedes-benz-india-record-94-sales-growth.html.
7. http://trak.in/tags/business/2012/01/27/nokia-grabs-19-of-dual-sim-mobile-phone-market-in-india/.
8. http://techcircle.vccircle.com/2013/05/30/india-has-67m-smartphone-users-desi-netizens-more-open-to-sharing-everything-online-mary-meeker/.
9. http://www.business-standard.com/article/companies/lg-india-eyes-rs-1-800-cr-sales-from-washing-machines-112101500155_1.html.
10. http://www.currentweek.com/top-washing-machine-brands-in-india-their-market-trends/.
11. http://www.adi-media.com/PDF/TVJ/annual_issue/008-Washing-Machines.pdf.
12. http://zh.scribd.com/doc/22761142/The-Survey-Report-on-Washing-Machine-Market-in-India.
13. http://www.currentweek.com/top-washing-machine-brands-in-india-their-market-trends/.
14. http://content.spencerstuart.com/sswebsite/pdf/lib/India_ConsumerRoundtable_web.pdf.
15. http://web.worldbank.org/WBSITE/EXTERNAL/TOPICS/EXTPOVERTY/EXTPA/0,contentMDK:20208959~menuPK:435735~pagePK:148956~piPK:216618~theSitePK:430367~isCURL:Y~isCURL:Y,00.html.
16. http://www.livemint.com/Politics/1QvbdGnGySHo7WRq1NBFNL/Poverty-rate-down-to-22-Plan-panel.html.
17. http://timesofindia.indiatimes.com/india/McKinsey-pegs-poverty-line-at-Rs-1336-per-month/articleshow/30691907.cms.
18. http://articles.economictimes.indiatimes.com/2014-03-03/news/47824075_1_billionaires-hurun-amancio-ortega.
19. http://timesofindia.indiatimes.com/india/India-to-have-4th-highest-number-of-billionaires-by-2023-Report/articleshow/31528448.cms.
20. http://www.mckinsey.com/insights/asia-pacific/the_bird_of_gold.

21. http://en.wikipedia.org/wiki/SEC_Classification.
22. http://www.dailymail.co.uk/indiahome/indianews/article-2317341/Indias-literacy-rate-rises-73-cent-population-growth-dips.html.
23. http://en.wikipedia.org/wiki/Literacy_in_India.
24. http://news.oneindia.in/2009/11/05/india-has-more-maths-science-graduates-than-us.html.
25. http://en.wikipedia.org/wiki/Tertiary_education_in_India.
26. http://www.fao.org/sd/wpdirect/WPre0108.htm.
27. http://qz.com/176658/india-has-the-lowest-workforce-participation-rate-of-women-among-the-brics/.
28. http://timesofindia.indiatimes.com/india/Women-account-for-just-22-of-workforce-in-India/articleshow/26548372.cms.
29. http://en.wikipedia.org/wiki/Women_in_India.
30. http://www.deccanherald.com/content/57119/women-ceos-india-inc-beats.html.
31. http://her.yourstory.com/5-powerful-women-ceos-tech-india-1120.
32. http://economictimes.indiatimes.com/features/corporate-dossier/india-incs-most-powerful-ceos-2012-top-women-ceos/articleshow/13409138.cms.
33. http://en.wikipedia.org/wiki/Women's_Reservation_Bill.
34. http://content.spencerstuart.com/sswebsite/pdf/lib/India_ConsumerRoundtable_web.pdf.
35. http://en.wikipedia.org/wiki/SEC_Classification.
36. http://www.dailymail.co.uk/indiahome/indianews/article-2317341/Indias-literacy-rate-rises-73-cent-population-growth-dips.html.
37. http://www.accenture.com/SiteCollectionDocuments/PDF/Accenture-Masters-of-Rural-Markets-Selling-Profitably-to-Rural-Consumers.pdf.
38. *Kisan* is the Hindi word for farmer.
39. The largest selling car brand in India (majority owned by Suzuki).
40. http://in.reuters.com/article/2014/02/03/india-autos-foreign-rural-carmarket-idINDEEA1200A20140203.
41. http://en.wikipedia.org/wiki/List_of_countries_by_number_of_mobile_phones_in_use.
42. Teledensity relates to the number of landline telephones per 100 individuals living in a given area.
43. http://archive.indianexpress.com/news/indian-telecom-cos-lose-1.7-mn-mobile-subscribers/1028216/.
44. http://en.wikipedia.org/wiki/Telecommunications_statistics_in_India.
45. http://techcircle.vccircle.com/2013/08/06/india-has-143–2m-mobile-internet-users-total-net-connections-stand-at-164–81m/.
46. http://cmrindia.com/india-overall-tablet-shipments-in-july-september-2013-touch-1–20-million-units-recording-a-growth-of-9-yoy-and-a-modest-4–7-increase-qoq/.
47. http://trai.gov.in/WriteReadData/PressRealease/Document/PR-TSD-Oct–13.pdf.
48. http://techcircle.vccircle.com/2013/09/25/trai-recommends-inter-circle-mobile-number-portability-in-6-months/.
49. http://techcircle.vccircle.com/2013/12/04/whatsapp-crosses-30m-users-in-india-inks-deal-with-tata-docomo/.
50. http://techcircle.vccircle.com/2014/02/25/whatsapp-to-add-voice-calls-after-facebook-acquisition/.
51. http://pib.nic.in/newsite/erelease.aspx?relid=85669.
52. http://timesofindia.indiatimes.com/india/200-million-Indians-have-no-TV-phone-or-radio/articleshow/12253614.cms.
53. http://www.thehindu.com/business/Industry/mobile-subscribers-largest-in-uttar-pradesh-tamil-nadu/article4686257.ece.

54. http://en.wikipedia.org/wiki/Television_in_India.
55. A conditional access system gives the consumer choice over the pay channels beamed to his or her home.
56. Audience metrics (measurement) measures the number of people in an audience, usually in relation to radio listenership and TV viewership.
57. http://www.livemint.com/Consumer/jEqqaSB8aVWmsdjmJmvryI/TV-ratings-system-set-for-a-shakeup.html.
58. http://geert-hofstede.com/india.html.
59. http://www.firstpost.com/fwire/print-media-in-india-bucks-trend-set-to-grow-tewari-1058847.html.
60. http://timesofindia.indiatimes.com/business/india-business/INS-wants-higher-FDI-ceiling-in-print-media/articleshow/23327919.cms.
61. http://www.thehindubusinessline.com/industry-and-economy/info-tech/etailers-see-mcommerce-as-the-next-big-thing/article5444588.ece.
62. http://www.researchandmarkets.com/reports/2408089/mobile_commerce_market_in_india_20122016.
63. http://articles.economictimes.indiatimes.com/keyword/mobile-commerce.
64. http://articles.economictimes.indiatimes.com/2008–09–16/news/28401857_1_m-commerce-mobile-commerce-mobile-subscribers.
65. http://globenewswire.com/news-release/2013/11/22/591951/10059221/en/Mobile-Commerce-Market-in-India-2012–2016-Features-Giants-Axis-Bank-Ltd-Vodafone-India-and-PayMate-India-Pvt-Ltd.html.

Strategies adapted to Indian needs

"The differences are the breadth and depth of the Indian market and the fact that India has undergone much more social and economic change in the last generation than the US has. Therefore Indian consumers and marketers are probably facing a far more intense and highly contrasted situation."

David Daniel, CEO, Spencer Stuart

The reader should by now have a good understanding of the serious economic and social transition that India has experienced in the last two decades. Such an understanding is critical to multinational corporations (MNCs) developing their strategy for winning in India's markets. First, the institutional landscape in India has evolved rapidly in recent decades bringing about unprecedented change to the soft and hard infrastructure in the country. Some of this change is ongoing and far from complete. In many businesses and sectors, the required level of institutional intermediaries and business ecosystems falls short of what is adequate. This means such ecosystems need to be established before MNCs can begin to earn profits from their investment. The case example given in this chapter provides more details on the amount of time it has taken for the pan-India retail operation of one of the biggest business houses in the country to reach profitability. Second, the reader has seen the macroeconomic challenges faced by the country's administrators to manage non-inflationary growth and to hold fiscal deficits within control to ensure that operators can safely engage in business transactions. This requires prudently advancing the reforms agenda and is intricately intertwined with highly fragmented and cacophonous political realities on the ground. Although all major coalitions that have ruled the country since economic reforms were launched have consented to pushing the reform process progressively forward, the devil is always in the detail of such processes. Legacy laws and erstwhile regulations need to be modified in many instances, requiring constitutional amendments in some cases. The federalist nature of India's democracy makes some of these problems more complicated than in other nations. It requires MNCs engage independently with multiple governments in their efforts to target the whole country with their products and services. Finally, India's consumers are more varied and unique in their preferences than is the case elsewhere. The presence of a huge informal economy also necessitates competing with unknowns in a market that is already complex in other ways. We use these basic fundamentals of the macro-context to delve deeper into the specifics of several different sectors in an effort to highlight those strategies that are likely to be effective.

Irrespective of the type of business, be it the imaginary rent-to-own business, a fast food operation, an airline business, automobile manufacturing, or an e-commerce business in India, you cannot escape but note that these businesses operate in embryonic or high-growth industries. Although MNCs have experienced similar industry environments in other places, such experiences are likely to have been in the distant past for many. Most MNCs enter emerging markets to counter stagnating or even declining growth in their home and other markets where they have an established presence. Thus, recent experiences dominate human psyches and necessitate significant unlearning to be able to operate in new and growing industries all over again.

The earlier discussion on the imaginary rent-to-own business noted that such a business does not exist outside the informal economy in India. Thus, this represents an embryonic industry, one that consumers (not to mention regulators) have no experience of. Hence, the key challenge would be to develop the concept and get consumers to try it. The next challenge would be to generate enough exposure to and excitement about the concept that it becomes standard and acceptable. In fact, this is the major challenge faced by such companies as Reliance Retail in organized retailing in India. Some reports suggest that the seven or more years it has taken for this company's organized retail operations to span the whole country are primarily a result of the difficulty in converting neighborhood shoppers into organized retail shoppers.[1]

In addition to opposition from different stakeholders, the fast food operations of McDonald's faced a number of hurdles in the form of logistics and distributions systems, for which the country lacked sophisticated ecosystems. This was a problem for Reliance Retail as well, as will become clear in the case example. Thus, McDonald's not only had to present its concept for customers to try and accept as standard, but it also had to create the back operations necessary for it to be done, while facing a political challenge from stakeholders on sensitive issues. If the industry considered is not embryonic, as in the cases discussed so far, it is then more likely than not a high-growth industry, complete with its own unique problems. Take the case of the airline business discussed earlier (see Chapter 4). Although India is geographically bigger than most countries, it is definitely not the size of China or the United States. Despite this, the airline industry is highly fragmented, with a large number of players, not many of whom are profitable. Although lack of profitability in a rapidly growing market could be blamed on nonsensical regulation, as some have done, there are other structural features in the industry that are at the cause. What does it take to succeed in a fragmented industry, while quickly ramping up operations to profitable levels? Perhaps it is a question of offering exactly what consumers want and in building a strong and differentiated brand in the process. Product proliferation and brand loyalty are the two main barriers to entry in an industry that is likely to be attractive to many new competitors as a result of its high growth. While these are sound business-level strategies to earn competitive advantage, they need to be supported by corporate acquisitions, as part of a well-formulated strategy, to establish a strong and vibrant business for the future. Fragmented industries need to consolidate and go through a shakeout in which the weaker competitors are left behind by the stronger ones.

In all the above cases it is imperative to keep in mind that this would all be done in a marketplace that is broader and deeper in terms of the number and nature of customer segments and their unique needs. The level of diversity in this country of 29 states and

7 union territories is likely to be of phenomenal proportions for most strategic managers. For instance, cultural sensitivity is an issue that many MNCs (e.g., McDonald's, Pizza Hut, KFC) have not only overcome but managed delicately to achieve the level of success that they have. No amount of strategizing can overcome cultural insensitivity, especially in industrial sectors such as food, where cultural specificities are the highest. While the common misconception of India among non-Indians is that a significant majority are vegetarian, many of these companies discovered the reality through successful groundwork. Such groundwork helped them develop menus suited to Indian needs by developing options based on chicken, mutton, fish, and even pork in some cases. More importantly, McDonald's took great care to ensure each of its restaurants had both vegetarian and non-vegetarian sections in light of India's unique cultural sensitivity. Additionally, McDonald's offers only vegetarian food in both sections during *Navratri*, a nine-day religious festival, when even meat eaters and their families avoid its consumption. Going even further, they developed mayonnaise and ice cream with no eggs to satisfy the needs of vegetarians. Pizza Hut and KFC (operated by Yum! Brands) offer menus that are divided into vegetarian and non-vegetarian sections to ensure that there is something for everyone. Although not all Indians are vegetarian, the majority eat vegetarian food more often than not. Additionally, religious practices dictate avoiding meat consumption on different days and times of the week, a practice that varies from one state to another and one region to another only in when exactly the restrictions apply. Thus, the necessity to handle cultural sensitivities as a prerequisite to any business strategy formulation cannot be overemphasized.

Industry life cycle and stages

To get a better feel for challenges that are unique to India, it is important to understand the concept of the industry life cycle and the different stages through which industries evolve. This is especially true because India launched major economic reforms only in the early 1990s when it decided to move towards a market-oriented economy. This makes it different from other countries where the reform processes were launched much earlier or were by nature capitalist and free-market oriented. Thus, in addition to analyzing institutional, political, economic, and market factors, as done so far, there is a need to look more closely at the structural features of specific industries and how they are evolving over time. Figure 6.1 (see p. 104) shows the typical sales and profit curves for industries across different stages of the life cycle.

Embryonic industry

When new business models are used to introduce products and services of which a market has no prior experience, the industry can be classified as embryonic. The rent-to-own furniture and fast food industries are good examples in the Indian context. To be sure, people in India have had experience of and exposure to embryonic and growth industries, mainly in the informal economy and the unorganized sector. There are entrepreneurs, mostly running tiny establishments, who engage in the renting of furniture for special occasions. These businesses are mainly in the informal economy where there are no formal practices for assessing creditworthiness or for insuring services, etc. Thus, cultural factors embedded deep within the psyches of buyers and sellers dominate these business transactions. When an MNC launches nationwide in the formal economy, perhaps in the organized sector, an embryonic industry can be seen to emerge. In the case of the fast food business, there are a wide variety of Indian foods that vary greatly from one region to another and thus constitute a very fragmented industry. If people consume *idli* and *vada* in one part of the country, it is *kachori* and *jalebi* in another, *vada pav* in another, *samosa* and *chutney* in another, and so on and so forth. Thus, any business that plans to open restaurants across the whole country would find itself in an embryonic industry.

Growth industry

Once the products and services, along with the business models of an embryonic industry, have had time to establish themselves as standard and acceptable forms of businesses, they slowly move into the growth stage. The rate of industry growth in such cases is fairly high as a result of few competitors slowly but surely entering the industry. The airline industry in India is a good example of a high-growth industry. India has the world's second largest growth rate in domestic passenger traffic and is among the five largest in cargo traffic.[2] International air traffic in and out of India has recently outpaced the growth in domestic passenger traffic as a result of the economy slowing but is expected to grow at higher levels than most other countries.[3] Growth is also reflected in the number of airlines flying to India and those flying within its borders. Thus, increased capacity is a reflection of high-growth industries. The nature of competition in high-growth industries is very different from that in other stages of the industry life cycle. Investments in capacity building make it difficult to engage in long-drawn-out price wars to steal customers from one another. Higher levels of differentiated services, uniquely catering to specific and unmet markets needs, are critical for success. The Indian airline company Kingfisher learned this the hard way. Even after acquiring a low-cost competitor so that it could serve both ends of the market, the company has been incurring huge losses and has defaulted on several debt payments, leading to bankruptcy. All other private air carriers in the market are losing money and are looking for investment from international carriers. While this is typical in high-growth industries, some of it is unique to the airline industry.

Mature industry

Once companies become well established in the marketplace along with their business models and products/services, the market slowly becomes saturated and growth begins to slow down to normal levels. However, profits reach healthy levels at this stage of the life cycle. Companies try to complete some of the consolidation efforts begun in the growth stage or begin the task of industry consolidation by engaging in mergers and acquisitions. This strengthens the position of strong companies and weeds out the weaker ones. The nature of competition is different from previous stages in that the focus shifts from designing better products and services to meet unique customer needs in different segments to industry consolidation activities. Companies try to erect stronger barriers to entry into the industry and at the same time try to strengthen established lines of products and services. The industry becomes less fragmented than before as a result of the needs of different customer segments being easily met by the few companies that remain in the industry. By virtue of the fairly recent liberalization and opening up of the economy, many industries subject to global competition have not reached the mature stage in India. The automobile industry in India can perhaps be quoted as the best example of an industry that is on the brink of entering the mature phase. Even then, it is perhaps the two-wheeler segment of the industry that is in the mature phase – not the one for passenger (cars) and commercial vehicles.

Declining industry

Finally, in industry's decline stage sales and profits begin to fall as a result of customer needs being met by other industries and more technologically advanced products. Companies begin to exit the industry as a result of declining demand, with a few engaging in harvesting strategies. There are few examples of declining industries in India. Automobile manufacturers would certainly hope to outstrip motorcycle sales in the not too distant future – whether or not that happens remains to be seen. The market for black-and-white televisions has been declining in favor of color televisions for a long time now, although this is happening in India much later than elsewhere.

Overall, many of the industries in India that interest MNCs are either in the embryonic stage or in the growth stage. Very few such industries would be in the mature stage and fewer still in the decline stage. This creates a competitive environment different from that of the home markets of most MNCs. The presence of global and domestic competitors makes for very intense competition in a market that is very broad and deep in terms of the number of different consumer segments and the variation in needs across these segments.

Operating in embryonic industries

In the embryonic stage, products/services are very unfamiliar to consumers, market segments are not clearly defined, and features of products/services are not entirely clear. Competition is likely to be limited in this stage. Although the thousands of traditional fast food vendors from the unorganized sector are likely to pose competitive threats, companies like McDonald's have the advantage of providing American-style fast food across the whole country. A combination of rapid urbanization, increased exposure to Western media, and the Internet revolution has led Indians to embrace American-style restaurants such as McDonald's, KFC, Pizza Hut, Domino's, and TGI Friday's. The situation of widely varying regional food preferences and the absence of a single dominant food preference is at one and the same time a hurdle and an opportunity for companies like McDonald's. The challenge is customizing the menu to cater to Indian tastes while ensuring that such customization does not become too different from one region to the next. Such standardization is critical to McDonald's chaining strategy of opening restaurants across the country and to being recognized all over the country for its menu. Under these circumstances, it was imperative for McDonald's to create a menu that would be acceptable to Indian palates. It was more important for McDonald's to get customers to try their products. In the initial phases the company even offered half-sandwiches for people to try. Even today, the company has only been able to tap into the upper middle class and richer class segments rather than the middle and lower portions of the middle class. This is a major change for the company from its home market and most other Western markets it operates in. However, McDonald's experience is likely to be similar to most other MNCs (from developed markets) that enter the country. Definitions and conceptions of what constitutes the middle class in India are likely to be different from the ones in the West. Moreover, there is a lot a variation even within the middle class that can make for different consumption choices and patterns, as emphasized in Chapter 5.

Customizing the menu to local cultural sensitivities and actually succeeding in getting consumers to try their products meant several things for McDonald's. First, they had to replace their traditional beef-based burgers with the Maharaja Mac (mutton-based burger), which had to go through rigorous testing and product development phases. From an industry life cycle point of view, the critical activities in an embryonic industry are research and development (R&D), product design, and differentiation strategies. In addition to the Maharaja Mac, the company also developed a veggie burger after a long process of testing and development. The restaurant chain also strictly segregated vegetarian and non-vegetarian lines in the restaurants to get Indian consumers to be comfortable dining there. Chicken kebab burgers, McAaloo tikki burgers (patties made of breaded potatoes and peas), vegetable nuggets, and Pizza Puffs were some of the additions to McDonald's menu in India. The company also used a creative pricing strategy with these menu options to get customers to visit repeatedly.

To cater successfully to a wide section of the middle class, McDonald's has as many as seven different price points for value meals (from INR29 to INR89, in steps of INR10). This value-laddering strategy is aimed at moving people gradually from the lower end of the ladder to the higher end. It is essential in this embryonic industry for consumers to come in and try their products, especially since the restaurant chain is perceived to be expensive. As far as the differentiation strategy goes, which is critical for embryonic industries to grow market share, McDonald's focuses on family-centric and child-centric strategies. It calls its restaurants family restaurants, showers knick-knacks on kids who walk in, provides special low-height counters to enable kids to place orders, promotes birthday parties and uses them in advertising targeting children, and provides a hassle-free environment for children and teenagers. This helps the company to grow market share by building a unique brand image among the Westernized elite in India. All these have helped the company focus on their branding, differentiated image, and achieve success in their efforts to get their products accepted as standard. All these elements in McDonald's strategy are necessary for other MNCs regardless of industry sector – appropriate and wide price range options, cultural sensitivity, clear focus on market segments, R&D and product design to cater to specific needs – for them to succeed in embryonic industries. The detailed case study of Reliance Retail offers a clearer glimpse into the reality of getting new concepts acceptable and standard in situations where consumers lack such experience.

Operating in India's high-growth industries

High-growth industries are characterized by increasing intensity of competition, as new players enter into the industry eyeing growing demand. The airline industry in India is an excellent example of such a stage of the industry life cycle, although there are others. The number of airlines flying into and out of India has increased, with a larger portion of the market share captured by international air carriers than domestic carriers. Some of this has been attributed to the 5/20 rule of the Directorate General of Civil Aviation (DGCA), which stipulates that any domestic carrier should have been in operation for five years and have a fleet of at least 20 aircraft before being allowed to fly to international destinations. With AirAsia, Tata-Singapore Airlines, and Tiger Airways entering Indian skies, the competition in this industry sector is heating up. These new competitors are pointing up the presence of significant customer segments with unmet needs and indicating their intention to target these segments. Differentiation, brand building, and product proliferation are not only key to competing in such high-growth industries but also to creating barriers to entry to prevent more newcomers from entering. In addition to differentiation, cost leadership also becomes a viable strategy in this stage of the industry's life cycle and one that is quite necessary in India, given the limits on disposable incomes. AirAsia and Tiger Airways are low-cost and to a certain extent ultra low-cost carriers, trying to convert people from taking trains to taking planes. Tata's ultra-low-price Nano automobile is also an example of the effort to convert families with two-wheelers to upgrade to the automobile segment. Cost leadership is also a very effective strategy to create barriers to entry for newcomers into the industry and strengthen a company's position within it. Domestic companies may use non-business strategies (such as lobbying the government) to raise objections and prevent the entry of newcomers into the industry on various grounds. An example of this was given in Chapter 4 when the Federation of Indian Airlines was discussed. Many of the domestic airlines in India are starved of the capital necessary for the expansion and implementation of refined strategies. This is typical of high-growth industries where the financial resources to sustain different value chain activities are imperative. A cost leadership strategy may help companies with financial resource availability. AirAsia, for instance, is known to operate with the world's lowest unit cost of INR1.25 or USD0.02 per available seat kilometer and a passenger breakeven load factor of about 52 percent. A financial strategy of 100 percent hedging for fuel requirements provides the financial boost to the company's ultra-low-cost strategy and makes it very difficult for new entrants. Further, the airline is making all out efforts to achieve an aircraft turnaround time of 25 minutes to optimize aircraft utilization, which contributes to the cost structure.[4]

The increasing number of competitors in a high-growth industry is likely to trigger price wars as is expected in the case of the airline industry as a result of AirAsia's entry. Both differentiation and cost leadership strategies can help withstand price wars under these circumstances. A differentiation strategy is likely to help as long as the unique needs of different segments of customers are catered to successfully. Meeting customers' needs precisely is likely to help strengthen brand loyalty and reduce price elasticity in specific segments. Cost leadership, on the other hand, can help withstand price wars by ensuring that sufficient margins exist even after lowering prices to sustain profitability over the long run. A combination of both differentiation and cost leadership is perhaps the best strategy to pursue in high-growth industries, although it is not without challenges. Tata Sons, for instance, has entered into a joint venture with AirAsia for an ultra-low-cost airline, while at the same time announcing plans to enter into another joint venture with Singapore Airlines for a full-service airline. India's leading carrier Jet Airways also has both a full-service arm and a low-cost arm in its operations, as did Kingfisher before its bankruptcy. This in fact is more or less standard practice in the airline business around the world. Although the strategy of combining cost leadership and differentiation is likely to be difficult to imitate by competitors, it also poses challenges to the company trying to implement it. Companies may be stuck in the middle as a result of underestimating the challenges involved in coordinating the value chain activities that create value. As reported in Chapter 5, Levi Strauss in India is an example of a company that is increasingly stuck in the middle as a result of its attempt to ladder down the price pyramid and target the mass market segment with its Denizen brand. When this initiative met with a lukewarm response, the company decided to discontinue this and move back to a focus on its core brand in the premium segment. As the company chooses to sell through its own stores, this creates confusion among customers about the company's positioning and brand image. Although Denizen is the company's most successful brand elsewhere in Asia, its launch has not been consistent with its premium positioning in India in consumers' minds. In the airline business, for example, it is important to coordinate (a) hedging strategies for fuel, (b) aircraft utilization rates, (c) distribution and sales of tickets, and (d) market research for better identification of changing needs in different segments. These varied activities can become overwhelming if not managed well.

In addition to triggering price wars, the growing number of competitors is also likely to bring about consolidation in the industry. Companies must therefore be conscious of strengthening their fundamental value proposition to customers as part of an overall strategy. This will give them power to engage in acquisitions or strategic alliances from a strong basis. The ability to access financial resources on a global scale is a strong advantage for global players in such industries in these circumstances.

Operating in mature industries

When the market becomes saturated and demand begins to slow, it signals the onset of the maturity phase of the industry life cycle. The few remaining competitors compete more intensely with each other, and early on in this phase they engage increasingly in acquisitions to further consolidate their position. Although very few industries in India belong in this category, the market for 2G feature phones or even black-and-white televisions (TVs) can be identified as good examples. Companies like Nokia that were leading players in emerging markets, especially in India, are now rapidly losing market share to a host of low-cost smartphone competitors. Similarly, dozens of Indian TV manufacturers were forced to upgrade their technologies to color TVs as a result of the economy opening up and the resulting flood in the market of cheaper color TVs. It is important to prepare for the maturity phase of an industry before it is reached to ensure survival in the longer term. Consistent investments in R&D and technological enhancements in the phases leading to the maturity phase are likely to evolve into a focus on process design in the mature phase of industry. The process design focus should yield increases in productivity and lower cost structures to better withstand higher competitive intensity. The collaboration between Microsoft and Nokia is an example of reflective strategies (as opposed to proactive ones) not only in India but on a global scale. Samsung, a leader in the mobile phone market in India, has used a value-laddering strategy by virtue of its strengths in both feature phones and smartphones. The company has successfully graduated its feature phone customers into smartphone customers over a period of time.

An understanding of the factors involved in the institutional, political, economic, and consumer profile dimensions in India is critical to formulating successful strategies in this context. It is equally essential to be aware of cultural preferences and trends in India not only to avoid culturally insensitive strategies but also, on the positive side, to take advantage of increased understanding in this domain. By means of examples from different business sectors, the importance of these factors and potential best practices in addressing them have been discussed in this chapter. The importance of recognizing the stage of the industry life cycle and using appropriate business strategies in each of the stages has also been highlighted. It is perhaps more important to be focusing on future stages in the evolution of industry in India and proactively prepare for this. As consumers in India catch up with the rest of the world on several fronts, many industries are likely to go through the different stages more quickly or make quantum leaps and skip an entire stage. The detailed case example of Reliance Retail provides a glimpse of the challenges faced in establishing consumer awareness and gaining acceptability from the different stakeholders involved in the process. As this sector is even more open to foreign direct investment (FDI) and soon to see an increasing number of global retailers, many of the lessons identified in this chapter are likely to help MNCs and their managers better formulate their strategies and adapt them over time.

Case example: Reliance Retail[5]

"I think it has been proven that nowhere in the world does the international retailer take everything. In China, which actually opened FDI [foreign direct investment] 20 years ago in a gradual manner, many of the top 10–20 retailers are still the local Chinese. Carrefour, Tesco, Walmart, you name it, everyone is there. You must remember that Walmart is not the winner in every country. It has withdrawn from Japan. It has withdrawn from a number of countries. So deep pockets really don't guarantee you success. What it guarantees you is access for sure. But, in reality, it is the customer-connect that is very important." Govind Shrikhande, MD, Shoppers Stop Ltd. (Bhaskar, 2011).

It was a warm May morning in Mumbai with an early cool breeze blowing in from the bay. It would get downright hot in a couple of hours. It was already quite hot in the business suite in Mukesh Ambani's office in one of the skyscrapers at Nariman Point overlooking the bay. Ambani, the richest Indian and the chief of a vast empire of petroleum, petrochemicals, textiles, retail, and a host of other subsidiaries, was particularly troubled by the phone call he just had with Raghu Pillai, one of his top retail executives. "Damn it," he cursed under his breath. "Why now? Why this? Couldn't he have chosen a better time for this," he thought, calmly trying to include all possibilities in his calculations for the next course of action. He remembered having announced a huge foray into retail four years ago to his shareholders at the annual meeting in 2006, one that envisaged an outlay of Rs. 25,000 crore (INR250 billion) over the next five years, with a grand accompanying vision of a farm-to-fork business model. He had pulled off a great coup when he poached Pillai away from the Future Group, the biggest domestic competitor in the retail business. He had always been able to draw inspiration from his father's vision and belief that made people work beyond their capabilities. It showed in his very successful top-down approach to recruiting the best talent in the world for the different verticals within the retail business, which was barely four years old. Once he had these top executives in place, he counted on them to do the rest within each of their respective businesses. These last four years had been filled with exciting times and remarkable progress in the retail business amid stiff opposition from different groups such as FDI Watch forcing the closure of a number of retail stores. There was also the huge global financial crisis and a recession in many parts of the world, which led to a global slowdown making it impossible to reach the full quota of investment initially planned for. To top it all, now, this news about Pillai's departure for personal reasons. "What personal reasons could there be? Is this really a counter punch from the competition in response to my initial poaching away of their executives? The war for talent in retail here is really getting hot." A number of thoughts ran through his mind. He had always kept a cool head and had shown investors his company's ability to implement big projects. Now was not the time to cower and back away. "Perhaps it is time for me to cast my net wider and bring in talent from outside India. After all modern retail is a Western concept and there is plenty of talent out there," he thought to himself. "But whatever I do, I need to do it quick. There's no time to waste." He picked up his phone and called his secretary to come in.

Introduction

Reliance Retail is an unlisted and wholly owned subsidiary of the oil and gas giant Reliance Industries Limited (RIL), the largest Indian private sector conglomerate, ranked 264th in the Fortune Global 500 in 2009, and 126th in the Forbes Global 2000 in 2010. The activity of the conglomerate spans such sectors as textiles, garments, petrochemicals, petroleum, and oil and gas, in addition to its recent foray into retail. Ambani, the chief of this vast empire is the son of the entrepreneurial and visionary founder Dhirubhai Ambani, whose rags-to-riches story is the stuff of Bollywood legend, and has actually been made into a movie. The firm (RIL) has seen both sides of the liberalization and massive deregulation in India that started in the early

1990s, having been firmly established long before this process started. Seeing the severe fragmentation of Indian retail, characterized by millions of mom-and-pop stores, and the eagerness of globally spread multinational retailers to enter India, Ambani decided to take advantage of the firm's excellent knowledge of Indian consumers and their behavior by entering the retail sector. Although his company was a huge conglomerate spanning several critical sectors such as petroleum and oil and gas, the company had no experience whatsoever in the retail sector. But Ambani, true to the spirit of his family, had a grand vision for a pan-India retail network that would be truly "Reliance".

Based on an assessment of the opportunities in the retail sector, the Board of Directors gave its consent to pursue the retail business, and approved an initial outlay of $750 million to set up a variety of store formats such as hypermarkets, supermarkets, convenience stores, and specialty stores.[6] The Chairman and CEO Ambani, announcing his intention to invest Rs. 25,000 crore[7] (INR250 billion) over a period of five years, also outlined his vision of inclusive growth and prosperity for farmers, vendor partners, small shopkeepers, and consumers. Ambani's vision also outlined a business model that is commonly called "farm to fork", and envisioned significant enhancements and involvement in the entire value chain to provide a solid footing in the organized retail sector. He and his top management team knew full well that top executive talent in the retail business would be critical for a company like theirs with no experience whatsoever in retail, especially if they had to compete against the likes of Walmart and Metro. Dhirubhai Ambani's vision and inspiring beliefs of harnessing human capability to the hilt was already firmly institutionalized at Reliance Industries. Now Mukesh had been strengthening this culture oriented on human resources and had been drawing on it for their already vast empire. For his grand foray into retail, Ambani wanted to have a solid bunch of top executives that would represent a capable human capital, full of knowledge and experience in the nitty-gritty of the retail environment in India. The average per capita retail space is the lowest in India, and Indian consumers have not really experienced modern retail, with such consumption not being part of their routines. Thus, it would take a miraculous effort to convert purchasing preferences and behavior to be successful in creating a pan-India organized retail network. To meet this challenge, Mukesh had looked at recent competitors and their executives representing success stories in this challenging environment. He lured away a number of these executives from the somewhat fragmented retail environment within the country, of which Pillai was one of the foremost. But, this morning's phone call signaled Pillai's departure in a few months and the retail foray would face a significant setback.

Rapid growth of Indian retail market

Today, Indian retail is dominated by a large number of small retailers, consisting of the local *kirana*[8] shops, owner-manned general stores, chemists, footwear shops, apparel shops, *paan* and *beedi*[9] shops, and handcart and pavement vendors, which together make up the unorganized market (see photographs). Business Monitor International Ltd. (BMI) estimates that this fragmented offering still accounts for about 95 percent of the country's grocery retail sales.

However, this is changing fast, as multinationals begin to seek opportunities to enter India and as local organized players accelerate their own expansion and business activity efforts in preparation for greater competition. The emergence of organized retail formats is transforming the face of retailing in India, as domestic and foreign players challenge the dominance of the country's traditional mom-and-pop stores by opening chain and speciality stores across the country to satisfy increasing consumer demand.

A.T. Kearney, in its 2011 Global Retail Development Index (GRDI), stated that "the time to enter (India) is now." India's strong growth fundamentals – 9 percent real GDP growth in 2010, forecast yearly growth of 8.7 percent through 2016, high saving and investment rates, fast labor force growth, and increased consumer spending – make for a very favorable retail environment and fourth spot in the GRDI.[10]

As has been the case for several years, Indian consumers continue to urbanize, have more money to spend on non-food purchases, and have more exposure to brands. The result is a powerful, more discerning consumer class. India's population of nearly 1.2 billion – forecast eventually to overtake China's – is also an attractive target.

Nevertheless, India attracted the most new retailers in 2010, according to CBRE's 2011 report. CBRE is the first independent international real estate consultancy, established in New Delhi in 1994. In addition, there are signs that multi-brand retailers should have the same (legal) rights as single-brand retailers (although they will have to dedicate at least 50 percent of their proposed investment to back-end supply chain infrastructure and commit a minimum FDI of $100 million).

The retail scenario in India

According to some official estimates, the retail sector contributes up to 27 percent of the world's GDP and is thus a significant contributor to global economic activity.[11] Some 20 to 55 percent of this global contribution is by organized retailing in many developing countries. Forty-seven Global Fortune 500 companies are retailers, most of them from developed countries such as the U.S.A., the EU, and Japan, constituting about 80 percent of world retail sales. Comprised of organized and unorganized retail sectors, the Indian retail industry is one of the country's fastest growing industries, especially over the last few years. According to many reports the Indian retail industry is pegged at $500 billion a year and growing at about 25–30 percent per annum, making it the fifth largest in the world and a very attractive market. Of this huge retail market, only about 7–8 percent is contributed by organized retail (Sharma, 2012). In contrast to the huge retailers of the world such as Walmart, Tesco, Carrefour, and Metro AG, the Indian retail scenario includes approximately 12 million mom-and-pop outlets, of which only 4 percent have floor space larger than 500 ft^2. This makes for the lowest per capita retail space in the world of about 2 ft^2 per person, compared with about 16 ft^2 per person in the U.S.A. Thus, the potential of the Indian retail sector is significant and has attracted global leaders such as Wal-Mart and Carrefour to enter either the complete retail value chain or significant parts of it.

Although the retail industry in India has mostly been unorganized historically speaking, recent trends in the tastes and preferences of consumers suggest that the industry is getting both more popular these days and organized. In this industry food and groceries is the most dominant sector accounting for 60 percent of the market and growing at a rate of 9 percent annually (Sharma, 2012). Clothing and fashion accounts for about 17 percent of this huge market.

Competitors

Although the Indian retail market is huge and attractive, it is one of the toughest to survive and compete in as a result of the severe inefficiencies of the retail supply chain. This is also complicated by the lower levels of purchasing power among Indians, with the average spending per month on fast-moving consumer goods (FMCGs) languishing at around $50 compared with $107 in China and $390 in Hong Kong.[12] In recent years, several domestic players such as the Future Group, the Aditya Birla Group, the Tata Group, ITC, and the Reliance group of companies have made significant attempts to capture an increasing portion of this unorganized sector and bring it into the fold of the organized sector (Satish, 2006). Many global leaders such as Wal-Mart and Tesco are waiting in the wings and developing their strategies to enter this sector, with key joint venture agreements in place (Kumar and Bhattacharya, 2006). There are key legal restrictions for FDI in the multi-brand retail sector that have prevented these companies from entering the market directly with wholly owned subsidiaries,[13] although these may be removed in the near future. While Tesco and Carrefour have somewhat significant sourcing operations in India, Wal-Mart has reached a joint venture agreement and mapped out a retail plan for India in association with the Bharti Airtel group of companies, and Tesco is in talks with the Aditya Birla Group for a similar purpose (Lakshman, 2006). Speaking after the Wal-Mart and Bharti deal was announced, Ambani said: "No one company, no one multinational, can help India realize its true retail potential. There is place for six to eight players. The government should allow foreign direct investment in retail, otherwise foreign companies will find their way into the country anyhow" (Kumar and Bhattacharya, 2006). All of these players are focusing on the favorable demographics of the country such as largest middle-class population (300 million), one of the youngest populations in the world (85 percent less than 45 years old), rising disposable incomes, and greater access to consumer financing. With this market being the target focus of many business houses, both domestic and international, the resulting retail market consists of a variety of retail store formats such as those in Table 6.1.

The India challenge for retail

In addition to severe inefficiencies in the supply chain and relatively lower levels of spending power, India poses many other challenges for aspiring retailers. Many analysts opine that the tax structure in India favors small retail businesses. Several analyses indicate that there is a serious lack of adequate infrastructure facilities. Complicating these problems is the high cost of real estate and serious restrictions in foreign direct investment (FDI) for multinational retailers, especially those not in single-brand retailing. As with many other consumer products, the huge social and cultural diversity of Indians leads to significant dissimilarities in consumer groups across the different states of the country. People in these different states speak

Table 6.1 **Classification of retail formats in India**

Mom-and-pop stores: family-owned businesses catering to small sections; they are individually handled retail outlets and have a personal touch
Department stores: general retail merchandizers offering quality products and services.
Convenience stores: located in residential areas they offer slightly higher priced goods due to the convenience offered
Shopping malls: the biggest form of retail in India offering customers a mix of all types of products and services including entertainment and food under a single roof
E-tailers: retailers providing online buying and selling of products and services
Discount stores: factory outlets that discount the maximum retail price (MRP)
Vending stores: relatively new in the retail sector, they sell beverages and small snack items through vending machines
Category killers: small speciality stores that offer a variety of categories; known as category killers they focus on specific categories, such as electronics and sporting goods
Speciality stores: retail chains dealing in specific categories and providing a wide range

Source: www.greenwood-management.com

different languages, have different cuisines, and have different preferences in traditional clothes and apparel. The relative newness of modern retail also has caused a serious shortage of trained manpower in the industry with relatively low levels of retail management skills in the labor market.[14]

These challenges have proven difficult even for companies with excellent local knowledge such as Vishal Retail. In a recent interview, Ram Chandra Agarwal, the erstwhile promoter of this retail company highlights the top 10 mistakes made by his company. Although some of these mistakes, such as reliance on cash and not having an adequate technological backup, can be attributed to inexperience in modern retail, a vast majority of these mistakes pertain to the shortage of skilled manpower and severe lack of trustworthy management skill in retail (see Table 6.2).

Table 6.2 **Lessons from Indian retail failures: top 10 mistakes**

No.	Mistakes
1	A company continuing to be known by the people it keeps
2	Lack of management bandwidth
3	Lack of planning
4	Overconfidence
5	Failure to learn how to manage scale
6	Downmarket image
7	Unprofitable growth
8	Reliance on cash
9	Lack of management skills
10	Inadequate technology backup

Source: Ram Chandra Agarwal on what he learned from Vishal Retail's ten big mistakes, 9 March 2012, 10.11 AM IST, ET Bureau.

Table 6.3 **Seven lessons from A.T. Kearney's 2011 GRDI**

No.	Lesson
1	Market selection is both an art and a science
2	Global expansion is a portfolio game
3	Consumers in developing markets are discerning
4	Local competition is often stronger than it appears
5	The rules are different for global and national organizations
6	Local talent is crucial
7	Global expansion requires a long-term view

Source: The Global Retail Development Index™: lessons learned from a decade of retail expansion. Available from: *http://www.atkearney.com/index.php/Publications/grdi-a-10-year-retrospective.html*

Seen in the context of management lessons derived from A.T. Kearney's extensive study of the retail scenario around the world, the lessons of this failed Indian retail venture suggest the importance of local talent and the discerning nature of consumers in developing markets such as India. In addition to talent shortages and manpower issues, this global study also highlights the importance of not ignoring local competition and the differential treatment of global v. national companies in this sector (see Table 6.3). These lessons apply to India as much as they do to other developing nations.

In summary, past experience points to the necessity of developing a comprehensive long-term strategy specifically suited to the Indian market, perhaps focusing a great deal of attention on people issues, both from the standpoint of employees and consumers. However, for companies that successfully manage these challenges, the future in Indian retail looks very bright indeed. The retail industry here is currently growing at a great pace and is expected to go up to $833 billion by 2013, with the organized sector alone expected to grow at a cumulative annual growth rate (CAGR) of 40 percent. The total retail sector (both organized and unorganized) is further expected to reach $1.3 trillion by 2018 at a CAGR of 10 percent.[15]

India: a growth story grown old?

India's economy is the 11th largest in the world by nominal GDP and 3rd largest by purchasing power parity (PPP). The country is one of the G20 major economies and a member of the BRICS (Brazil, Russia, India, China, and South Africa) group of emerging markets. In 2011, the country's per capita income stood at $3694 (in PPP terms), 129th in the world, thus making India a lower middle income economy.[16]

India recorded the highest growth rates in the mid-2000s, and is one of the fastest growing economies in the world. The growth was led primarily by a huge increase in the size of the middle-class consumer base, a large labor force, and considerable foreign investments. India is the 19th largest exporter and 10th largest importer in the world. Economic growth rates were projected at around 7 percent for the 2011–12 fiscal year.

India's economic growth was expected to remain robust in 2012 and 2013, despite a likely headwind of double-dip recessions in Europe and the U.S., according to the U.N. annual economic report – *World Economic Situation and Prospects 2012*. The Indian economy was expected to grow between 7.7 and 7.9 per cent in 2012–13, as per the report. As predicted by Goldman Sachs, the Global Investment Bank, by 2035 India would be the third largest economy in the world just after the U.S. and China. It will grow to 60 percent the size of the U.S. economy. Today's booming economy will have to pass through many phases before it can reach such a milestone, however.

In the midst of debates characterizing India metaphorically as either a Hindu elephant or an Asian tiger (Panagiotou and Story, 2004), India is the second most preferred destination for foreign investors, according to the report *Doing Business in India* by Ernst & Young. The report explores India's key sectors, investment climate, funding scenario, laws, and regulations to aid companies that are doing or plan to do business in India.

Reliance Retail Limited (RRL)

Reliance Retail Ltd. (RRL) is one of the major subsidiaries of RIL and started operations in 2006. Reliance Retail continued to expand the presence of its value and specialty formats. During the most recent reporting year, Reliance Retail opened 90 new stores spanning the value and specialty segments. In-store initiatives, wider product choice, and value merchandizing enabled the business to achieve robust growth during this period.[17]

Early vision and strategy

Reliance Retail is an unlisted and wholly owned subsidiary of the oil and gas giant RIL, the largest Indian private sector conglomerate, ranked 264th in the Fortune Global 500 in 2009 and 126th in the Forbes Global 2000 in 2010. The activity of the conglomerate spans such sectors as textiles, garments, petrochemicals, petroleum, and oil and gas, in addition to its recent foray into retail. Based on an assessment of opportunities in the retail sector, the Board of Directors gave its consent to pursue retail, and approved an initial outlay of $750 million to set up a variety of store formats such as hypermarkets, supermarkets, convenience stores, and specialty stores.[18] Chairman and CEO Ambani, announcing his intention to invest Rs. 25,000 crore over a period of five years, also outlined his vision of inclusive growth and prosperity for farmers, vendor partners, small shopkeepers, and consumers. This vision outlined a business model that is commonly called "farm to fork", and envisioned significant enhancements and involvement in the entire value chain to provide a solid footing in the organized retail sector.

The plan envisaged the company opening nearly 6000 outlets in 784 town and cities by 2010–11, with around 6400 procurement centers around the country, each with cold storage for fresh produce (Sinha, 2007). The company thus planned to connect farmers to end consumers and to *disintermediate* the whole distribution chain for these products. The company thus aimed to build a huge logistics network to support the national chain of retail stores, with some of this being outsourced. Another aim of this huge logistics network was to serve corner store shopkeepers (external customers) to help them derive maximum benefits. The company went into acquiring mode to help build the logistics infrastructural backbone of the entire network by (a) leasing 300 warehouses from the Himachal Pradesh Marketing Corporation (HPMC), best known for its apple juice concentrate, using them as rural retail hubs (RRHs), and buying into HPMC's equity; (b) buying the Sahakari Bhandar chain of cooperative stores in Maharashtra, mainly for access to retail real estate and infrastructure; (c) buying an exclusive fleet of 40 aircraft to bolster the logistics network (Bhattacharya, 2006); (d) engaging in talks to take over the defunct cooperative chain run by the central government called Kendriya Bhandar for its employees, with 112 stores around the country and 42 fair price shops in Delhi; and (e) planning to take over Super Bazar, another defunct chain of cooperative stores with prime real estate in Delhi such as Connaught Place (Bhattacharya, 2006).

The company's pan-India retail network currently operates nearly 1150 stores in 86 cities across 14 states (Table 6.4), and had retail sales of about Rs. 4,500 crore (INR45 billion) in the year ending March 2010.[19] There is continued and growing optimism and enthusiasm on the part of top management and the executive leadership at Reliance Industries for the future of its pan-India retail network. Ambani, the CEO of this group, said, "Over the next five years, I can realistically foresee this business growing 10 fold from current levels, and becoming a significant value creator for Reliance in the coming years . . . Your company is well equipped to be a national leader in this space."

But for initial resistance from some states and stakeholder groups (Bhattacharya, 2007; Srivastava, 2007a), the company's initial plans and roadmaps would have been

Table 6.4 Reliance Retail's presence in India

Year	No. of stores	States	Cities
2006–07	96	4–5	Jaipur, Chennai, NCR, Guntur, Vijayawada, Visakhapatnam

2007–08	590	13	57 cities
			First digital store (April 2007)
			First hypermarket, Ahmedabad (August 2007)
			Also launched many speciality stores
			    (Reliance Trends, Reliance Footprints,
			    Reliance Jewels, Reliance Timeout,
			    Reliance Autozone, Reliance Wellness,
			    Reliance Super, Reliance I Store)

2008–09	900	14	80 cities Reliance Super, iStore (Apple products), Reliance Living
2009–10	1150 stores	14	86 cities
2010–11	1240	14	86 cities

more successfully accomplished. A group of protesters including farmers' unions, trade union members, and a group called FDI Watch (calling for a national retail policy in FDI) were protesting in the state of Maharashtra, following earlier protests in Uttar Pradesh, West Bengal, and Orissa. According to reports, these protests were against all large retail groups, but some were targeting Reliance Retail specifically (Bhattacharya, 2007). As a result of these protests, Reliance Retail closed more than 50 stores and all procurement centers in many northern states (Layak, 2009; Srivastava, 2007a). But, despite these roadblocks and other hurdles, the company and its top managers, including Ambani, the CEO, are very optimistic and determined to continue with their expansion plans. During the slowdown caused by the global recession, which coincided with these protests across many states, the company held many Town Hall–style meetings with its employees. During one of these meetings, called Let's Talk Growth Meetings, the CEO vowed to make RRL a world-class retailer, and outlined a four-point strategy of continuation (Kamath, 2010).

Response to setback

This four-point strategy of continuation was Ambani's response to the series of setbacks his venture had faced in recent years, including this morning's news that Pillai was leaving for personal reasons. When he called in his secretary, he wanted an immediate meeting of the top executives of the retail business to ensure that he communicated with them directly about this key departure and to ensure that they in turn communicated clearly with their rank and file. He wanted to avoid wrong signals and rumors through the grapevine at all costs. More importantly, he also wanted to communicate the firm's continued strategic commitment to this business despite the hard times. In his words, "I never give up. I want to make a world-class retail chain and I am committed to this cause. I will support the venture throughout." The CEO of RRL's value formats, Gwyn Sundhagul (Subramanian, 2008), said at this meeting, "We have prepared a robust, sustainable and deliverable business plan that will help us achieve the ambitious growth and returns that we have set for our business. We have also built a very strong and experienced top leadership team to ensure we can implement the plans." Moreover, in response to the departure of Pillai, who would eventually go back to his erstwhile employer and key competitor of Reliance Retail (i.e., the Future Group), Ambani also disclosed his plans to cast his net wider in the hunt for talent. He communicated this intent clearly to his group of top executives sending the message that reinforcements were to arrive soon. He kept his promise by bringing in two veterans from Wal-Mart's China operations, with Rob Cisell coming in as CEO to replace Pillai and Shawn Gray coming in as COO. Thus, Ambani ensured that strong generals were in place to oversee the success of the retail venture. Backing up his early beliefs in the importance of crucial top talent, Ambani stuck to his emphasis on strong vision and leadership commitment from the entire top management of the venture. No other Indian competitor had an investment as big as the one Reliance started with. All the other major competitor groups started with and envisioned an overall size much smaller than that of Reliance. For instance, the Aditya Birla Group, which is in talks with Tesco for a potential joint venture, planned for a total outlay of Rs. 4600 crore (Lakshman,

2006). But would Reliance Retail and Ambani be able to hold on and steer the ship when the FDI restrictions on multi-brand retail are relaxed? Would his team's efforts be sufficient enough to fulfill early promises and expectations of capturing 5 percent of the total retail market in India? Only time will tell.

Strategic intent and response to downturn

In addition to the size of the planned investment and expansion, Reliance Retail is different from the rest of the group in terms of its overall strategy of entering and occupying a dozen different segments of the retail sector from produce to apparel and footwear, and from books and music to jewellery and consumer electronics. There are those who believe that format proliferation as a strategy works (Layak, 2009). Table 6.5 provides a listing of the different store formats in different segments that have been opened by the company during the six years since its inception.

As can be seen from Table 6.5, Reliance Retail plans (1) to have a pan-India presence in multiple formats and in many different segments of retail, (2) to blanket the markets with a product proliferation strategy, which is known to be a very good

Table 6.5 Reliance's Retail offerings

Reliance's "Value" formats	
Reliance Fresh	A neighborhood concept
Reliance Mart	All-under-one-roof supermarket concept
Reliance Super	A minimart
Reliance's "speciality" formats	
Reliance Digital	Consumer durables and information technology concept
Reliance Trends	Apparel and accessories concept
Reliance Wellness	Health, wellness, and beauty concept
iStore by Reliance Digital	Exclusive Apple products concept
Reliance Footprint	Footwear concept
Reliance Jewels	Jewellery concept
Reliance Time Out	Books, music, and entertainment concept
Reliance AutoZone	Automotive products and services concept
Reliance Living	Homeware, furniture, modular kitchens, furnishings concept
Stores through joint ventures with global players	
Marks & Spencer Reliance Stores	Apparel and accessories
Vision Express	Joint venture with Pearle Europe for eyewear
Office Depot	Business-to-business joint venture for office stationery
Hamleys Toys	Franchisee stores for Hamleys Toys in India
Giorgio Armani	Franchisee boutique-style stores for Armani in India

Source: Reliance Industries Limited Annual Report 2010–2011.

strategy to increase barriers to entry into the industry, and (3) to provide solid positioning in the competitive marketplace for retail customers. Other competitors such as Subiksha, a chain of convenience-type supermarket stores, has struggled in recent times in the face of protests against large retailers, and the impact of the global recession caused by the financial crisis of late 2008 (Layak, 2009). The RP Goenka Group, running a chain of Spencer's stores, also had to close around 55 stores, although it says it is opening new ones as well (Layak, 2009). Multi-format retail competitors such as Pantaloon Group (owned by Future Group) are claiming to be unaffected by the downturn and have no bad news to share (Layak, 2009).

Joint venture strategy

In addition to its strategy of having a presence in multiple retail segments such as apparel, footwear, books, music, consumer electronics, wellness and health, home furnishings, jewellery, automotive products, and groceries, the Reliance Retail Group is also engaging in joint ventures with a number of global players. As a way of hedging its risks during the downturn and of increasing its presence in more segments of retail, it has entered into a joint venture with the U.K.'s Marks & Spencer to open more than 50 outlets selling apparel and accessories (Gopalan, 2008). Within a fortnight of signing the joint venture with Marks & Spencer, Ambani also signed another joint venture with Office Depot, the global retailer of office supplies, and together they announced the acquisition of eOfficePlanet, a company that supplies office equipment to corporate customers in India (Gopalan, 2008). Additionally, the company has entered into an equal joint venture with Pearle Europe to open a chain of 700 Vision Express stores selling optical goods and eyewear to an Indian market worth $900 million, which is expected to grow exponentially in the organized sector.[20]

Reliance Retail also established partnerships with several leading international brands aimed at meeting consumer aspirations. During FY 2012–13, RRL doubled the presence of its partner businesses and operated over 160 stores in various parts of the country. In the fashion and apparel segment, RRL now operates around 40 stores in association with leading brands like Marks & Spencer (19 stores), Diesel (7 stores), Paul & Shark (4 stores), Ermenegildo Zegna (6 stores), and Timberland (6 stores). Its presence in the optics business is in partnership with Grand Vision. Fifty-one new stores were added during FY11 taking the total presence to 100 stores across key markets in the country. The retail chain offers single-brand optical products including Vision Express frames, lenses, contact lenses, sunglasses, cleaning solutions, and accessories.

For the very first time, consumers in India had the opportunity to experience Hamleys, considered to be the world's most wonderful toy shop. The brand was launched in India with the opening up of two stores during FY11. Reliance Digital also launched iStore, a one-stop-shop for all Apple products and services; there are 17 such stores currently operational.

Reliance Brands also announced an exclusive licensing arrangement with two leading international brands: Steve Madden, a leading designer, wholesaler, and retailer of fashion-forward footwear and accessories for women, men, and children; and Quiksilver, a leading outdoor sports lifestyle company famous for its Quiksilver and Roxy brands. Across India, Reliance Retail serves over 2.5 million customers every week. Its loyalty program, Reliance One, has the patronage of more than 6.75 million customers.

Institutional legitimacy

A key underlying success factor of the Reliance Retail strategy and the reason for some of the opposition and protests in many northern states is the issue of institutional legitimacy and the related concept of liability of newness (DiMaggio and Powell, 1983). Many stakeholder groups – such as market middlemen, trader associations, and small-shop owners, whom Reliance seeks to ultimately replace with its farm-to-fork business model, as well as groups in the communist-ruled states of Kerala and West Bengal and other political groups like FDI Watch – have protested forcefully and stalled the progress of the Reliance juggernaut (Srivastava, 2007b). This is essentially an issue of institutional legitimacy and the appropriate way of doing retail business in a country that has been historically dominated by millions of unorganized mom-and-pop retailers. Reliance's strategy to confront this trouble has been one of working the system quietly but firmly, and achieving legitimacy in as many states of the country as possible, before bringing things to a head in those states where there is trouble. Eventually, even communist West Bengal and its constituent groups have been won over by Reliance's charm offensive, with the Agriculture Marketing Minister of the state saying, "We would like Reliance to apply for the APMC [Agricultural Products Marketing Control] licence all over again. We must be practical and look at things from the current perspective" (Chakraborty, 2009). Another piece of this institutional legitimacy puzzle is the silence of the Confederation of Indian Industry (CII), perhaps not helping Reliance because it is headed by a top manager of a key competitor.

Another aspect of institutional legitimacy, the Reliance strategy to counter the liability of newness (Hannan and Carroll, 1992), is another important underlying factor of the success achieved to this date. Reliance's petrol retail business struggled for a long time in the face of competition in a not-so-level playing field comprising primarily public sector petroleum retailers. Eventually Reliance closed down many of its petrol retail outlets.[21] Perhaps learning from this experience, and wanting to avoid legitimacy issues, Reliance started off with the strategic vision of opening outlets in multiple formats across many different segments to enable consumers to think of a Reliance store as an automatic (and therefore legitimate) option for sourcing their purchases. Customers and farmers have always been on Reliance's side throughout the protests from other groups. Regardless of Reliance's intentions, having a presence in multiple formats and segments of the retail business across many states of the country within a short span of time has given the company the required legitimacy to sustain itself in a tough political and competitive environment. Without such legitimacy, the forces of liability of newness would have taken over and consigned the company to obsolescence in a relatively short span of time. But would this proliferation of formats help in the long run? Will they all be profitable or will certain formats result in critical decisions being made about shutting them down? Would the demands made by these multiple formats on human capital and other resources be met with sufficient responses from the firm? These would be critical questions needing answers from the retail arm of this huge conglomerate if success and a position of leadership in this sector are to be achieved.

Human capital and retail in India

Retail is an emerging industry with unique talent challenges. There are many participants in the Indian retail business environment including both local and global players, which was not the situation two decades ago. In the early years of organized retail in post-liberalization India, the human capital challenge varied across established players in retail and those that had no experience in this sector, such as Reliance. This human capital challenge would also be very different for the likes of globally experienced Wal-Mart and Carrefour, as opposed to the fledgling Indian players, despite their being huge entities with deep pockets in other economic sectors. Thus, although it could be argued that the retail industry does not need highly specialized skills, as more than 70 percent of retail positions are at the frontline level for which people can easily be trained, the critical challenge for Reliance was in the top 30 percent of the organization.[22]

Selection of executives and organizational design

Realizing that the scale and scope of their strategic foray into the retail sector could not be achieved without key human resources in the form of executive leadership, the company began by recruiting well-experienced top executives in the retail sector and creating the necessary organization to make it a great success. Many of Reliance Retail's key generals were initially enticed away from the domestic competition (Nambisan and Lakshman, 2006) and then later from some global players as well (Subramanian, 2008). The recruitment of these top executives was the first shot fired by Reliance Retail, leaving the competition battered and bruised (Nambisan and Lakshman, 2006), and eventually led to some non-poaching agreements with key competitors (e.g., the Bharti–Wal-Mart joint venture).[23] This war for talent in a country that has a severe shortage of retail talent, as a result of decades of dominance by unorganized retailers, has at times negatively affected Reliance itself by triggering a poaching war, as illustrated by the opening situation in this case.

First, however, Reliance effected a coup by enticing away Pillai, who kicked off retail ventures such as Food World, Music World, and Health & Glow for the RPG Group of companies from Pantaloon Retail, where he had a strong presence. Pillai, who had been instrumental in spearheading the front-end operations of the retail venture as CEO of Reliance Retail eventually decided to leave the company and later announced his decision to return to his former employer Pantaloon Retail. He left the company after having firmly established Reliance Retail as a legitimate and successful player in India's retail sector, much as he had done for two other companies earlier. The company also arrived at an operating structure in which the retail division's chief executives would head the vertical profit centers and report to Ambani's right-hand man, Manoj Modi. The company also envisioned a geographical structure with a state-level CEO who would take charge of the area and all the formats therein. The heads of business verticals were to be entrepreneurial and responsible for driving profits within the vertical (Carvalho, 2008), whereas the geographical owners were to be responsible for individual store and geographical performance. Thus, the company essentially set up a matrix structure of operations in the country to handle the complexities of the different institutional environments in different states of the country.

Following the recruitment of Pillai, Reliance headhunted the former marketing head of Titan Watches (a Tata Group retail venture) Biju Kurien, who was to lend his expertise to lifestyle. Dipping into the multinational talent pool, Reliance then brought in the king of the supply chain, D. Saravanan, from McDonald's as well as Sanjeev Asthana from Cargill India Ltd. as the business head for grains and oilseeds. Rajeev Karwal, an ex-Onida LG Electrolux executive, was brought in to head the consumer electronics vertical. Table 6.6 provides a complete list of the experienced and knowledgeable executives brought in from leading national and multinational players to provide the think tank and operational power behind Reliance Retail's foray and to make its vision a reality.

Such strategic executive recruitment was supported by training, management development, and strategic retention practices that only a company the size of Reliance, not to mention its ambitious attitude, could handle effectively. A recent entry into this fold of top executives is Gwyn Sundhagul, after his successful career as Director of Tesco Lotus in Thailand (Subramanian, 2008). He is CEO of Reliance's value formats and a member of the board. Sundhagul soon unveiled his brand strategy of "Bettering the lives of Indians everyday" in one of the Let's Talk Growth Meetings mentioned earlier.

Such a level of poaching activity eventually led to a poaching war and later to a non-poaching agreement with the Bharti–Wal-Mart retail joint venture.[24] The agreement was supposed to last a year and would ensure that these two companies did not get into each other's talent pool. Reliance had poached a number of professionals from the Bharti–Wal-Mart combine just a year earlier, as a result of the talent shortage of retail professionals in India, compounded by the high turnover for such professionals. Among other factors, employee turnover, perhaps as a result of poaching by competitors, or as a result of a firm's declining capability to retain key employees, has long been considered a crucial matter of interest for people studying strategic human resource management (SHRM) (Griffeth et al., 2000; Lepak and Snell, 1999). At least two of the people in Table 6.3 have been enticed away from Reliance Retail in the last year, including Pillai and Karwal.

Human capital: the other 70 percent

Organized retail offers opportunities for people from multiple industries and varied backgrounds such as consumer durables, agricultural products, and real estate and operations including support functions (e.g., IT, marketing, finance, and HR). Organized retail also provides economic security to people in urban as well as rural areas.

Table 6.6 **Strategic recruitment of key executives**

No.	Name of executive	Past experience	Key responsibility at RRL
1	Rob Cisell	Former Chief Operating Officer of Wal-Mart, China. Senior Executive at Kingfisher Plc and Argos	CEO
2	Shawn Gray	Former Vice President in charge of stores, Wal-Mart, China	COO
3	Gwyn Sundhagul	Former CEO of Tesco, Thailand	Chief Executive of Value Format
4	Ajay Baijal	NA	President of Corporate Planning
5	Manu Kapoor	NA	Senior Vice President of Corporate Affairs Division
6	Darshan Mehta	NA	Head of Reliance Brands
7.	Raghu Pillai[a]	Food World, Music World, Health & Glow, Pantaloon Retail	CEO of Reliance Retail Ltd.
8.	Biju Kurien	Marketing Head of Titan Watches	CEO of Lifestyle Division
9.	D. Saravanan	Supply Chain and Quality Control at McDonald's	Supply Chain and Quality Control
10.	Sanjeev Asthana	Business Head, Grains at Cargill India	Head of Oilseeds and Grains
11.	Rajeev Karwal	Onida, LG, Electrolux	Head of Consumer Electronics
12.	Sriram Srinivasan	Indus League	Head of Apparel
13.	Suresh Singaravelu	Prestige Constructions and Forum	Development of Malls
14.	K.L. Muralidhara	Vice President and Country Head of American Express	Head of Financial Services and Travel
15.	Gwyn Sundhagul	Director of Tesco Lotus, Thailand	CEO of Value Formats
16.	Gunender Kapur	HUL executive head of Modern Foods and Unilever Nigeria	Head of Food and Grocery

Notes: NA = not available; HUL = Hindustan Unilever;
[a]Raghu Pillai left the organization in 2010.
Source: compiled from multiple sources (Subramanian, 2008; Pal, 2006; Nambisan and Lakshman, 2006).

As Bijay Sahoo of Reliance Retail Ltd. explains, "In Indian villages, there are very large numbers of people who are either unemployed or underemployed because of limited land resources for agriculture. Additionally, they have limited opportunity for employment in sectors other than retail, as most other industries require technical/professional education or training. Since the retail industry, at the store associate level and in many other back-end operations, does not require a high level of education, people can be trained for those operations." Thus, with the opening of the retail sector in India, over 2 million job opportunities are likely to be created in the country over the next four to five years. Reliance, a major organization in this sector, will play a significant role in creating employment for large masses of people, including many who are migrating from rural to urban areas to gain employment.

Since Reliance's inception in 2006, the company's expansion plan required a continuous supply of trained manpower to meet business requirements. To ensure this continuity, key initiatives were created and they have been highly successful in generating rapid growth. Such programs include "Each One Brings Ten" (EOBT), "Train and Hire Model for Frontline Manpower", and the hiring of expatriate subject matter experts. The company has also structured training and developmental programs that continuously build and upgrade the organization's human capital through inputs in various behavioral, technical, and techno-functional areas. Under the EOBT program, each new hire was encouraged to bring ten new people into the organization. Under the "Train and Hire Model for Frontline Manpower" the company partnered with several vocational training institutes across the country (i.e., industrial training institutes, ITIs) for frontline workers, where candidates are provided with training on soft skills and functional areas and then go through an assessment process. The company also hired expatriates as subject matter experts from across the world (where retail industry had reached levels of maturity) to support defining processes, identifying technologies, building capability, and enabling knowledge transfer. Through these programs, the company opened 700 stores in less than two years while educating, employing, and empowering nearly 30,000 people. As can be imagined, poaching and the talent war has not been restricted to just the top layers of retail management, they have extended down to the bowels of retail organizations as well. It would simply be much easier to recruit people with experience in retail, a relatively rare commodity in the Indian retail scenario, than to hire new people and train them to work with specific store formats and information systems. These factors have been critical to gaining competitive advantage for global retailers such as Wal-Mart in their home base and elsewhere.

All this serves to highlight the role of SHRM, in general, and strategic executive selection, in particular, for the success of ventures such as this. The presence of an army of generals and executives whose middle names are "Retail" also adds to the institutional legitimacy factors discussed earlier. Thus, SHRM in the form of executive recruitment and institutional legitimacy work hand in hand in contributing to the sustainability of the business model and its competitive advantage. Reliance does invest in training and managerial development in association with premier Indian institutes of management to build competencies in the retail sector.[25]

Framework for understanding success in pan-India retail

Based on the above case description, we present a brief framework of the success of Reliance's foray into retail showing the relationships between its strategy and vision, linked with institutional legitimacy, and strategic human resource management (HRM), as they impact sustainable competitive advantage (Figure 6.1).

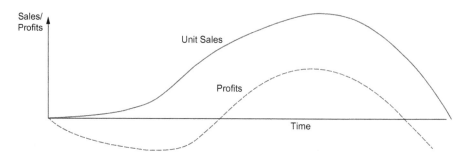

Figure 6.1 Sales/Profits curves over different stages of the industry life cycle

Figure 6.1 shows that the top few levels of Reliance's executive leadership has had a significant impact on both institutional legitimacy and on its strategic HRM practices. Its strategic HRM practices have in turn had an impact on institutional legitimacy, independent of their vision and strategy. All three of these factors have had a tremendous influence on sustaining the competitive advantage that Reliance Retail has already built and is continuing to establish more firmly in this emerging market.

Reliance's unique staffing strategy

Reliance Retail's hiring methods are pretty unique. The company starts off by hiring Presidents for all its verticals. Those hired for the retail venture were asked to recommend ten others and list five HR practices that they had experienced. In no time they had built a huge database. At the end of the first year of the retail venture, Reliance had 30,000 employees with virtually no hiring mandates or ads. In fact, Reliance Retail had hired 500 professionals without spending a penny.[26]

Reliance Retail's hunt for talent and skills

The massive talent shortage in the retail sector was the catalyst for the retail sector to gear up in its search for skilled employees for key positions. To this end Reliance asked the HR team to camp in Dubai and do gate interviews (high-speed walk-in interviews) for positions in sales, marketing, purchase, and merchandizing. But, what is attracting west Asians to move to India?

The Indian economy has continuously recorded high growth rates and has become an attractive destination for investments, which is creating and providing many job opportunities for employees. The compensation package is attractive and matches the position(s). This is attracting more west Asians to move to India.

Reliance's HRM and its transformation

Ambani created an aura that made people work seemingly beyond their capabilities. He believed that HR no longer related to packages and perks, incentives and facilities. It involved unshackling the latent energies of people. Top talent is hired first. When the company hires talent, its employees are told they are part of something that will change the world. The work environment is such that the senior employees stay and work at the office even beyond their normal hours. Yet Reliance is able to retain them long term.[27]

Reliance stresses the quality of life. The workplace environment is deliberately set up to proactively foster professional as well as personal growth. Reliance gives freedom to its employees to explore and learn, and there are opportunities inspiring initiative and intrinsically motivating the employees. Reliance thinks, behaves, lives, and thrives with a global mindset, encouraging every employee to reach his or her full potential by availing themselves of opportunities that arise across the group. With a presence in more than 38 countries, Reliance offers global opportunities. It offers possibilities for cross-organization, cross-discipline, and cross-country career opportunities.

Reliance ensures it has the world's best practices and processes by constantly reengineering them and adding to them.[28] In sum, Reliance's HR systems can be categorized as high-performance work systems (HPWSs) (Datta et al., 2005; Iverson and Zatzick, 2011).

Awards and achievements[29]

- Reliance Footprint received the Retailer of the Year Award in the non-apparel and footwear category at the Asia Retail Congress 2010.
- Reliance Time Out received the Retailer of the Year Award in the leisure category at the Asia Retail Congress 2010.
- Vision Express was bestowed the 2010 Award by the Netherlands India Chamber of Commerce and Trade.
- Reliance Trends received the Retail Marketing Campaign of the Year Award at the Asia Retail Congress 2010.
- Reliance Trends also received the Impactful Retail Design and Visual Merchandizing of the Year Award at the Asia Retail Congress 2010.

Prospects for the future

Although Reliance Retail has achieved tremendous success since its inception, it has not been able to achieve all its initial goals. Ambani wanted to have an eventual retail presence in 1500 towns, but 6000 outlets in 784 towns and cities by 2010–11, which is yet to be achieved (John, 2006). The company has still not been able to achieve its target investment levels as initially planned as a result of a number of setbacks to its expansion efforts. What factors have enabled Reliance to achieve the level of success it has had in this difficult market? What factors have impeded its progress and limited its expansion plans, making it difficult for the company to expend all of the outlay envisaged at the outset? Could there perhaps have been a different strategy for this effort? How critical is the role of HR in the implementation of this strategy? These were questions the top executive team at Reliance would ponder during their subsequent strategic meetings. However, nothing could put into question the continued commitment and attention of the very top levels of management at this firm.

Discussion questions

1. Although Reliance Retail Limited has succeeded in firmly establishing itself and making a profit, why has it been unable to achieve the level and scope of expansion objectives initially envisaged? Focus both on factors internal to the firm and critical environmental factors.
2. To what extent do you think that the role of strategic human resource management is critical to success in ground-up retail initiatives of such large magnitude? Could the company have used different strategies for executive recruitment and development? Would those alternative choices have eliminated or minimized the difficulties faced?
3. Does the Reliance strategy of format proliferation make sense in the context of institutional legitimacy in emerging markets such as India? What are the alternatives to having a simultaneous presence in multiple formats and a near simultaneous countrywide presence in this market? Would these alternative choices be more effective in overcoming roadblocks?
4. What approach to the market should global retailers take, knowing the experience of this formidable player in the Indian environment composed as it is of millions of unorganized mom-and-pop retailers?

Financial highlights

	2011	2010	2009	2008	2007
Turnover	Rs. 2586.51 ($58.0)	Rs. 2004 ($44.6)	Rs. 1463.28 ($28.9)	Rs. 1392.69 ($34.7)	Rs. 1183.54 ($27.23)
PBDIT	Rs. 411.78 ($9.2)	Rs. 330.41 ($7.4)	Rs. 257.43 ($5.08)	Rs. 242.01 ($6.03)	Rs. 205.24 ($4.72)
Cash profit	Rs. 345.30 ($7.7)	Rs. 279.33 ($6.2)	Rs. 223.65 ($4.4)	Rs. 252.05 ($6.28)	Rs. 176.78 ($4.07)
Net profit	Rs. 202.86 ($4.5)	Rs. 162.36 ($3.6)	Rs. 156.37 ($3.08)	Rs. 194.58 ($4.85)	Rs.119.43 ($2.75)
Net profit (10-year CAGR)	23%	21%	25%	30%	30%
Total assets	Rs. 2847.19 ($63.8)	Rs. 2510.06 ($55.9)	Rs. 2457.06 ($48.4)	Rs. 1497.92 ($37.34)	Rs. 1173.53 ($27)

Notes: All currency amounts are in billions (Indian rupees, Rs.; U.S. dollars, $). CAGR = compound annual growth rate; PBDIT = profit before depreciation, interest, and taxes.
Source: Annual Reports (2007–11).

Notes

1. http://articles.economictimes.indiatimes.com/2013–12–30/news/45711403_1_reliance-mart-reliance-retail-cash-and-carry-format.
2. http://articles.economictimes.indiatimes.com/2012–12–06/news/35647626_1_ceo-tony-tyler-iata-dg-and-ceo-iata-study.

3. http://www.livemint.com/Companies/95aM4EcmxJ0dXhdYCO9sxL/International-airline-traffic-beats-domestic-growth.html.
4. http://en.wikipedia.org/wiki/Air_asia.
5. I sincerely thank Sangeetha Lakshman for her significant contributions in compiling this case.
6. Reliance Industries Limited Annual Report, 2005–6, p. 61.
7. 1 crore = 10 million.
8. A *kirana* is a grocer.
9. *Paan* and *beedi* shops are small tobacconist shops selling chewing tobacco and tobacco-like herbs, respectively.
10. http://www.atkearney.com/index.php/Publications/global-retail-development-index.html.
11. http://www.atkearney.com/index.php/Publications/global-retail-development-index.html.
12. The Global Retail Development Index™: lessons learned from a decade of retail expansion. Available from: http://www.atkearney.com/index.php/Publications/grdi-a-10-year-retrospective.html.
13. Press Trust of India/New Delhi (9 May 2010). Retail FDI may come with stiff conditions.
14. www.greenwood-management.com.
15. www.greenwood-management.com.
16. Business Monitor International Ltd. India Retail Report Q3 2011.
17. Reliance Industries Limited Annual Report 2010–2011.
18. Reliance Industries Limited Annual Report 2005–2006, p. 61.
19. *The Economic Times*, 19 June 2010.
20. http://www.dnaindia.com/money/report_reliance-pearle-europe-plan-up-to-700-stores-of-eyewear-chain_1334716.
21. *Press Trust of India/New Delhi* (6 May 2008). Reliance shuts 1432 petrol pumps.
22. The Global Retail Development Index™: lessons learned from a decade of retail expansion. Available from: http://www.atkearney.com/index.php/Publications/grdi-a-10-year-retrospective.html.
23. http://www.dnaindia.com/money/report_bharti-reliance-enter-into-no-poaching-pact-for-retail_1085274.
24. http://www.dnaindia.com/money/report_bharti-reliance-enter-into-no-poaching-pact-for-retail_1085274.
25. Reliance Industries Limited Annual Report 2008–09.
26. Reliance Industries – Best company to work for by Sachin Darekar from Articlesnatch.com.
27. Reliance Industries – Best company to work for by Sachin Darekar from Articlesnatch.com.
28. Reliance Industries Limited Annual Report 2010–2011.
29. Reliance Industries Limited Annual Report 2010–2011.

Rural India and bottom-of-the-pyramid markets

7

> *"In the case of rural marketing's most celebrated story ITC's e-choupal, each of the 4,100 kiosks (containing a computer with a V-SAT connection) set up under the scheme cost between US$3,000 and US$6,000 to install and about US$100 for annual maintenance. That translates to an average initial investment of US$20.5 million and a variable cost of US$0.4 million each year."*
> **Sanjay Dawar, Managing Director, Accenture Management Consulting[1]**

As stated earlier, it is rural India that holds the key to future economic growth and many more opportunities for businesses. Rural India is going through significant transformation and economic change on an unprecedented scale. Many bottom-of-the-pyramid (BoP) markets are being converted into fully functioning and thriving marketplaces as a result of increased physical and digital connectivity. Rural India accounts for 50 percent of India's GDP and nearly 70 percent of its population (down from 80 percent in the 1950s). For the first time since independence, agriculture accounts for only one fourth of rural GDP. With nearly 75 percent of all new factories built in the last decade going to rural areas, approximately 55 percent of manufacturing GDP is rural and rural factories account for 70 percent of all manufacturing jobs in the country. Per capita GDP and consumer expenditure are both growing faster in rural areas than urban areas. With higher growth and a larger portion of India's population, it is not difficult to see why many companies, domestic and multinational, are increasingly targeting rural markets. That India's rural markets, with a staggering 12 percent of the world's population, offers huge opportunities for long-term growth should therefore not be surprising.[2]

These opportunities, however, are not without significant challenges associated with huge diversity in these markets, high dispersion of the population, and the fragmented nature of the markets.[3] If urban India lacks the institutional intermediaries required by MNCs and taken for granted by their managers in other markets, this problem in rural India is worse. High levels of dispersion and unsustainable population densities in rural areas make for highly undeveloped marketplaces in rural India, more so than anywhere else in the world. These characteristics have created traditionally high poverty levels and have forced people in rural India to operate in BoP marketplaces. People in BoP markets engage in economic transactions simply to make a living in the absence of the physical infrastructure to which their developed world counterparts are privy. Rural areas that are not electrified, are not connected by roads to other areas, do not have a supply of cooking gas and water, and do not have access to mobile phones are not integrated by any stretch of the imagination with the economy of the rest of the country and constitute BoP markets. According to a study by Credit

Suisse, there is a huge economic (productivity and wage gap) difference between rural areas that are connected by roads, are electrified, have a supply of cooking gas and water, and have access to mobile phones than those that do not benefit from them. Before the government's rural roads construction program, these areas were economically deprived and people had to travel significant distances to carry out economic activity. The Credit Suisse team discovered that in the connected villages they visited there were textile shops, packaged consumer food products, and stores selling a range of consumer electronics and white goods. These stores were absent in unconnected villages. Thus, although rural markets represent great opportunities, the challenges of serving these highly fragmented, dispersed, and rudimentary markets are many. These challenges are especially stark in rural areas that have neither physical nor digital connectivity. The presence of institutional voids, discussed in Chapter 2, is revisited here with a special focus on rural areas. The importance of a strong sales and distribution infrastructure and the challenges of establishing such an infrastructure are highlighted through a case example of one of the most successful attempts in India: ITC's e-Choupal. But, first, we take a look at the rural roots of India and the cultural connections to rural traditions and practices.

India's cultural roots

For centuries India has been predominantly rural. Rural life is the source of many of its cultural traditions, if not all. In fact, it would be very difficult to identify cultural practices that have been borne out of urban life in India. Urbanization began during colonial times and has intensified only since the onset of economic reforms and liberalization in the early 1990s. About 67 percent of Indians lived in rural areas as of 2001 according to the census reports of that year. Although agricultural land is the most productive resource and property for a great number of rural Indians, land ownership is highly dispersed with about 80 percent of households owning fewer than 2 acres of land. However, land ownership is not just a means of livelihood but a way of life for rural Indians. This way of life has led to the institutionalization of cultural practices over centuries. Cultural festivals celebrating harvests have been common across the country, but known by different names in different parts of the country. These festivals are also commonly confused with New Year festivals by many, as a result of the occasional temporal overlap (between the New Year and the Harvest) with the local calendar. Each major language-speaking region of the country has its own calendar and each is somehow different from the other in critical respects.[4] The Harvest Festival is called *Pongal* in Tamilnadu, *Bihu* in Assam, *Lohri* in Punjab, and *Sankranti* in Andhrapradesh.[5] The Harvest Festival usually lasts several days and is more or less at the same time of the year across the country. The New Year Festival, in contrast, is celebrated at different times in different regions of the country, depending on the local calendar. In addition to the Harvest Festival, many other festivals and celebrations arise out of rural life in India.

Caste system

Although agricultural work was most common in traditional India, there were many other occupations such as potters, carpenters, weavers, ironsmiths, and goldsmiths. Rural life supported many others such as storytellers, astrologers, priests, water distributors, and oil pressers. The huge diversity of occupations in India is captured by the caste system for which the country is infamous. The caste system is very ancient and is primarily based on occupation. In other words, the caste you belonged to signified the ancestral occupation your family was involved in. This ancient system classified people into four broad categories: *Kshatriyas* (rulers), *Brahmins* (priests), *Vaishyas* (business people), and *Shudras* (laborers). However, within these four broad categories specific occupations such as washermen, carpet makers, and oil pressers can also be found. Thus, the entire system consists of thousands of castes constituting a complex hierarchical tree from top to bottom. Although initially created to reflect occupation, this system evolved into a very rigid and inflexible system over centuries. Each of the four broad categories had multiple hierarchical levels within them, contributing to high levels of power distance in society. Caste membership was determined by birth and could not be changed just because an individual wanted to. Over time, the caste system became the root of many social evils, creating a category termed *untouchables* out of people who performed the most menial of jobs in society. Although it is illegal today to discriminate on the basis of a person's caste, the practice (caste system) is still prevalent in rural areas, much more so than in urban areas. In many ways the rural population is more conservative and traditional than its urban counterpart. Simultaneously, however, the rural population is the seat of most things cultural, much more so than its urban counterpart. The caste system prevents social mobility and makes it very difficult for the son (or daughter) of a potter, for instance, to become a teacher or a priest. The rationale for grouping people by occupation and having them work in a clustered community of people engaging in the same occupation works particularly well even today among goldsmiths and jewelers, for instance. But, the value of this historical rationale has lost its sheen for many other occupations, yet societal forces have prevented change in this regard.

When the fact that people traditionally marry within their specific castes and are extremely hesitant to cross even minor subdivisions in the caste system is taken into account, social mobility can be seen to be even more restricted. Simply go to any website proposing matrimonial services in 21st century India and conduct some preliminary searches to discover the number of caste categories from which a life partner can be chosen.[6] This centuries-old practice has ensured that the caste system has not only survived but strengthened. The basic Indian cultural practice of marriages being arranged by families rather than the two individuals in question needs to be understood. Heads of families choose life partners from other families of similar socio-economic status (oftentimes the same caste subdivision) and the key criterion in these cases is the compatibility of the two families rather than that of the two individuals to be united in marriage. Although this practice of having marriages arranged by families is declining, it is still prevalent even in urban India. In rural India there is a higher proportion of marriages conducted in the traditional manner. This further restricts social mobility across castes and strengthens the caste system.

In today's India many people choose not to use caste as a criterion in marriage-related decisions, although this is more the case in urban areas than in rural areas. Just look at the matrimonial section of the classified ads in any newspaper (either hardcopy or online versions) and the number of inter-caste options people can choose from become immediately apparent, thereby ruling out caste as a criterion. Although this trend is increasing, it is far from the ideal state – one in which caste plays no role in such decisions. Thus, until such time severely restricted social mobility has to be dealt with. This is critical to understanding rural markets because of the role of the caste system in deciding the agrarian social structure, and hence the socio-economic status of households and individuals in these areas. Traditionally, the higher castes were the major landowners, and thus represented a higher socioeconomic class. The relationship between caste and economic class is complex. Although *Brahmins* are the uppermost caste in India, they have rarely been landowners, and hence they do not form part of the agrarian structure despite their presence in rural life. However, most other upper castes and middle castes were traditionally major landowners, and therefore dominant in rural society. Despite changes introduced during British rule and reforms initiated by the government in independent India, this power structure has not changed much. Thus, land ownership is still highly dispersed and much of the population is wage dependent. However, the increase in rural industrialization has contributed to rising incomes in rural India. In conjunction with rural development programs (road construction, electrification, etc.), rural incomes and discretionary spending have increased and they are increasingly integrating with the rest of the country's economy. Thus, like urban India, a rural India where caste identity is no longer a major criterion in economic decision making can hopefully be envisioned.

BoP markets in rural India

Despite the progress made in connecting more and more villages by roads and electrification, much remains to be done. For instance, there are many in rural India who do not even have a bank account. According to recent reports, just 13 percent (30 million) of rural households have a bank account and are thus financially included in the country's economy.[7] Thus, a large proportion of rural households have little chance of getting involved in personal economic activity. This is typical of BoP marketplaces around the world. A major contributory factor is that banks have to contend with very low margins for serving these customers – low balances and low loan requirements – making it a difficult proposition for them. The push by many state governments and the central government to have all rural households covered financially will burden banks with a cost between INR250 and INR500 per account and little prospect of making profits until a number of years later.[8] This is a fundamental feature of BoP marketplaces – low margins, low profits, and long payback periods. The link between poverty and lack of access to financial services such as savings and loan accounts is well known.[9] People with no such access to financial services are at the mercy of alternative sources for money, such as money lenders who charge exorbitant interest rates (22–50 percent) to kickstart and sustain their economic activities. In many cases such high-interest-rate loans consign them to debt for the rest of their lives.[10]

The high cost of doing business in rural India extends to all spheres of economic activity and is by no means restricted to banking or financial services. However, a network economics effect can come into play in that the greater the number of different service providers entering rural markets the faster the likely growth in volumes to offset low margins. Physical and digital connectivity, in addition to electrification and provision of cooking gas and water to all villages and households in them, can lead to a situation in which such network economic effects can take hold. Until such time these markets remain BoP markets in many ways. An illustrative comparison between two villages in the state of Madhya Pradesh conducted as part of a study by Credit Suisse throws more light on this phenomenon (Credit Suisse, 2013). The Credit Suisse team contrasted two villages 15 km apart, each of which was only 50 km from the largest city in that state, Bhopal. Whereas Mograram was connected to this city by a road built in October 2009, Sukhila Hansraj (the other village) was not connected and the nearest access road was 4 km away. The two villages matched in terms of two important criteria: mobile phone penetration among males (100 percent in both cases) and household electrification (100 percent in both cases). The connected village performed well regarding land prices, labor mobility, wages, and alternative employment avenues; however, the unconnected village performed poorly in all these areas despite being electrified and having access to mobile phones. The cumulative annual growth rate in land prices during the 2007–13 period in Mograram was 31 percent but was only 20 percent in the unconnected village. The move to clearer land titling by the federal government and many state governments, after intense criticism from abroad, has had a very positive impact. It has made land a more easily tradable commodity than other financial instruments available to rural Indians. Land prices are critical to the well-being of most rural Indians as it is their most productive resource along with property and allows them to put the land to alternative uses, thus giving them more economic flexibility. Farmers with *Kisan* credit cards, for instance, use their land as collateral for loans exceeding INR100,000. With travel times to regional markets cut down significantly by road access, poultry farming and vegetable farming in Mograram became alternative economic avenues, whereas they were absent in the unconnected village. People in Mograram were commuting on a daily basis to pursue economic activities whereas people in the unconnected village were not. There were more *pukka* houses (those built of brick and mortar, with cement walls, floor, and roof, making them safer and more secure) in Mograram (80 percent of all houses) than in the unconnected village (40 percent). The off-season wage rate in the connected village was between INR150 to INR200 per day while it was at a low of INR120 in the unconnected village. Dairy farming started in Mograram with the help of a regional milk cooperative, whereas such assistance from the regional cooperative was absent in the other village.

There were also clear differences in terms of consumption in these two and many other similar villages. Those that were connected had more textile shops selling pre-stitched (readymade) clothes, as opposed to simple fabric in earlier times. Connected villages had a number of small grocery stores (*kirana* shops) selling a variety of packaged consumer food products hitherto unheard of. A whole range of consumer durables and white goods were sold by ITC's retail stores (see the case example for more details) in connected villages. Companies selling products such as televisions, refrigerators, and air conditioners had also set up service networks to cater to their rural clientele in these areas. Additionally, ecosystem advantages (network economic effect) can also be seen in the increased consumption of rural households with *Kisan* credit cards (interest rates of 4–7 percent), allowing villagers to hold inventory until better prices could be achieved. Price discovery has become possible as a result of mobile phones and ITC's e-Choupal[11] (see the case example for more details), and reasonable interest cost inventory financing has become possible as a result of the scheme of credit cards for farmers set up by the banking system. Thus, farmers can afford to wait for better prices to sell their products, which otherwise would have been impossible. Thus, although the contrast between these two villages shows the relative power of physical connectivity (roads), the ecosystem effect of financial services, mobile connectivity, digital connectivity through e-Choupal, electrification, and the supply of cooking gas and water is increasing the quality of life of rural Indians to much higher levels than before. With about 60 percent of all villages with a population above 100 having been electrified, many major problems have been resolved.[12] However, ensuring a continuous supply of electricity to all these villages and households is an altogether different matter and, put mildly, challenging. Improvement in the quality of life in rural India is a fundamental requisite for MNCs to engage in business activity in this area; work can then begin on efforts to change consumption patterns from bare necessities to more discretionary spending.

Special challenges in rural markets

Having seen the transformation undergone by rural areas and having considered the growth in consumer spending in rural India, we now turn our attention to the special challenge posed by rural areas to businessmen and marketers. First, many companies mistakenly assume that the rural consumer represents a single homogeneous market and thereby ignore the diversity within these regions.[13] By virtue of lower levels of integration with the national economy, lower literacy levels, and lower levels of physical and digital connectivity, rural Indians are more diverse than urban Indians. Rural Indians lack knowledge of the common language that connects urban Indians and have widely different life styles, each unique to their region of origin. Although urban Indians are a diverse group as well, rural Indians are more so. What is probably common across all rural markets in India is the level of geographical dispersion; the inadequacy of the physical, digital, and social infrastructure; and the high costs of distributing goods and services to people in areas where transaction volumes are much lower.[14] The keys to overcoming these common barriers to success in rural markets are likely to be different from one region of the country to another, something that is also true of the actual mix of products and services. When Zee TV partnered with Turner Broadcasting International in an effort to increase penetration in rural areas, they realized the complex challenge of creating programming in multiple languages. It was not enough to create the same programming choices and simply dubbing them into different languages for the company to have higher levels of viewership in a current market of 15 million rural cable and satellite households.[15] Instead, creating programming choices based on local content and values was more important to increase viewership, and hence viability as an advertising medium. After years of using national celebrities and nationally standardized advertising, Coca-Cola launched its first regional TV commercial in India, as part of a larger effort to target different rural Indian markets with a multi-pronged campaign.[16] "We are also connecting with local festivals and culture to reach out to the semi-urban and rural consumers. The consumer acceptability differs from area to area and it is in the domain of product acceptability that the company will now focus on," a senior public communication official of Coca-Cola India said. These and other examples suggest that focusing on common themes will help companies skim the market but deeper penetration is only possible with a complete understanding of the regional, language, social, and economic diversity that exists in different parts of the country.

Trust plays a greater role in rural markets than in urban areas when it comes to economic transactions. However, creating this trust necessitates different responses in different rural areas of the country. Many companies that have succeeded on this front use an effective ecosystem of trustworthy stakeholders (value chain partners) and a sales force comprising local talent. It is important to speak the language of the consumer in the local accent and to possess a sociocultural profile that the consumer can relate to. This necessitates the recruitment of local individuals who are both respectable and trustworthy when it comes to social status or possess a socioeconomic profile similar to the consumer. When ITC and Monster.com teamed up to launch their rural job portal, they found themselves limited to specific regions of a few states simply because their portal *rozgarduniya.com* was only available in Hindi and English.[17] Unilever's Indian arm, HUL, tried multiple approaches to tackle the diversity of consumer segments while seeking cooperation from other businesses to handle common barriers.[18] To match the larger range of consumer purchasing habits, varying from daily purchases to monthly purchase frequency, HUL successfully packaged premium products like Dove soap and Pond's anti-aging cream in a variety of smaller stock-keeping units in this roughly $9 billion rural fast-moving consumer goods (FMCG) market. To leverage trust, HUL also uses *Shakti Ammas*,[19] women who sell their products to rural consumers and double up as customer service providers and saleswomen for companies like the State Bank of India (SBI) and some mobile phone companies. These saleswomen help customers open bank accounts, in addition to selling mobile phones and services as well as consumer products. This serves not only to leverage trust but also to offset the higher costs resulting from lower transaction volumes. Independently, SBI and Bharti Airtel, a mobile service provider, teamed up by combining their sales forces to help customers open more bank accounts in areas where the penetration of mobile services was significantly higher.[20]

Trust is also important when trying to communicate to rural customers the benefits of new technologies. Communication is more effective when it is initiated by people who are respected locally or by people to whom the end user can relate. Manufacturers of consumer durables are increasingly targeting rural Indian households with a whole range of products from the most basic to the most advanced in terms of base technology.[21] Telecom companies are striving to move their rural customers from basic feature phones to smartphones. In all these cases companies hire local talent that are both respectable and similar to the end user. Companies like Whirlpool with an established market presence in urban India are increasingly moving into rural markets in the search for growth in this very competitive market. They are learning that the customer service needs of rural consumers are broader and involve customer education, gearing up for which is a huge challenge.[22] Rural folk, like anywhere else, are more down to earth and trust people who genuinely care for them. Demonstrating this care and commitment to rural consumer needs is a far more important issue than in urban India.

The high cost of serving rural markets is the biggest challenge facing most of the successful companies in rural India. These success stories have always involved innovation,[23] as exemplified by the case example of ITC's e-Choupal. A large part of these high costs relates to the extensive network of distribution and service centers for products like consumer durables, agricultural machinery, commercial and passenger vehicles. Costs become excessively burdensome when low transaction volumes are taken into account, at least in the initial stages. Therefore, leveraging physical and digital resources and using technology innovatively are critical components to overall success. Tata Motors succeeded in this tough market by using a variety of direct and indirect approaches. First, through extended and face-to-face interviews with owners of small commercial vehicles, the company developed a good understanding of the different customer segments within this market. Second, it used a feet-on-the-street network approach to access rural customers, much like the FMCG companies mentioned earlier. They also leveraged a network of channel partners like some of the companies already mentioned and like the company in the case example did to access rural customers.[24] For instance, ITC, the most celebrated success story in this regard, leverages its partnership with 160 different companies by means of its information infrastructure highway (e-Choupal) to reach and tap into a wide variety of customer segments in rural areas. This allows each company in the partnership to keep the unit cost of distribution and services low, while benefiting from the long-term growth potential in rural areas.[25] But what ITC does so much better than any other company in this regard is that it uses its enormous physical and digital infrastructure to engage in buying (sourcing) as well as selling, and thus manages to keep its costs down on both sides of the profit equation.[26] In addition to what ITC has already achieved in its core agribusiness, the company is also using this urban–rural transaction highway to diversify into a number of other related businesses: building rural manpower skills, advisory business in agricultural commodities, ecotourism projects, and selling fruit and vegetables in cities.[27]

ITC differs from most other companies in achieving success in rural markets by creatively managing a stakeholder ecosystem and establishing trust in the bilateral and multilateral relationships involved. This is explained in more detail in the case example. Briefly, ITC successfully recruited individuals of high standing to run their e-Choupals to facilitate the acceptability of the messages conveyed through the information infrastructure. Additionally, they appointed key stakeholders from the erstwhile distribution system to run the stores which comprised their physical infrastructure of retail stores. They also partnered with 160 companies who made their products available for sale to rural consumers through the information highway established by ITC. Thus, the most celebrated success story in rural India involved innovatively leveraging the stakeholder ecosystem.

Another aspect of success in rural markets is being perceived as socially responsible and making efforts at community development. This plays a much larger role in rural areas than anywhere else. Here again, as shown in detail in the case example, ITC has done much more than any other company so far in rural India. Since trust plays a very large role in rural India, it needs to be addressed at multiple levels. Investing in community development and demonstrating genuine commitment and care for the rural community, as well as the individuals and households within them, are all equally important. It is critical to remember that it is possible to make profits while doing good and being responsible. Each of these aspects is now addressed in a little more detail in the case example. It is also worth remembering that most lists of examples of socially responsible businesses do not include any companies from India, and hence this case example is truly unique and revealing in that sense.

Case example: ITC and India's BoP markets

"e-Choupal goes beyond mere knowledge-connectivity and enables farmers to exercise the informed choice by connecting them to local and global markets. Thus, the human and the digital infrastructure at the village is complemented and completed with a physical infrastructure in the form of 'Choupal Saagars', each at the centre of a cluster of 40 e-Choupals. Saagars offer multiple services under one roof – a marketing platform, store front for agri-equipment and personal consumption products, insurance counters, pharmacy & health center, agri-extension clinic, fuel station and a food court ... ITC has innovated a win–win situation for the farmers and the shareholders of ITC by linking the farm operations directly to their agri-export business through e-Choupal. The system has avoided the middlemen and also ensured quality product reaching the national and international markets with quality certification needed by the importing countries."

(Dr. A.P.J. Abdul Kalam, National Symposium on Agriculture)

Corporate social responsibility, especially in the context of globalization, has been a very widely discussed topic in recent times, with attention to it growing slowly but steadily (Bies et al., 2007). Although this domain is growing rapidly, not much of it is focused on Asia and almost none on India (Bruton and Lau, 2008). In fact, experts have noted that most broader management knowledge seekers, both at the micro and macro-organizational levels, have not focused as much on Asia as they have on North America and Europe. This is very surprising given that Asia contains one of the global economic powerhouses (i.e., Japan) and two of the most rapidly growing economies of the world (i.e., China and India), the former of which could become the world's biggest economy in the not too distant future. Recent debates on corporate social responsibility (CSR) have focused to a certain extent on the differences in CSR across countries (Matten and Moon, 2008), but still with very little to no emphasis or focus on countries within the Asian region. Moreover, as experts point out, Asia is a very broad region with a wide variety of cultures within its boundaries. These experts specifically make the suggestion that there is a strong need to study countries other than Japan and China (e.g., India) within this Asian region. This case example examines CSR in an Indian context, thereby providing the initial spark for such focus on India within this vast Asian region. This case example serves to demonstrate successful actions in rural markets in India while simultaneously focusing on community development issues.

The 2008 list of the world's most ethical companies (93 companies in all), compiled by U.S. companies Ethisphere and Forbes, does not have a single Indian representative, although earlier lists have had one or two such representatives (e.g., Tata and Hindustan Lever).[28] Going beyond legal minimums, bringing about innovative ideas for public well-being, and working on reducing a company's carbon footprint are among the key criteria used in this compilation of most ethical companies. The fact that no Indian company is mentioned on this list and very few over a period of time is worrisome because there are companies that excel on these criteria. The situation may simply be a result of something akin to the country-of-origin effect and the association of high corruption with India (according to the Corruption Perceptions Index). Hence, there is a need to have discussions in the public domain about Indian companies that do excel on these criteria. This case example focuses on providing details of consistent triple bottom line reporting (for over three years) according to global standards by one Indian company (i.e., ITC Ltd.).

Instead of merely providing details of Indian companies that are socially responsible, this case example focuses on identifying gaps in knowledge on CSR around the world and aims to fill some of these knowledge gaps by providing a case description and analysis of ITC and its activities in the social responsibility realm. First, this case example contrasts the different (etic and emic) conceptualizations of CSR across countries by focusing on how CSR is conceptualized in India. Second, it focuses on an examination of leadership of a certain form (i.e., knowledge leadership; Lakshman, 2007; Viitala, 2004) and its role in influencing CSR as an organizational state of being. Although leadership has been associated with and examined in the context of CSR (Basu and Palazzo, 2008), experts suggest that examination of the role of leadership in the emergence of social change activities has high potential for unique insights. Third, this case description and analysis of ITC also provides valuable lessons on how resources have been configured in an innovative fashion to create value in BoP markets (Prahalad, 2004), which is challenging to say the least. Experts suggest that our collective knowledge of configuring and creating value from resources in BoP markets is very limited because of the likely complexity and lack of clarity in the cause-and-effect relationships in such regions (Prahalad, 2004). Thus, this case example serves to throw light on the innovative building of a business model through knowledge leadership in rural and other markets of India and in so doing meet an Indian conceptualization of social responsibility.

This case example is organized as follows. First, the uniqueness of India in both a global and Asian context is highlighted by focusing briefly on its culture, economy, and nature of markets (BoP). The discussion then moves on to address the role of leadership in the social change initiatives that address CSR, since such a role has not been adequately addressed before. The subsequent section focuses on the challenge in BoP markets of establishing appropriate business models, especially those that fulfill both profit and social responsibility objectives. The next section provides an analysis of ITC's actions in fulfilling economic, social, labor, human rights, and environmental objectives, consistent with the triple bottom line approach to reporting, which the company has done now for many years.[29] The focus is largely on the e-Choupal initiative, which highlights the role of knowledge leadership and the building of business models in BoP markets, while providing the minimal coverage required on ITC's other activities comprising its broader CSR initiative.

For the sake of clarity, let us define CSR. The social responsibility of business encompasses the economic, legal, ethical, and discretionary (philanthropic) expectations that society has of organizations at a given point in time (Carroll, 1979).

India

India's culture, economy, and nature of markets differs greatly from those of China and Japan, the Asian countries that have received the most attention from experts. A study of the CSR practices of Dutch companies in India found that Indian conceptions of CSR differed greatly from Dutch conceptions.[30] One of the strongest findings of the study was that Indian companies thought of community development as a critical part of CSR, whereas Dutch companies thought of it as charity. This held true for a number of stakeholders such as NGOs, employees, and outside observers. Many small and medium-sized enterprises (SMEs) – Indian subsidiaries of Dutch parent companies – in this Dutch study had very negative perceptions of trade unions and resisted them, many of them being non-unionized. Although many of these Dutch subsidiaries met legal minimums they did not go much beyond them (according to the trade unions) by way of wages and working conditions.[31] Additionally, the study failed to focus on the environmental performance of the subsidiaries, simply noting that these companies met the legal minimum and did not go much beyond that as far as product integrity and meeting consumer needs were concerned. This is typical of most SMEs that do not have adequate resources, intellectual or material, to conceive of and support CSR strategies. However, this state of affairs does convey something about the Indian approach to CSR.

Economy

India is one of the few countries in the world where the knowledge economy operates side by side with an industrial and agrarian economy, each operating within its own rules of business. This is a huge challenge facing emerging economies such as India. India's rural market is a potentially huge market with 720 million consumers

(>65 percent of the population), but constitutes less than 30 percent of the country's GDP (Annamalai and Rao, 2003). Adding to the problem of small wallets, the rural market is also characterized by high levels of dispersion and unsustainable population densities from a marketer's perspective. The farmer's plight is no less in that land ownership is dispersed and fragmented (average 1.5 hectares), plagued with a weak infrastructure, heavily dependent on the monsoon, and subject to numerous inter-mediaries. Much like two other cases in Bangladesh (Seelos and Mair, 2007), this situation is characteristic of the complexity and uncertainty surrounding BoP markets, where little collective knowledge exists on how to build appropriate business models. How ITC and its Chairman Yogesh Deveshwar configured the corporation and the resources available in this highly unmunificent environment to build a business model that would bring in profits and meet society needs is the subject of this case example. Being able to look at this picture and seeing the tremendous opportunity for integrating, sharing, leveraging, and managing information and converting it into a business model would take unique skills on a par with the ITCs and knowledge leaders (visionaries) of the world such as Deveshwar. According to G. Ramachandran, a financial analyst and member of the Shankerlal Guru Committee on Agricultural markets, "E-choupal has correctly regarded India's agrarian and rural poverty as the result of a cruel situation faced by India's small and poor farmers, which forces them to operate and transact in 'un-evolved' markets. Farmers and rural households remain uninformed or inadequately informed in these 'un-evolved' markets because of adverse societal and economic structures."[32]

Leadership and CSR

In addition to the tendency to view community development as a critical part of CSR in India, there is also another subtle side that views this as the primary responsibility of the government. More specifically, according to one Indian company in the Dutch study, "Sustainable development implies optimizing financial position while not depleting social and environmental aspects and CSR implies supporting issues related to children, women and environment."[33] Thus, CSR typically evokes community development and issues related to children, women, and the environment, but not the "planet" or "profit" part of the triple bottom line approach. Thus, good labor prac-tices that go above and beyond the legal compliance minimum as well as the achieve-ment of profits and servicing financial capital would both fall outside a comprehensive conceptualization of CSR. It is in this context that executive leaders and their concep-tualizations of what is within the realm of CSR for their corporation take on higher importance.

Although experts on CSR have paid some attention to examining the connection between leadership and the establishment of values (Carlson and Perrewe, 1995), much more work needs to be done into how people are influenced and how they con-ceptualize CSR, especially from the point of view of bringing these viewpoints into line with global conceptualizations of CSR, such as the all encompassing triple bottom line approach. Moreover, existing knowledge on CSR also focuses on a preponder-ance of either instrumental (e.g., transaction cost economics) or institutional theory approaches to why firms behave in a socially responsible manner, to the exclusion of a "leadership and corporations as social agents" approach (Aguilera et al., 2007). In other words, existing knowledge suggests that companies and their leaders engage in socially responsible actions because they are likely to yield positive outcomes or because not being socially responsible can hurt them in an environment where many companies engage in such actions. This case example focuses on examining leader (CEO) espoused values on his conceptualization of CSR and demonstrating his knowledge leadership (Lakshman, 2007) in the building of a business model that would operationalize his conceptualization of CSR in this BoP market. This case is remarkable because of the success the business model has had amid the generally challenging conditions attested to by experts with special knowledge of BoP markets (Seelos and Mair, 2007). The ITC case is also remarkable for achieving both business success and successful accomplishment of social performance (see the following sections on BoP markets and the e-Choupal for details). Knowledge leadership involves leader-initiated and leader-influenced actions pertaining to organization-wide managing of knowledge including the creation, sharing, leveraging, and dissemination of knowledge for the benefit of the entire corporation (and society, in this case) (see Lakshman, 2007 for more details). This case example highlights the use of knowledge leadership in building a business model to achieve both financial (profit) and social objectives, while not forgetting the environmental objectives.

BoP markets

Our knowledge of BoP markets generally suggests that there is a high level of complexity in such environments making the disentangling of cause-and-effect relationships very difficult. Such high levels of causal ambiguity also lead to high levels of uncertainty in such environments. The configuring of resources in such an environment to building business models that could become effective is therefore a very challenging task, with very low net present values for these projects and delayed future cash inflows from such resource investments. This uncertainty and complexity is so high that BoP experts suggest that there is very little collective knowledge about how to accomplish this task in such environments. This case example highlights one such instance of highly fragmented and dispersed rural markets in India, complicated by poor infrastructural problems and other social inadequacies. ITC's e-Choupal (a combination of sociocognitive and technological knowledge networks) has successfully demonstrated the building of a fruitful business model under such conditions. Hence, this case example throws some light onto what is known about CSR from this perspective, in addition to focusing on uniquely Indian conceptualizations of CSR as well as on (knowledge) leadership–guided approaches to making corporations social change agents.

ITC's triple bottom line approach to CSR

ITC is the first and only one of seven Indian companies to adopt the Global Reporting Initiative's (GRI) triple bottom line reporting on a voluntary basis. Incidentally, it is also one of only 700 corporations worldwide to adopt the initiative.[34] The ITC group of companies is one of India's largest private sector companies with a market capitalization of approximately $4 billion and annual sales of $2 billion. The ITC group of companies has the distinction of being water positive for at least three successive years, in addition to becoming carbon positive in its most recent reporting year.[35] It is also making rapid strides toward becoming a zero solid waste company. Once this third objective is accomplished, it will become the first company in the world to claim such a distinction, thus justifying the selection of ITC for this analysis.

Leader's cognition and language

Leadership experts suggest that the way in which top managers (CEOs and their top teams) conceptualize, think about, and frame issues has an impact on the nature, intensity, longevity, stability, and success of CSR activities carried out by their firms (Basu and Palazzo, 2008). In an environment where people (Indians) are likely to think of CSR as mainly social and community-oriented actions (most importantly, excluding profit and labor objectives), such managerial cognition and espousal of values becomes very important. The following quote captures the essence of Deveshwar's thinking on the concept of CSR and how it applies to ITC.

> *"Envisioning a larger societal purpose ('a commitment beyond the market') has always been a hallmark of ITC. The Company sees no conflict between the twin goals of shareholder value enhancement and societal value creation. The challenge lies in fashioning a corporate strategy that enables realization of these goals in a mutually reinforcing and synergistic manner."*
>
> *(Y. Deveshwar, CEO, ITC[36])*

As suggested by this quote, Deveshwar and his team do not see social and economic objectives as being different or as competing for managerial attention. Instead, the way they think and talk about it reinforces these objectives and leads the team to operationalize them in appropriate business models such as large-scale IT intervention in the form of e-Choupals, which are discussed in detail in the following sections. The results (in some cases goals) of the other initiatives comprising the broader social, economic, and environmental initiatives of the ITC group of companies can be found in the appendix to this chapter. In addition to building business models meant to achieve economic and social objectives in BoP markets (the component most discussed here), the ITC group of companies engaged in the following initiatives: (1) to manage natural resources including wasteland, watershed, and agricultural development; (2) to generate sustainable livelihoods including the economic empowerment of women (social entrepreneurialism) and the genetic improvement of livestock; and (3) to develop communities with a special focus on primary education, health, and sanitation. These three initiatives were grouped under the umbrella of Mission *Sunehra Kal* (A Bright Tomorrow), details of which can be obtained from ITC's sustainability report. We now move our attention to a discussion of the role of knowledge leadership and business models for BoP markets.

The e-Choupal

Fighting against the conventional wisdom of the Western world of focusing on one core business, in a situation where 33 percent of ITC is owned by BAT, the British tobacco behemoth, Deveshwar wanted to excel in several other consumer goods besides tobacco: flour, cooking oil, matches, salt, hotels, paper, paperboard and packaging, and agribusiness (the source of e-Choupals).[37] Arguing that the concept of focus is a Western fixation, Deveshwar has gone on to create strategies for ITC in a multi-business environment. In a context within which ITC was concerned about social responsibility, triple bottom line reporting, and national development, Deveshwar and his team of executives developed the concept of the e-Choupal, which could integrate, leverage, share, and manage information in a fragmented and dispersed rural marketplace. The overall objective of the organization is to balance investor interests with those of the communities in which they operate and that of the government. A business model for development within the context of the international business division ($150 million in revenues) was created with an agricultural trading company providing the immediate context for the e-Choupal. The e-Choupal was simultaneously conceived as a more efficient solution for the company's supply chain as well as an e-commerce platform for selling the company's goods and services to farmers.

e-Choupals were established as a business platform consisting of a set of organizational subsystems and interfaces with the potential of connecting farmers to global markets.[38] The purpose of establishing such an organizational system that makes use of IT was to utilize it for both the procurement of supplies from the farmers and for providing a host of services and products to them as consumers. The e-Choupal business platform consists of three broad layers. The first layer consists of village-level kiosks with Internet access (e-Choupals), managed by an ITC-trained local farmer called a *sanchalak*. These e-Choupals are located within walking distance of each target farmer, with approximately one e-Choupal located per cluster of five villages. The second layer consists of a bricks-and-mortar infrastructure called "hubs" managed by a traditional intermediary with local knowledge and skills. This person, a former commission agent in the traditional *mandi*[39] system, which the e-Choupal system partly substituted, is called a *samyojak*. The *samyojak* in this second layer is located within the premises of a large mall targeting rural farmers and their families. These malls called *Choupal Sagar* are spread over 7000 ft^2 and stock all the leading brands of clothes, home appliances, consumer goods, and a variety of farm-related supplies needed by the farmer like fertilizer, pumps, and pesticides. The third layer consists of the various product and service providers (today numbering about 160 companies), in addition to ITC itself as the procurer of farm output.

Today, the e-Choupal initiative comprises 6400 e-Choupals that are transforming the lives of over 3.5 million farmers in 40,000 villages in 16 states of India. Although the company had set a target coverage of 20,000 e-Choupals for 10 million farmers in 100,000 villages worth $2.5 billion in business (Deveshwar, 2007), it had to slow down the process as a result of regulatory changes by the Agricultural Produce Market Committee (APMC). At the end of 2005, there were about 50 *Choupal Sagar* spread across four states, with more planned for the other states.

The e-Choupal business platform is an excellent illustration of the knowledge transfer mechanism and the utilization mechanism at work. The computer with Internet access located within a *sanchalak*'s home becomes the means through which ITC channels information and knowledge in a number of different domains to farmers. This information and knowledge ranges from daily prices for grain and crops at the *mandi* (the traditional outlet for sale of grains), to weather information, information on cropping practices, and healthcare information, in addition to open information available on the Internet. For instance, *sanchalak* have been known to use the system to track prices at the local *mandi* as well as on the Chicago Commodities Exchange. The use of trained *sanchalak*, local farmers with local knowledge and skills, forms a key constituent of the reverse movement of information and knowledge from villages to the multinational corporation (ITC). The same system can be used as a two-way transaction-processing system for farmers to sell their output to ITC and use it to order a variety of supplies they themselves require for use in their farms or households. The need of the day for both farmers and the ITC (as well as a variety of rural marketers) was disintermediation. The numerous intermediaries in Indian rural markets have a history of earning trading profits by undermining the structure and magnitude of rewards accruing to poor farmers owning small tracts of land.[40] The system was such that farmers were not getting an adequate price for their output, while at the same time consumers were not getting their produce at a fair price. The intermediaries were blocking information and market signals and using these activities as the basis of their profit making. Thus, the movement of information and knowledge, sharing knowledge between the producer and value-adding intermediaries such as the food-processing companies, and leveraging such knowledge would benefit all the people in the value chain. Understanding the motivation and vested interest of the *mandi* traders and utilizing many of them as *samyojak* was a stroke of genius on ITC's part, although not completely without resistance. In December 2004 soya bean trading at the *mandi* in Madhya Pradesh came to a grinding halt as a result of an indefinite strike observed by traders in various locations.[41] The strike was in protest at the e-Choupal direct marketing system. With much more information about price trends, farmers were holding on to their produce waiting for better prices, lowering trade volumes in the *mandi* and leading to a stir among traders. Farmers are able to make better decisions about who best to sell their output to and at what price, not to mention their decision-making ability in planting, irrigation, and other cropping practices as a result of the increased information flows made available to them.

It is a win–win situation as far as ITC is concerned, since it has carefully invested its time and effort in a multilayered organizational system, under the able knowledge leadership of Deveshwar, and by doing so obtain valuable information from farmers, offer them prices for their output at prevailing market levels, and using the system to sell them a bundle of products and services, in coordination with about 160 or so corporations. ITC has hooked up with *Intellect*, the research and technologies wing of the Lintas Media Group, to launch Bharat Barometer – the primary information source on all aspects of rural consumer behavior.[42] Surampudi Sivakumar, CEO of ITC

International Business Division, says, "The enthusiastic response from farmers has encouraged us to plan for the extension of the e-choupal initiative to 11 other states across India over the next few years. There are plans to channelize services related to micro-credit, insurance, health and education through the same e-choupal infrastructure."[43] Having established the rural information infrastructure highway, the company is awaiting the many other potential users: state governments putting their services online, consumer goods firms (whose distribution networks rarely get to the smaller villages), microcredit providers, and so on. Deveshwar jubilantly says, "We are owners of the road and, of course, we will charge a toll."[44] Attesting to the success of ITC's e-Choupal initiative, a few other firms are planning to roll out similar initiatives.

The village level

The village's Internet-connected computer is usually housed within the *sanchalak*'s house and connectivity is through either a phone line or through a satellite connection. Each of these e-Choupals serves approximately 600 farmers located in five to ten nearby villages, with the ultimate aim of ITC (strategic intention) to provide one such location within five kilometers of any farmer in rural India. Each of these e-Choupals takes an approximate investment by ITC of 2 lakh[45] rupees, on top of which there are the yearly operating and maintenance costs borne by the *sanchalak*, who receives a commission in return for his "aggregating" services. The *sanchalak* also receives a certain level of social prestige as a result of being selected, hired, and trained by a multinational corporation. ITC channels all its communications through *sanchalak*, knowing full well that farmers have historically been taken advantage of and that trust is a very critical element in any transaction for the villagers. All *sanchalak* take a public oath vouching that their actions will benefit the village community. Understanding that trust is a critical element of all knowledge-sharing activities, the effective knowledge leadership of ITC builds its core knowledge network component (village e-Choupal) by carefully selecting and training the individual who runs it. All *sanchalak* are selected for their ability to communicate and build trust by virtue of actions and status, literacy, willingness to try new things, risk-taking ability, and availability. In addition to accessing daily closing prices, farmers use the e-Choupal to order seed, fertilizer, and consumer goods from ITC or its partners. At the time of harvest, ITC usually offers to buy the crop at the previous day's closing price. Farmers willing to sell at that price transport their goods to the ITC processing center (in many cases the *Choupal Sagar*), where the produce is electronically weighed (a process subject to farmer complaints and pilferage in the traditional *mandi* system) and assessed for quality. Farmers get their price and a transport fee. Thus, farmers minimize transaction costs, which would otherwise go to an intermediary with added margins. Some farmers do sell directly to the crushers (in the case of soybean) and others sell their produce at the *mandi*, the traditional system set up to enable farmers to get the best prices, which has ended up benefiting traders more than farmers.

The Choupal Sagar

When farmers collect their money at the *Choupal Sagar*, they are tantalizingly close to the shopping aisles of the mall, where they can access products ranging from motorcycles to fertilizers, branded clothes to farm equipment, and diesel to home appliances; ATMs are available as are other outsourced retailers. The intention is to capitalize on both the impulsive and planned buying habits of farmers and their families. First, though, the farmer stands to benefit by being provided the transportation costs of bringing the crop to the warehouse located at the *Choupal Sagar*, and by not being cheated in the process of weighing and assessing quality. The combined system of buying and selling provides checks and balances to ensure fraud does not take place. Moreover, the *samyojak* running the *Choupal Sagar*, although disadvantaged like traders in the traditional *mandi* system, are now part of the value chain run by a larger entity, the multinational corporation. They provide bridge financing by paying the farmers and later collecting it from ITC. They manage storage, transportation, and other logistics for a commission. Many *mandi* traders have agreed to work as *samyojak* as a combined result of a desire to work for a global company and the fragmented nature of *mandi* agents, who compete amongst themselves to a certain extent. These *samyojak* provide working capital rather than the major infrastructure investment provided by ITC for the mall, the warehouse, and the electronic infrastructure. Such investment also sends powerful signals to traders who realize that they are dealing with a significantly powerful entity in the business. In the final analysis, it seems like a win–win situation for all. The *samyojak* are another crucial element in the information and knowledge-leveraging network component of the e-Choupal. They bring years of experience of handling the system and are able to provide crucial inputs on markets and trends in the e-Choupal system. In return for taking an agent's role v. the earlier principal's role, the *samyojak* benefits by managing the mall, selling consumer goods, household provisions, etc. and by finding work for himself and his staff throughout the year rather than just during the harvest season. The dynamics of the e-Choupal system, which includes the powerful motivating features of the traditional system and the alternative e-Choupal system, provide an excellent illustration of knowledge leadership at work, similar to the motivational problems faced by Toyota's knowledge-sharing network (Dyer and Nobeoka, 2000). Toyota had to face such motivational issues among its network of suppliers; the success of its supplier knowledge-sharing network eventually came down to its excellent management of the multifaceted motivational challenges it faced.

ITC and providers of products and services

Choupal Sagar stock the products of about 160 companies who pay a fee to ITC for using the channel to gain access to difficult-to-reach rural consumers.[46] The fee serves as a toll to use the physical infrastructure built by ITC. A similar possibility for charging a toll exists in the virtual realm as well for direct sales through the e-Choupal, which are serviced through the *Choupal Sagar* acting as warehouses, thereby forming a clicks-and-mortar infrastructure. All the providers of products and services benefit by leveraging the physical infrastructure built by one company over the offerings of all companies, thereby bringing down distribution costs. ITC benefits because it can get better quality delivered to its doorstep at better prices compared with the conventional option of obtaining grain from the *mandi*. Sivakumar proffers the example of the company Aashirvaad Aata to explain the success of the e-Choupal system. He says, "If under two years ITC's *Aashirwad aata* [flour] has become the No. 1 brand in the country with nearly 15 percent of the market share, it is because of quality, which is the result of the choupal infrastructure. Because we now buy from the farmer directly and we are able to store different varieties of wheat separately. When farmers sell in mandis or the FCI, all the wheat gets aggregated. And after that it can't be segregated. So sometimes the aata quality is very good, sometimes it is quite bad, and the consumer has to deal with it. But today when we store wheat separately, we have different blends. What is sold in Kolkata, Mumbai, or Chennai is very different as consumer preference is different in terms of level of coarseness, colour, usage patterns, the water absorption capacity, and so on. Earlier, consumer preferences were not matched with the wheat grown, and the farmer didn't get the right value for his produce. But that is changing now."[47] Thus, as can be seen, the process of creating, sharing, and leveraging information extends all the way from the farmer to the consumer as a result of the e-Choupal system, thereby making it an excellent illustration of the concept of knowledge leadership along the entire value chain. The company is working on the traceability of farm produce aimed at adding value by providing buyers with products of their choice.[48] Traceability is the ability to track the origin of a product and its attributes. Such a feature would help add value and get higher returns for farmers. The traceability option is extended to some produce and aquaculture products as well as being backed by insurance. The concept of traceability not only adds value from the perspective of information and knowledge of sources of products but also the resulting value in the marketplace. Wheat from Punjab and some parts of Madhya Pradesh is valued more than wheat from other sources, and rice from certain locations is more valuable than others. The e-Choupal network leverages this fact by helping identify and track the source of various products, which would otherwise not be possible under the traditional system with intermediaries oftentimes muddling information and blocking signals. Seeing the potential value of the e-Choupal system, more and more companies are aligning themselves with ITC in their efforts to reach the rural consumer, thereby enhancing the efficacy of the e-Choupal network and further lowering distribution costs. Motorola India recently joined the growing list of companies that are aiming to use the retail space provided within the e-Choupal network. Dukes Consumer Care Ltd., the Hyderabad-based confectionery maker also recently tied up with ITC to market its products through the e-Choupal network.[49] Direct-to-home (DTH) player TataSky is another company that has recently tied up with ITC's e-Choupal initiative to reach cable-dry rural areas and expand its business. Overall, this is likely to make consumerism more available to rural consumers and bring economic benefits to all participants.

ITC has won the Development Gateway Award, the TERI[50] Award, and the Golden Peacock Award for its e-Choupal initiative, which all goes to show the value of the e-Choupal network and the knowledge leadership underlying it. The Development Gateway Foundation recognized ITC's initiative of giving farmers access to market information by awarding the company the Development Gateway Award in 2005 (worth $100,000). Deveshwar said, "By delivering essential healthcare and educational information, we can extend the benefits of e-choupal more deeply into the fabric of our communities across India. And by recognizing programs like ours, the Development Gateway Foundation is spurring on the use of information technologies in communities worldwide, to build grassroots capacities and enhance the quality of life." The Development Gateway Foundation, based in Washington D.C. with operations in 60 countries, gets the Internet to work for developing countries, helping improve lives by enabling more effective development worldwide. Awards such as this further attest to the efficacy of such initiatives and to effective knowledge leadership in this context. Imitation is the best form of flattery. When the National Alliance for Mission 2007 proposed creating a massive network of information kiosks in 600,000 villages in India by August 2007 and acknowledged the importance of "village knowledge centres", the knowledge leadership initiative is clearly validated. "Village knowledge centre (VKC) is one of the essential components for realizing our goal of graduating into a knowledge society," said A.P.J. Abdul Kalam, speaking at the second annual convention of the National Alliance.[51]

The company was also bestowed the 2004 Corporate Social Responsibility Award from TERI for its e-Choupal initiative.[52] The award is given to companies providing impetus to sustainable development and encouraging ongoing social responsibility processes within the corporate sector. ITC's social responsibility initiatives (e-Choupal and social and farm forestry) were also recognized with the receipt of the Golden Peacock Global Award for social responsibility in emerging economies in 2005.[53] The award was presented to the company in London by Ola Ullsten, former Prime Minister of Sweden, who headed the jury. Capping it all was the induction of Deveshwar into the Hall of Pride of the Indian Science Congress.

Harvard Business Review ranked ITC's chairman the seventh best performing CEO in the world in 2013 based on the company's consistent triple bottom line performance for over 15 years. In his 2013 annual address to the stockholders, Deveshwar noted that the company's market capitalization, which had stood at Rs. 5570 crore in 1996, had multiplied 50 times to Rs. 290,000 crore in 2013. Total shareholder returns had grown in this period by an annual compounded growth rate of 27 percent. The company has been water positive for 11 consecutive years, carbon positive for 8 consecutive years, and solid waste recycling positive for 6 years. Renewable energy constitutes over 41 percent of all energy consumed by the company, with several factories and 5 premium luxury hotels run by the company meeting 100 percent of their energy requirements from wind energy. The company's businesses and associated value chains support the livelihoods of more than 5 million people from some of the weakest sections of society (Deveshwar, 2013).

Conclusion

The case example of ITC's triple bottom line approach to CSR highlights a number of issues and gives insights into CSR. It highlights the role of leadership in accomplishing the challenging task of building effective business models that simultaneously accomplish social and other (e.g., environmental) goals. The business goals served by the company's e-Choupal initiative could be easily lost on readers. Given that more organizations, both in the private and public sector (including some NGOs), are mimicking the e-Choupal initiative for rural marketing and development objectives, respectively, it should be clear that such initiatives achieve a great blend of both kinds of objectives. The case example highlights the role of leader cognitions and leader (and others) use of linguistics in reinforcing the CSR-oriented actions of the company. Conceiving the problem as one that requires the management of information and knowledge – thereby sharing, integrating, and leveraging knowledge – is the first critical step in the knowledge leadership process illustrated by Deveshwar and his team. Thus, the case example also highlights the role of leadership (i.e., knowledge leadership) in making such business models successful in BoP markets. Utilizing local farmers as *sanchalak*, and making them take public oaths as though they were occupying public offices, serves as a crucial element building trust in the farming community. Use of the system in the absence of trust would have been highly doubtful. Managing the motivational challenges of other key stakeholders in the process, (i.e., the commission agents, or traders, in the traditional *mandi* system) serves as the other crucial element in the building of a sociocognitive network of knowledge, a crucial requirement for such knowledge leadership initiatives (Lakshman, 2007; Viitala, 2004). The strength of vision possessed by the team of leaders in overcoming the many infrastructure difficulties (lack of power, lack of bandwidth) and other obstacles, delaying the materialization of potential returns, is another critical element of the knowledge leadership initiative. Balancing both the technological and sociocognitive knowledge networks and channelizing them for optimum effectiveness is another critical feature of this initiative. Using the knowledge network to manage both the supply side and the distribution side of the value chain is perhaps what is unique about this knowledge leadership initiative. Future conceptualizations of CSR in the globalized world, specifically within Asia, would do well to include *local* as well as *global* conceptualizations of CSR within their models, while also not forgetting the critical role of top executive leaders in such models.

An increasing number of domestic and global companies are targeting India's rural markets and transforming this marketplace. Home to a staggering 12 percent of the world's population and showing signs of increasing incomes and discretionary spending, this market provides significant opportunities for interested companies. Both the opportunities and unique challenges involved in operating in this arena have been highlighted in this chapter. The rural consumer is down to earth and simple in nature, quite unaware of the wiles and guiles of his or her urban counterpart. Trust, respect, social status, and a host of related characteristics are important for people employed in this sector to win the hearts of rural consumers. Physical and infrastructural challenges need to be converted into opportunities to be exploited, as adequately demonstrated by the case example and other company examples in this domain. In addition to trust, companies may need to demonstrate care for the rural community and its development to win not only the hearts of rural consumers but also their wallets.

Appendix   ITC's triple bottom line achievement

Economic performance	• Total shareholder returns, measured in terms of increase in market capitalization and dividends, grew at a compound rate of over 30 percent per annum • Gross turnover for the year 2005–06 grew by 21.5 percent to Rs. 16,224 crore driven by good topline growth across all businesses • The ITC scrip gained 118 percent during the year outperforming the benchmark BSE Sensex by 44 percentage points
Environmental performance	• ITC is now a carbon-positive corporation • ITC continues to be a water-positive corporation • ITC is rapidly moving towards zero solid waste • Many constituent business units have obtained the ISO 14000 and SA 8000 certification in addition to other quality certifications
Social performance	• Labor practices and fair work: sufficiently empowered trade unions • Occupational health and safety: award-winning, accident-free performance. ITC's leaf-threshing plant at Chirala has won a staggering 12 swords of honor, the only plant in the world to achieve this distinction
Human rights	• Human rights consideration across the supply chain and when making significant investments • Prevention of discrimination at the workplace • Freedom of association • Prohibition of child and forced labor
Society	• Community development: Mission *Sunehra Kal* (Bright Tomorrow) • Web enablement of the Indian farmer through the e-Choupal initiative • Natural resource management to develop wasteland, enhance soil and moisture conservation, and promote improved agricultural practices • Genetic improvement of livestock productivity • Sustainable livelihood creation by the economic empowerment of women • Community development with a focus on the universalization of primary education, health, and sanitation • Patronage of classical music, art, and heritage
Product responsibility	• ISO 9001, ISO 14001, and OHSAS 18001 certifications • Full compliance with appropriate laws • ITC follows voluntary codes on marketing communications

Source: http://www.itcportal.com/sustainability_report_2006/ [accessed 25 August 2008].

Notes

1. http://archive.indianexpress.com/news/understanding-indian-rural-markets-the-challenge/1110153.
2. http://archive.indianexpress.com/news/understanding-indian-rural-markets-the-opportunity/1105969/.

3. http://archive.indianexpress.com/news/understanding-indian-rural-markets-the-challenge/1110153/1.
4. http://en.wikipedia.org/wiki/Hindu_calendar.
5. http://en.wikipedia.org/wiki/Makar_Sankranti.
6. *http://www.bharatmatrimony.com/* is a good example but there are many others.
7. http://archive.indianexpress.com/news/at-3-crore-rural-accounts-banks-set-global-record/1042470/.
8. http://in.reuters.com/article/2013/01/21/india-banks-cash-transfer-sbi-idINDEE90K00M20130121.
9. http://blogs.wsj.com/indiarealtime/2012/11/01/why-few-indians-have-bank-accounts/.
10. http://in.reuters.com/article/2013/01/21/india-banks-cash-transfer-sbi-idINDEE90K00M20130121.
11. e-Choupal enables ITC to link directly with rural farmers via the Internet for the procurement of agricultural products.
12. http://en.wikipedia.org/wiki/Rural_electrification.
13. http://www.business-standard.com/article/management/marketing-to-rural-india-113070700506_1.html.
14. http://articles.economictimes.indiatimes.com/2012-02-24/news/31095227_1_rural-banking-kisan-credit-cards-bank-branches.
15. http://articles.economictimes.indiatimes.com/2004-07-28/news/27375366_1_rural-markets-zee-turner-rural-areas.
16. http://articles.economictimes.indiatimes.com/2004-05-13/news/27409925_1_coca-cola-india-rural-markets-cola-giant.
17. http://articles.economictimes.indiatimes.com/2010-03-12/news/28416354_1_rural-job-job-portal-choupal.
18. http://articles.economictimes.indiatimes.com/2011-05-25/news/29581830_1_hul-plans-hemant-bakshi-rural-markets.
19. *Shakti Ammas* literally means power-women.
20. http://articles.economictimes.indiatimes.com/2004-06-28/news/27398249_1_rural-markets-mobile-marketing-urban-markets.
21. http://articles.economictimes.indiatimes.com/2004-04-05/news/27398708_1_rural-markets-durable-majors-sales-in-rural-areas.
22. http://articles.economictimes.indiatimes.com/2009-06-04/news/27663836_1_rural-markets-shantanu-das-gupta-whirlpool.
23. http://www.accenture.com/SiteCollectionDocuments/PDF/Accenture-Masters-of-Rural-Markets-Selling-Profitably-to-Rural-Consumers.pdf.
24. http://www.accenture.com/SiteCollectionDocuments/PDF/Accenture-Masters-of-Rural-Markets-Selling-Profitably-to-Rural-Consumers.pdf.
25. http://articles.economictimes.indiatimes.com/2012-07-25/news/32848625_1_fmcg-business-e-choupal-network-fiama-di-wills.
26. http://articles.economictimes.indiatimes.com/2011-12-07/news/30485918_1_choupal-aashirvaad-agri-commodities.
27. http://articles.economictimes.indiatimes.com/2010-04-12/news/27612204_1_choupal-itc-plans-agri-reforms.
28. http://timesofindia.indiatimes.com/Business/Intl_Business/Indian_firms_not_among_worlds_most_ethical_cos/articleshow/3103816.cms#write#write.
29. ITC Annual Report 2008.
30. CREM-report nr. 03.650 (2004). *Corporate Social Responsibility in India: Policy and Practices of Dutch Companies.* Consultancy and Research for Environmental Management, Amsterdam, The Netherlands.

31. CREM-report nr. 03.650 (2004). *Corporate Social Responsibility in India: Policy and Practices of Dutch Companies*. Consultancy and Research for Environmental Management, Amsterdam, The Netherlands.
32. *Businessline* (17 May 2005). ITC wins "Golden Peacock" award.
33. CREM-report nr. 03.650 (2004), p. 13.
34. http://www.newindpress.com/NewsItems.asp?ID=IEA20060119013321&Page=A&Title=Southern%2BNews%2B-%2BAndhra%2BPradesh&Topic=0.
35. ITC Sustainability Report, 2006. Available from: http://www.itcportal.com/sustainability_report_2006/.
36. ITC Sustainability Report, 2006.
37. *The Economist* (5 June 2004). Business: cigarettes and virtual cathedrals – face value.
38. *Businessline* (26 August 2007). ITC e-choupals to focus on product traceability.
39. *Mandi* is Hindi for marketplace.
40. *Businessline* (26 November 2004). Ryot choice.
41. *Businessline* (17 December 2004). Soya trading grinds to halt on mandi stir: traders protest against e-Choupal.
42. *Businessline* (4 January 2006). ITC to invest $1 billion in e-choupal infrastructure.
43. *Businesswire* (3 May 2004). Gilat Satellite Networks announces milestone in ITC-IBD "e-Choupal" Project in India.
44. *The Economist*, 2004.
45. A lakh corresponds to 100,000.
46. *Businessline* (19 November 2004). Give them empowerment first.
47. *Businessline* (28 December 2004). Broadband versus narrow elitism.
48. *Businessline* (26 August 2007). ITC e-choupals to focus on product traceability.
49. *Businessline* (2 May 2007). Marketing: Dukes expanding in northern, eastern regions.
50. TERI stands for The Energy and Resources Institute.
51. *Businessline* (12 July 2005). Village knowledge centres vital for rural development.
52. *Businessline* (3 June 2005). ITC's e-choupal bags TERI award.
53. *Businessline* (17 May 2005). ITC wins "Golden Peacock" award.

Competitive advantage of India

"The real treasure of India is its intellectual capital. The real opportunity of India is its incredibly skilled work force. Raw talent here is like nowhere else in the world."

Jack Welch, CEO, General Electric

The service sector in India, the biggest contributor to the nation's GDP, has leveraged the treasure trove alluded to in the above quote by building a strong base for business. Knowledge-based services form part of India's distinctive competencies and real competitive advantage. In strong contrast to the country's literacy levels, lack of technological sophistication, and bottom-of-the-pyramid nature of India's rural scenario, India presents a totally different face to the world with its strengths in knowledge-based services. India is unique both among emerging economies of the world and developing countries in terms of its strength in this domain. Unlike most other developing countries of the world, India possesses a very strong competitive advantage in a whole range of knowledge-based services including but not limited to (a) software development, (b) information technology–enabled services, (c) product/project engineering and design, (d) biotechnology, (e) pharmaceuticals, (f) media, (g) entertainment, and (h) healthcare services. As noted earlier, seven Indian companies are listed in the world's top 15 companies for IT outsourcing. Knowledge process outsourcing (KPO) services in India are particularly strong in the areas of business and market research, legal services, intellectual property research, and research and development (R&D).[1] India is the leading destination for multinational corporations (MNCs) to invest their R&D dollars with about 870 MNCs operating R&D centers (up from 836 in 2011).[2] Such business has seen consistent growth over the years across a wide range of industries. Top names in international business including General Electric, Lucent, Hewlett-Packard, IBM, Microsoft, Eli Lilly, and Cisco are among the many other firms that have set up R&D centers in India. India is truly a sweatshop for brains, in addition to being a sweatshop for hands.[3] On top of providing huge markets for interested MNCs, India also provides huge value through its human resource pool, which is increasingly cost effective as well. In the pharmaceutical industry, for instance, there are very few global players that have not offshored their R&D to Asia. Such offshoring of R&D services is expected to grow 16 percent annually with India much better placed than most other Asian nations to grab these opportunities. Such an advantage accrues from similarities and compatibilities in many parts of the R&D value chain such as the patent registration process, legal protection, law enforcement, and significant improvements in India in terms of cultural and governmental attitudes to intellectual property rights (IPR) protection.[4] The Indian market for R&D services in product engineering is expected to grow at a 14 percent compounded annual rate from $14.7 billion in 2012 to $42 billion in 2020, despite stiff competition from China and Russia.[5]

Doing Business in India.

Consider the following instances of investment offers from both domestic and multinational companies made to technology business startups in India at a recent industry event. Bangalore-based startup Thinkflow Software received an offer for strategic investment and three offers from potential customers for their product which helps companies build and deploy business applications faster.[6] The Chennai-based startup Unmetric was successful in attracting interest from Proctor & Gamble (P&G), Colgate-Palmolive, and Kroger, among others, for their innovative use of artificial intelligence technology to help companies understand their competitors' strategic moves by collating data from social media platforms. Capillary Technologies attracted interest from Xerox and P&G for their products which help retailers understand customer purchase behavior. Bright young startups engaged in business intelligence and analytics, using technology to recruit talent and making use of employee productivity software, among others, presented their products at various stages of development, beginning with proof of concept, to interested investors and customers at the event. More than a dozen offers for investment and other deals with potential customers were made at the event, which was organized by an industry think tank. The event demonstrated not only the potential for knowledge-based products and services in India, but also the institutional mechanisms facilitating these players in getting exposure to global players and acquiring investment interest. Many reports suggest that the 25-year-old Indian ecosystem for R&D and knowledge-based services provides huge cost arbitrage to MNCs, in addition to their capability to provide high-value-addition work on innovation and leadership.[7]

For instance, in healthcare services the availability of low-cost, good (international) quality medical facilities, and English-speaking doctors and service staff contribute to a rapidly growing (30 percent per annum) medical tourism industry.[8] The most popular treatments that medical tourists seek in India pertain to areas of advanced medicine such as cardiac bypass, bone marrow transplants, and eye surgery, in addition to alternative medicine in the form of traditional Indian medicines. While some other developing countries and emerging economies may also provide such healthcare services, Indian industry players feel that India is the only medical tourism destination that can provide comprehensive mainstream solutions for a wide range of medical needs.[9] Additionally, although a growing number of Indian students go to Russia or China for medical education,[10] only between 10 and 25 percent of these returning graduates are able to pass the Medical Council of India's (MCI) screening test to qualify for practice in India.[11] India is but one of a few countries where a large number of medical graduates leave the country to work abroad in places like the U.S.A. and U.K., thereby worsening the shortage of doctors in the country.[12] The MCI decision not to dilute the screening test despite the shortage of doctors is critical in the face of challenges to the legality of the test, which have been turned down by the Supreme Court of India. Instead, the MCI has decided to require all Indian medical graduates to serve at least one year in rural India,[13] where the shortage is at its worst. Thus, despite a number of challenges, the quality of medical graduates in India is maintained at relatively high levels. There are 18 hospitals in India that are already accredited by Joint Commission International, a U.S.-based non-profit body that uses rigorous standards to certify hospitals.[14] There are many more hospitals seeking such certification at different stages of the process.[15] Concerted efforts by leading hospitals, the Confederation of Indian Industry, the Central Government, the Ministry of Health, and the Ministry of Tourism have ensured the presence of adequate infrastructure and appropriate levels of support from institutional intermediaries to help sustain growth in the industry.[16] Hospital chains in developed countries can seize opportunities in this high-growth sector by entering India and helping the government address issues related to uniform health coverage for all Indians, while still profiting from the growth. While the healthcare sector is expected to grow at around 30 percent, India simultaneously suffers from poor and inadequate coverage in rural areas.[17]

The software industry is India's best-known sector with a large number of players in the global market. It forms part of the larger knowledge-based services sector that is the focus of this chapter. In addition to many domestic companies, there are many multinational software companies that choose to locate in India because of the competitive advantage India possesses in all knowledge-based services. In turn, many Indian companies have overseas offices in the U.S.A., Europe, and Japan, which are respectively the largest consumer markets for these services. The software industry in India is so strong that Bill Gates once commented that India is likely to be the next software superpower of the world. Valued at $8 billion in 2000 (Kapur and Ramamurti, 2001), the software industry in India has grown at approximately 50 percent per year and is today a $100 billion industry.[18] About 70 percent of the revenue generated from this industry is from exports. Even the domestic market constitutes $30 billion and is growing at about 15 percent per year. In the face of cutbacks in global markets, the growing domestic market for IT spending is increasingly sustaining most providers of software services. Whereas there were a little more than 800 software firms, mostly small and medium sized, in 2000, there were 141 billion-dollar firms in 2010, a number expected to grow to around 700 by 2020.[19] The top 4 players in this industry account for around $35 billion and are aggressively competing with each other and a host of other firms in this sector. According to some estimates, the software industry employs around 10 million people. Hundreds of firms in this industry are listed on NASDAQ in the U.S.A., which has one of its few non-U.S. offices in Bangalore, India. Thus, by all accounts the Indian software industry, in particular, and the Indian knowledge-based services industry, in general, have tremendous competitive advantage in the world.

Most stereotypical conceptions of India portraying it as one of the poorest countries in the world, with one of the highest illiteracy rates and scoring low on the Human Development Index, fail to comprehend this truly contrasting picture of strengths in knowledge-based services. Why does India possess such a huge advantage in knowledge-based services? How is a country that fails to provide educational coverage to millions of its population able to provide such advanced services to some of the best companies in the world? Some analysts have tried to use Harvard Business School Professor Michael Porter's Diamond model of competitive advantage to try and understand the reason behind India's strength in software (Kapur and Ramamurti, 2001). More than a decade after Kapur and Ramamurti's attempt to analyze India's software strengths, the analysis presented here focuses on India's competitive advantage in broader knowledge-based services and identifies opportunities for global players in this sector. In addition to the economic sectors described so far in this chapter, one of the largest film industries in the world, Bollywood, and India's growing sports businesses could be added to the broader services sector in India. We described the evolution in Indian cricket as a rapidly growing sport business in Chapter 2. Bollywood is the Hindi-language film industry. However, it is only a part of the Indian film industry, in which films are made in a total of 22 languages. Bollywood, in particular, and the larger Indian film industry, in general, are immensely popular around the world today.[20] While there is greater strength in the entire service sector in India, we focus our attention here on knowledge-based services.

Factor conditions

India has tremendous strength in knowledge-based services as it enjoys a huge advantage in human capital, a key resource in this industry. In contrast to the sometimes serious deficiencies in primary education, the country has experienced an immense amount of investment in higher education across various disciplines related to knowledge-based services. India's output of scientists, engineers, doctors, and IT professionals is not only large it is among the highest in the world. These professional graduates constitute a labor pool that is among the cheapest in the world. One of the major reasons India was able to successfully launch its *Orbiter* towards Mars at one tenth the cost of NASA's mission to Mars is the cost of engineers in India relative to the U.S.A. (Neuman, 2013). MNCs can (purchase) hire the services of three to four engineers in India for each one they employ in a developed country, making it a much better cost proposition. Many global high-technology players such as GE, Honeywell, IBM, Microsoft, Intel, Motorola, and Google have operations in India because of the availability of this cost-effective labor pool. Many of these MNC centers as well as domestic firms are quality certified at the highest levels in the world. The English language capability of these graduates makes for easy interactions with people all over the world, regardless of whether they are customers or end users of services such as medical services. The high cost-effectiveness of the labor pool in conjunction with the language capabilities provides very high levels of comparative advantage over most other nations for India. Not only is this base of human capital highly cost-effective and conversant with the rest of the world it is also rich in entrepreneurial spirit. This human capital has been responsible for the entrepreneurial activities of hundreds of firms in the knowledge-based services sector in the last few decades. Nowhere else in India is the entrepreneurial spirit among its people more evident than in this sector.

Related and supporting industries

Although historically richer in teaching as opposed to research-type activities, today's India consists of a huge network of educational institutes across science, medicine, and engineering. This sophisticated network of universities and colleges supply the raw talent and human capital required for the entire range of knowledge-based services, including but not limited to those discussed earlier in the chapter. Institutions such as the Indian Institute of Technology and the Indian Institute of Management have admission ratios that mean a great majority of those who apply for admission (more than 90 percent) are rejected. This means they only admit the cream of the crop that have graduated from the previous level of education. The large number of institutions and the many medical graduates managing to meet the tough educational requirements provide the necessary human capital for the medical tourism sector. Other institutions such as the Indian Institutes of Information Technology, Indian Institutes of Science, a network of regional engineering schools, and a host of private educational institutions ensure this large supply does not run out. Culturally speaking, there is a huge entrepreneurial spirit in the country, which helps channeling these graduates into appropriate business firms, especially when there are no restrictive governmental regulations. Additionally, most Indian families, not only historically but even today, want their children to become either scientists/engineers or doctors. Today, inspired by the IT boom, many families want their children to be IT professionals. In other words, strong cultural patterns fuel this trend of valuing and establishing higher educational institutions in increasing numbers. These cultural traits also ensure that students flock to these institutions not only in large numbers but with high degrees of motivation. This cultural preference for "professional education" is so strong that many parents end up putting undue pressure on their children. This large and sophisticated network of educational institutions has been made possible as a result of deregulation in the education industry which preceded the national economic reforms and liberalization of the early 1990s.

The government has had a role to play in the establishment and growth of these related industries. The activities undertaken within such a role only served to fuel the cultural preferences of an increasingly larger number of students for this type of education and knowledge acquisition. Before such deregulation, and even after, many Indian students went abroad for higher education in science, engineering, and medicine among other knowledge domains. While the government's initiatives to strengthen the physical infrastructure have historically not kept pace with the country's needs, this has not been the case so far by the knowledge-based services industry. The combination of historic lack of attention to infrastructure development has led to the surge of the knowledge-based services sector being greater than the manufacturing sector. Moreover, the reduction of import barriers and tariffs on IT hardware accompanying national economic liberalization fostered a growing breed of entrepreneurs keen to plunge into this sector with their competencies. Several state governments established software technology parks providing the raw infrastructure necessary for these firms to build on.

Entrepreneurial firm behavior

Although the industry was pioneered by companies like Tata Consultancy Services (TCS), the largest (and oldest) player in the sector today, companies like Infosys were the result of entrepreneurial actions of groups of engineers and IT professionals. Infosys, the second largest player in the sector, was established in 1981 by a group of six people who had quit well-paid positions in computer firms that had a modest capital base. The story of Infosys' struggle through issues ranging from raising capital to fighting corruption and finding customers is one that is replayed countless times by all the other players in the industry today. That there are more than 140 billion-dollar firms in the industry today is credit to the indomitable entrepreneurial spirit in India. Many of these entrepreneurial Indian firms were among the first globally to obtain appropriate international quality certification critical to the growth and viability of the industry as it stands today. According to the founding entrepreneur of the third largest software services company, Wipro, many of the people entering the industry in the 1980s had a strong professional orientation in which they always put the customer first (Ramamurti, 2001). This business attitude of putting customers first was unheard of in India's business culture in those days. This entrepreneurial leader is also quick to point out that pioneering firms in this industry cut their teeth in the business by serving domestic customers and by using carefully developed human resource management practices to build a strong competence base. In fact, in the lists of best employers in the country today and over the last decade, there is a higher proportion of IT and knowledge work firms. Thus, the incredible human capital in the knowledge-based services business brings entrepreneurial spirit, professional orientation, and fosters a business culture conducive to global long-term growth.

Domestic rivalry

Rivalry among the hundreds of players has been particularly strong in the software services industry and is currently even more so across the broader knowledge-based services industry. Such rivalry is critical for the best practices in the industry to evolve and for business to emerge as world-class operations, providing the nation with competitive advantage. Although TCS, Infosys, and Wipro, the top 3 in the software industry, are relatively large today, they began modestly and were relatively small in size. There are hundreds of firms today that are very small and few are likely to win out against their competitive rivals and become big. As indicated earlier, the number of billion-dollar firms is likely to increase from its current level of 141 to about 700 in 2020. Thus, it is not difficult to imagine just how intense the competitive spirit is and how long-lasting the entrepreneurial spirit is in the country, some of it fueled by overseas Indians. The software industry is going through a special phase of its business cycle with an incredibly large number of contracts coming up for renewal. Deals worth nearly $50 billion (about half the size of the entire software industry) are coming up for renewal and driving increasingly extreme competitive behavior among firms.[21] With the industry coming out of a particularly slow period of growth in the last few years, people are expecting the competition to reach a peak this time around. Some industry observers are also raising the prospect of companies becoming irrational in their efforts to steal contracts away from competitors. Among the long-term software-outsourcing contracts coming up for renewal are Proctor & Gamble's $3 billion contract with Hewlett-Packard (HP), Bank of America's $4.5 billion contract with HP, and American Express's $3 billion contract with IBM. The industry could very easily take on a new restructured look once all these contract agreements are done and dusted. Like the more aggressive behavior of MNCs, in general, many Indian software firms are engaging in mergers and acquisitions across the globe, indicating their global strategic ambitions. According to one industry observer, "The Indian software industry is in the middle of a multi-year cyclical transition as organizations are focusing investments on technologies to support existing system structure."[22] TCS, for instance, merged its Japanese operations with the IT arm of Mitsubishi in the second largest IT market in the world.[23] The fifth largest Indian IT firm,[24] Tech Mahindra, recently acquired an American startup in the data analytics business run by overseas Indians, estimated to boost its global revenues.[25] Overall, therefore, the nature and intensity of the competition in the knowledge-based services business among Indian firms is healthy and continues to contribute to India's global competitive advantage.

The role of overseas Indians

Although much of the initial growth and competitive strength of knowledge-based services came from Indians in India, much of the later growth and entrepreneurial activity has been fueled by overseas Indians. These overseas Indians brought not only their technical expertise and competence but also their global mindset and social capital to bear on the success of these efforts. The Indian diaspora is estimated to be about 30 million strong and spread over more than 150 countries.[26] To formally recognize the contribution of overseas Indians, the country has started celebrating the 9th of January each year, the day Mahatma Gandhi returned to India from his overseas stint in South Africa, as Overseas Indians' Day. The vast majority of overseas Indians live in North America and Europe, from where they leverage their social and intellectual capital to contribute to knowledge-based services, in particular. For instance, there are more than 300,000 doctors of Indian origin living abroad, many of whom want to contribute in various ways to the country, in this instance in the medical tourism sector.[27] Historically, MNCs have coordinated with overseas Indians in their initial forays into various sectors of India's knowledge-based services sector. MNCs interested in the Indian knowledge services sector can tap into this resource for more insights on how to go about establishing a presence in this rapidly growing sector. The Indian government has established mechanisms such as the Overseas Citizen of India (OCI card) and the Person of Indian Origin (PIO card) to facilitate the movement of overseas Indians into and out of the country, among other objectives.[28] Thus, although much of the credit for India's strength in the initial years of knowledge-based services should go to domestic Indians, it is increasingly being apportioned to those overseas, especially for quantum changes in the industry.

Global demand

Unlike Porter's conventional focus in his Diamond model on domestic demand for national competitive advantage, the situation in this sector for Indian firms has been different. However, although domestic demand for knowledge-based services has been historically slow-growing, it was noted earlier that about 30 percent of the total market for such services comes from domestic clients. Still, the knowledge-based services sector in India would not have been as strong in the absence of demand from the U.S.A., Japan, and Europe, the three largest markets, respectively, for these services. Some analysts have explained this departure from Porter's model by noting that a key difference between knowledge-based services and other sectors is the possibility of digitizing both work in process and final output to be eventually moved across the world, based on demand characteristics (Kapur and Ramamurti, 2001). This feature has minimized the need for colocation, which is critical in most industries, and allowed knowledge-based services to conduct operations away from the location where they are typically consumed. This ease of moving work across locations has allowed Indian firms to make comprehensive and effective use of every hour in a day by only having minimal physical locations across key time zones, especially close to consumption sites in the largest markets. The very feature of being able to digitize work has facilitated the involvement of overseas Indians in leveraging both ends of their social network to enhance the quality and volume of business. India has rapidly moved up the value chain in the knowledge services business by importing raw talent and human capital in this sector from many of the markets in which these services are eventually consumed. Having achieved prominence in global markets, Indian firms are poised to take advantage of the changing situation in India with IT spending expected to reach record levels of growth.[29] After all, India is one of the fastest growing markets in the world, including for knowledge-based services, with such growth expected to extend long into the next 50 years.

Opportunities for MNCs in this sector

If it has not been evident so far, it should be made clear that all major firms in this sector enjoy the benefits provided by the various elements contributing to India's competitive advantage in this sector, regardless of whether they are Indian or multinational. A footnote to the industry association's ranking, which we have been using thus far, reads as follows:

> "Note: This list does not include some companies whose corporate headquarters are located outside India, but have significant India-centric delivery capabilities, and have not shared their India-centric revenue figures. Had they been ranked based on their India revenues, companies such as Accenture, Cognizant, HP, Capgemini, Oracle and IBM would also have appeared in this ranking."[30]

Thus, established MNCs and up-and-coming startups in this rapidly changing industry can and have in the past entered India for their global operations, if not for final sales and marketing. Independent reports suggest that Oracle has recently pipped IBM to become the second largest software player in India, with Microsoft continuing as leader with nearly $5 billion in revenue in 2013.[31] There is no reason new technology startups from around the world should not target Indian markets or establish a base in India for their global operations. Once a new technology is commercialized, it requires scale to be globally effective, which is where India comes in. As amply described above, both large MNCs and new startups can rapidly establish large-scale operations in the country to take advantage of the business opportunities.

Additionally, the evidence of Indian firms' capabilities in high value–added products and services in this sector should reveal significant opportunities for multinational firms to use India as a base for such operations as well. Although one report suggests that only 26 percent of the numerous MNCs having established R&D operations in India provide for a strategic role,[32] these companies have succeeded in establishing what could be conceived as a launching pad for more high value–added services in this sector. Another report suggests that a significant portion of foreign direct investment (FDI) in R&D flows into the software and IT sector, but very little FDI in high value addition work flows into the rest of the knowledge-based services sector.[33] This represents another strategic opportunity for investment by MNCs who should be targeting the higher value addition work that comes from having an India base while the currency and labor cost differentials are still favorable. The demographics in India (young) also favor continued sustenance of the human capital pool well into the future, a critical component in this business. Perhaps this is why McKinsey lists "Leverage India for global products, services, and talent" as one of its keys to winning in India.[34] The opportunities that India provides in a wide variety of business sectors, knowledge-based services in particular, cannot be overemphasized. This represents India's true strength and the good news is that it is open to all.

Most stereotypical conceptions of India as one of the poorest countries in the world, with one of the highest illiteracy rates, and scoring low on the Human Development Index fail to comprehend the truly contrasting picture of competitive advantage in knowledge-based services. Unlike other emerging market economies of the world, India possesses very strong competitive advantage in a whole range of knowledge-based services. India is truly a sweatshop for brains, in addition to being a sweatshop for hands. One knowledgeable observer of India suggests, "We are confident that India will continue to maintain its competitive advantage over other emerging markets for a long time."[35] This advantage accrues from similarities and compatibilities (vis-à-vis developed nations) in many parts of the R&D value chain such as patent registration, legal protection, law enforcement, and significant improvements in terms of India's cultural and governmental attitudes to international property rights (IPR) protection. Many factors – such as the conditions prevailing in India, the strength of related and supporting industries, the nature and intensity of domestic rivalry, the entrepreneurial behavior of Indian firms, the role of overseas Indians, and global demand conditions – fuel India's competitive advantage in knowledge-based services. This advantage benefits domestic as well as multinational firms, regardless of their size. Many untapped opportunities continue to exist, and the domestic market in India continues to grow rapidly in the face of declines elsewhere. As with any other sector, this growth is expected to last well into the future. Many reports suggest that India is the second most competitive market in the world. Nowhere is this more evident than in the knowledge-based services industry, which is going through a critical phase in its business cycle. Whatever happens in this industry is likely to be a result of the competitive actions of multiple players. In addition to deciding their competitive strategies, firms in this and other sectors in India have to face up to the issues of managing talent and establishing organizational practices for winning in this country. We now turn our attention to these issues.

Notes

1. http://www.outsource2india.com/why_india/articles/KPO.asp.
2. http://knowledge.wharton.upenn.edu/article/india-continues-to-attract-multinationals-research-dollars/.
3. http://www.gurgaonithub.com/services/kpo.
4. http://www.pharmoutsourcing.com/Featured-Articles/125941-Offshoring-of-Chemical-Pharmaceutical-R-D-to-Asia/.
5. http://knowledge.wharton.upenn.edu/article/india-continues-to-attract-multinationals-research-dollars/.
6. http://economictimes.indiatimes.com/news/emerging-businesses/startups/startups-receive-offers-for-investment-from-worlds-biggest-corporations/articleshow/33755905.cms.
7. http://knowledge.wharton.upenn.edu/article/india-continues-to-attract-multinationals-research-dollars/.
8. http://en.wikipedia.org/wiki/Medical_tourism_in_India.
9. http://www.medicaltourisminindia.org/.
10. http://timesofindia.indiatimes.com/india/Aspiring-doctors-flock-abroad-as-education-cost-surges-in-India/articleshow/21609211.cms.
11. http://en.wikipedia.org/wiki/Medical_Council_of_India_Screening_Test.
12. http://en.wikipedia.org/wiki/List_of_medical_colleges_in_India.
13. http://student.bmj.com/student/view-article.html?id=sbmj.g1681.
14. http://www.jointcommissioninternational.org/.
15. http://www.indian-medical-tourism.com/.
16. http://www.who.int/bulletin/volumes/85/3/07-010307/en/.
17. http://en.wikipedia.org/wiki/Medical_tourism_in_India.
18. http://www.livemint.com/Industry/9NgcztgP98azLAAwqfQNeI/Indian-domestic-IT-market-to-grow-at-1518-in-2013-report.html.
19. http://www.nextbigwhat.com/domestic-software-market-india-297/.
20. http://en.wikipedia.org/wiki/Bollywood.
21. http://articles.economictimes.indiatimes.com/2013-01-21/news/36463209_1_software-exporter-hcl-technologies-information-technology.
22. http://www.thehindubusinessline.com/features/smartbuy/tech-news/software-market-in-india-up-10-to-47-b-microsoft-tops-tally/article5892241.ece.
23. http://economictimes.indiatimes.com/tech/ites/mitsubishi-deal-to-add-375-million-incremental-revenue-for-tcs-in-fy15/articleshow/34055687.cms.
24. http://www.nasscom.in/industry-ranking.
25. http://economictimes.indiatimes.com/tech/ites/tech-mahindra-acquires-big-data-start-up-fixstream-networks/articleshow/34050553.cms.
26. http://en.wikipedia.org/wiki/Non-resident_Indian_and_person_of_Indian_origin.
27. http://articles.economictimes.indiatimes.com/2011-01-09/news-by-industry/28433428_1_indian-doctors-indian-origin-diaspora.
28. http://timesofindia.indiatimes.com/nri/other-news/Over-12-lakh-PIOs-have-overseas-Indian-cards-10-fold-rise-in-7-years/articleshow/21720421.cms.
29. http://www.rediff.com/business/slide-show/slide-show-1-tech-infosys-sees-up-to-9-sales-growth-in-2014-15/20140415.htm.
30. http://www.nasscom.in/industry-ranking.

31. http://www.thehindubusinessline.com/features/smartbuy/tech-news/software-market-in-india-up-10-to-47-b-microsoft-tops-tally/article5892241.ece.
32. http://www.firstbiz.com/corporate/survey-shows-only-26-of-mncs-have-global-roles-from-india-39288.html.
33. http://www.currentscience.ac.in/Volumes/105/06/0767.pdf.
34. http://www.mckinsey.com/insights/winning_in_emerging_markets/how_multinationals_can_win_in_india.
35. http://knowledge.wharton.upenn.edu/article/india-continues-to-attract-multinationals-research-dollars/.

Leadership of Indian intellectual capital

> "So, what comes next for leadership? Absolute honesty, fairness and justice – we are dealing with people. Those of us who have had the good fortune of commanding hundreds and thousands of men know this. No man likes to be punished, and yet a man will accept punishment stoically if he knows that the punishment meted out to him will be identical to the punishment meted out to another person who has some Godfather somewhere. This is very, very important. No man likes to be superseded, and yet men will accept supersession if they know that they are being superseded, under the rules, by somebody who is better than they are but not just somebody who happens to be related to the Commandant of the staff college or to a Cabinet Minister or by the Field Marshal's wife's current boyfriend. This is extremely important, Ladies and Gentlemen. We in India have tremendous pressures – pressures from the Government, pressures from superior officers, pressures from families, pressures from wives, uncles, aunts, nieces, nephews and girlfriends, and we lack the courage to withstand those pressures. That takes me to the next attribute of Leadership – Moral and Physical Courage."
>
> **Field Marshall Sam Manekshaw on leadership**

Once managers have understood the diversity of Indian markets and consumers, and have formulated an appropriate business strategy for India, it is imperative to establish a strong system of leadership in the local organization. As noted in the opening quote on the lack of leadership in India, one of India's top military leaders argues against nepotism and lack of moral courage, which have so often plagued the country. It is thus important to ensure good leadership to prevent the breakdown of otherwise good systems. One of the world's top corporate leaders, Jack Welch of GE, preferred to use the term "business leader" over the term manager for most of his managerial cadre. Keeping this spirit in mind, the chapter focuses on what sort of leadership is required of managers at different levels in an Indian organization, and the overall leadership systems required for winning in India. With this purpose in mind, the chapter focuses on the stories of four political leaders from different corners of India to obtain an understanding of what leadership means to people in India and the desired qualities and values of leaders in the country. Globally popular models of leadership such as transformational and charismatic leadership began with a focus on political leadership. Thus, the managers of multinational corporations (MNCs) interested in doing business in India have much to gain from an understanding of political leadership in India. Such an understanding will help them recruit and train the managerial cadre to be employed in the country. By walking the reader through four stories of Indian political leadership, the chapter develops a profile of the qualities and values that are likely to be successful in Indian business.

Diversity in India is multi-dimensional and spans religion, language, geography, and politics. We came across some of this diversity in Chapter 4 on the federalist system of government and some broad principles used in the formation of states post independence. The overarching principle in the federalist system is "unity in diversity", which has been facing tough tests from separatist movements over the last few decades. The four stories of political leaders in this chapter introduces the reader to different protagonists (leaders) and their political movements and elaborates India's challenge in progressing as a nation in the face of these movements. An analysis of this struggle reveals the core underlying values of the people of India pertaining to desirable leadership qualities. According to a large ethnographic study by the Anthropological Survey of India, about 75 percent of the more than 4000 communities examined in the study followed Hinduism, about 12 percent followed Islam, 7 percent followed Christianity, 2.5 percent Sikhism, 2 percent each followed Jainism and Buddhism, and 0.2 percent followed Judaism and Zoroastrianism. Several hundred of these communities followed two religions and more than a dozen communities followed three. The survey also identified 325 languages, belonging to 12 different language families, and 24 different scripts that are commonly used. The study noted that the incidence of bilingualism among these communities was high at 65.51 percent (Palrecha et al., 2012). The initial division of the country into different states on language lines is made all the more complex as a result of these characteristics, as is evident from the most recent instance of state bifurcation, Telengana. This broad and multi-dimensional diversity highlights the importance and need for local leadership in local cultural contexts that are difficult to capture with one broad theory. Through the comparative analysis of four political leaders, the chapter will identify leadership lessons for MNCs and their business leaders in India.

Having focused on India's competitive advantage in Chapter 8, this chapter begins with the story of political leader Rajiv Gandhi, who is often credited with having sown the seeds of the Indian government's facilitation of the development of this competitive advantage. In addition to technological and economic progress, Gandhi had faced challenging situations with separatist movements in different parts of the country. The chapter focuses on the story of one such separatist movement from the southern part of the country, spearheaded by the political movement led by C.N. Annadurai. The third story focuses on a politico-economic ideological movement that differed from the mainstream. Headed by J.P. Narayan it resulted in breaking the stranglehold of the Congress Party in India as the single best representative face of the country's democracy. As noted earlier, coalitions made up of dozens of parties form today's Indian government, and this has been the case for the last few decades. This is very different from the first four or more decades after independence when the Congress Party was almost always in power. Finally, we focus on the story of the current Prime Minister of India Narendra Modi, someone who has brought religious issues to the forefront more than ever before. Each of these leaders represents a different political party and comes from a different part of the country: north, south, east, and west, respectively. These stories will take the reader through a historical journey beginning in the 1950s and ending in contemporary India, while highlighting the different ideologies and political bases on which these leaders sought the support of the Indian people. Each of these leaders has been a regional as well as a national representative in his own right. Although diverging in terms of the core values of the political movements they represent, there are a number of common qualities and values that the analysis provided here highlights. In essence, there is a unity-in-diversity principle of leadership that comes to the surface as a result of this analysis.

Leadership for technological progress in India

"India is an old country, but a young nation; and like the young everywhere, we are impatient. I am young and I too have a dream. I dream of an India, strong, independent, self-reliant and in the forefront of the front ranks of the nations of the world in the service of mankind."

(former Prime Minister Rajiv Gandhi addressing a joint meeting of the
U.S. Congress)

Rajiv Gandhi, a rank outsider in Indian politics, became the youngest Prime Minister of India in 1984 on the death of his mother and former Prime Minister Indira Gandhi. The young Rajiv expressed no interest in politics, unlike his younger brother Sanjay, and became a commercial airline pilot in India after spending time at Trinity College in Cambridge and Imperial College in London, without getting a degree. While he was in the U.K. he married Antonia Maino, an Italian waitress, who took the name Sonia Gandhi. She is currently a senior Congress Party official and Member of Parliament in India. He only entered politics at the behest of his mother, following the death of his brother and trusted lieutenant of his mother in an aviation accident. The 1984 elections at the end of the then five-year term of parliament resulted in a landslide victory for the Congress Party and Rajiv Gandhi as a result of a huge sympathy vote following the assassination of his mother by her own Sikh bodyguards. His youth, progressive views, and outsider image (corruption free) helped him obtain an 80 percent majority in the parliamentary elections. He utilized all of these qualities to good measure and led India along a completely different path from the socialist policies of previous governments including his mother's. In a big departure from the past, he dramatically improved bilateral relations with the West, in general, and the U.S.A., in particular. Despite later allegations of having received funds from the KGB, Rajiv Gandhi's policies were predominantly progressive on both the technological front and the economic front. His policies, which predated the liberalization of the early 1990s, are often credited with having sown the seeds of the IT and telecommunications revolution in India, providing the building blocks of the competitive advantage discussed in Chapter 8. The economic reforms and liberalization programs were launched by the Indian government that took the helm soon after the 1991 elections, during the campaign for which Rajiv Gandhi was assassinated in a bomb explosion. Rajiv Gandhi and his ideological vision were critical factors in India becoming one of the largest emerging markets of the world.

While battling separatist movements in several parts of the country, one of which led to his mother's assassination, Rajiv Gandhi instituted several economic policies that advanced the buildup of the technology and education sectors in the country.

Whereas previous separatist movements in the country had been by and large peaceful and ended up simply as demands for more regional autonomy, the Sikh separatist movement ended in a lot of violence and the Prime Minister's assassination. These events provide the reader with a glimpse of the significant political movements in India, many of which were a result of the policies of earlier federal governments. Thus, the unfavorable policies of earlier governments – mainly in terms of language imposition and centralization of economic power – led to the birth of many politically rebellious movements, as we will see in more detail in the other three stories. Ironically, the measure of success he achieved in settling some of these disputes led to his own eventual assassination in May 1991 during the campaign leading up to the elections.

Regardless of his swing in fortunes in the battle with separatists, Prime Minister Rajiv Gandhi achieved plenty of success with his vision of a progressive, strong, and self-reliant India on the education and technology frontier. Armed with a vision and foresight to make information technology a critical feature of twenty-first century India, he made a valuable contribution to modernizing the Indian administration and developing India's capabilities. He is credited with promoting the introduction and use of computers in India. He increased government support for science and technology and related industries. He reduced import quotas, taxes, and tariffs on technology-based industries such as computers, airlines, defense, and telecommunications. His efforts created MTNL, the state-owned organization responsible for increasing the penetration of modern telephone services across the country, especially in rural areas. As part of his efforts to reduce red tape and bureaucracy in the federal government, he introduced several measures to reduce the Licence Raj (Permit Raj), allowing businesses and individuals to import capital goods without restrictions.[1] These were fundamental in bringing about the entrepreneurial spirit in the software services and knowledge-based services industry, as noted in the previous chapter. These steps preceded the formal economic liberalization and privatization programs of the early 1990s. In 1986 he announced a national policy on education to modernize and expand higher education programs across India. He founded the *Jawahar Navodaya Vidyalaya* system in the same year, aimed at uplifting rural education.[2] These initiatives in the education sector were soon replicated in many progressive states of the country, as education is subject to both central and state jurisdictions. The country was put on course to achieve competitive advantage in knowledge-based services as soon as the policies were aligned with natural cultural patterns and preferences. In honor of his contributions to science and technology-related institutions, several technological universities and research centers in India have been named for him. It is interesting to note that he himself was sent to the U.K. to obtain an engineering degree by his mother and grandfather, both former Prime Ministers. That he did not obtain the degree but became a commercial airline pilot is testimony to the excessive pressure on kids in India alluded to in the previous chapter. Thus, the core values of Indian culture of obtaining and disseminating valuable knowledge for practical use were aided by his knowledge leadership initiatives. Knowledge leadership pertains to the establishment of technological and sociocognitive mechanisms for creating, sharing, leveraging, and disseminating knowledge by executive leaders, once the importance of such knowledge management became clear. Knowledge leadership manifests itself along two dimensions, one internal and the other external (Lakshman, 2008b). Rajiv Gandhi, as Prime Minister, undertook a variety of measures to facilitate such knowledge management across the whole country. Such leadership, needless to say, was well received and appreciated by most Indians, evidenced by the fact that the Congress Party under his leadership won an unprecedented majority in parliament not only in 1984 but also in 1991. That his party lost in the 1989 elections as a result of serious and large-scale corruption scandals is testimony to his personal fight against the corrupt political system. Although he and his party benefited from popular sympathy following his mother's assassination, his values, vision, and actions were truly appreciated by most Indians, who were dissatisfied with the existing system. That his policies were continued more formally and continue even today is testimony to the existence of core underlying values in this domain among Indians. As will be shown in the other three stories, a broad set of knowledge leadership behaviors are common to most successful political leaders in India. But, first, it is important to make a note of the regional disparities and minority religious tensions that had prevailed in India for a while and were at their peak at the time Rajiv Gandhi first became Prime Minister. The political movements associated with these tense events link this story to the other three.

By all accounts, minority religious tensions were high when Rajiv Gandhi became Prime Minister. His mother had just been assassinated by her two Sikh bodyguards as a result of a separatist movement in the state of Punjab (where Sikhs are in the majority). Prime Minister Indira Gandhi's decision to have the Indian Army enter the holiest of Sikh religious sites, the Golden Temple in Amritsar, upset the feelings of all Sikhs and angered many. Thus, her decision to smoke out extremists, allegedly hiding with a large cache of arms inside the temple, backfired on her and ended her life. Rajiv Gandhi, as Prime Minister, made several symbolic efforts at reconciliation with different aggrieved groups in different parts of the country, including neighboring Sri Lanka. In the case of Punjab and the Sikhs, he released many extremists held as prisoners and ordered judicial investigations into cases of violence against Sikhs in the riots ensuing his mother's assassination. The state of Punjab is one of the most economically productive and advanced in the nation. The average participation of Sikhs in the Indian armed forces is much higher than any other state, with Sikhs historically endeavoring to contribute at least one person per family to the armed forces of the country. Thus, many analysts argue that the separatist movement in the state of Punjab was merely the result of poor governmental decisions made on political grounds. These decisions, as in other parts of the country, ended in usurping state autonomy and granting more power by the Central Government, leading to widespread dissatisfaction. In addition to this, Rajiv Gandhi engaged in several other symbolic efforts at reconciliation for past disputes by entering into peace agreements with several regional parties. In the high-profile case of a divorced Muslim woman who was granted maintenance (alimony) by the Supreme Court, his actions were interpreted by critics as intended to appease minorities and ensure their votes would not be lost. In this case the highest court decided to bypass Islamic personal law, which does not allow such payments, and ordered her husband to pay her maintenance. This upset Muslim organizations who viewed the court decision with alarm, interpreting it as an instance of an overall attempt to undermine Muslim personal law. In an alleged effort to appease these Muslim organizations, Rajiv Gandhi, armed with an absolute majority in parliament, enacted a law that would nullify the Supreme Court decision. All such symbolic efforts at appeasement were regarded with contempt by the Bharatiya Janata Party (BJP), a Hindu fundamentalist party, whose leader Narendra Modi was to become Prime Minister in May 2014. The protagonist of the second story, C.N. Annadurai, was also involved in earlier federal attempts to impose the Hindi language on everyone in the country and to similar attempts at centralization of power. The concept of unity in diversity is at the core of all four stories. The men in the next two stories played important roles in the economic and religious issues associated with the unity-in-diversity concept and the gradual development of an alternative to the Congress Party as the single best representative of Indians in parliament, which was true for more than four decades after independence. The protagonist of the next story attempted to battle central dominance over states in the 1960s.

Leadership for the rights of self-determination

> "Dravidians want the right of self-determination ... We want a separate country for southern India ... To make the Dravidian state a separate state was our ideal. A situation has arisen where we can neither talk nor write about this ideal. Of course we can destroy the party by undertaking to violate the prohibition. But once the party itself is destroyed there will not be any scope for the ideal to exist or spread. That is why we had to give up the ideal."
>
> (C.N. Annadurai, before and after the enactment of a law prohibiting proponents of separatism from contesting elections)

> "The movie Velaikari [Servant Maid] made it clear that greed and avarice of the rich did not pay in the long run. [...] Some of the elementary principles of socialism and stressed that we should depend upon our own labor for our progress and well being and not some unknown factor."
>
> (C.N. Annadurai on the movie made from his novel)

The protagonist in this story, C.N. Annadurai, was so popular that a record 15 million people attended his funeral on his untimely death due to cancer in 1969. The funeral attendance made it into the *Guinness Book of Records* as being the highest ever recorded. While the protagonists in the next two stories represent the efforts of a movement that would eventually lead to the first non-Congress Central Government, Annadurai's story deals with efforts that would lead to the first non-Congress government anywhere in India. It is important to note here that the Congress Party was previously called the Indian National Congress and was instrumental in achieving independence for India. However, subsequent policies of the Congress Party in independent India caused serious dissatisfaction among many regional political movements, as noted earlier in Chapter 4. It was Annadurai who raised the voice of the downtrodden and those of the Dravidians, in general, and Tamils, in particular. Dravidians have historically populated the four states of southern India, which were grouped together into what was called the state of Madras immediately after independence. Dravidians were considered different from the Aryans in the north. Apprehensions that independent India would be dominated by Brahmins and north Indians of Aryan descent were quite common in the immediate aftermath of the British decision to free India. Even as early as 1928, and later in 1938, efforts to suggest Hindi as a suitable language for all Indians, and making Hindi compulsory in school education in the State of Madras, respectively, caused serious levels of anxiety among Tamils in the current state of Tamil Nadu. The predominant fear, expressed articulately by Annadurai was that Tamils would become second-class citizens in their own country. In the first instance, 1928, it was Rajiv Gandhi's great-grandfather Motilal Nehru who headed the committee that suggested Hindi would be an apt language for official purposes in India. Not surprisingly, Motilal Nehru's son, granddaughter, and great-grandson, all Prime Ministers of India, would follow the same policy of using Hindi as a suitable language across India. However, this caused a great deal of anxiety among the Tamils. Annadurai entered politics in 1935 by joining the Justice Party, which was later renamed *Dravidar Kazhagam* (Dravidian Organization). This party was openly atheist and founded by non-Brahmin elites for the purpose of uplifting the lower-caste masses in an environment that was perceived to favor the upper castes and at the same time discriminate against the lower castes. In a context where superstitions and religious (exploitation) beliefs were used as vehicles of domination by the upper castes over the lower castes, Annadurai and many in his party made a stand in the fight against these evils. He was forced to interrupt his schooling during high school to work as a clerk and help with the family finances. At the age of 25 he graduated with a BA degree and later obtained an MA degree in Economics and Politics. He worked as an English teacher in a high school before turning to a journalistic and political career.

Imposition of Hindi in the second instance in 1938 involved the head of the Madras Presidency, C. Rajagopalachari, promulgating an order requiring the use of Hindi as a compulsory language in schools. Annadurai and his party participated in the protest demonstrations and in the first Anti-Hindi Imposition Conference held in that same year. Two of the protesters died later that year as a consequence of police beatings, following which the Madras government withdrew the order. Annadurai also protested against Chief Minister Rajagopalachari's 1953 educational scheme that indirectly encouraged traditional caste-based occupations. That same year Annadurai also protested against Prime Minister Jawaharlal Nehru's description of DMK[3] activists defacing Hindi letters on official name boards as "childish nonsense". In 1950, the newly formulated Indian constitution gave special status to Hindi, putting it on course to obtaining official language status in 1965. Arguing against the notion of giving Hindi official status just because it is spoken by the majority,[4] Annadurai is reported to have said, "Why should we then claim the tiger as our national animal instead of the rat which is so much more numerous? Or the peacock as our national bird when the crow is ubiquitous?" With protests mounting on the issue of language imposition, Prime Minister Nehru promised in parliament that English would continue to be the official language of India as long as the non-Hindi-speaking people desire. A planned black flag protest was withdrawn following this promise in parliament. However, when the expected constitutional amendment to follow through on the promise was not forthcoming, Annadurai declared 26 January 1965, India's Republic Day, as a day of mourning. Amid voices that called this move blasphemous, Annadurai made a bid to shake off the secessionist image and amended the protest slogan to "Down with Hindi, long live the Republic". The result was rioting and violence throughout the state. Annadurai was arrested for instigating the violence despite the absence of evidence directly linking him to the rioters (Hardgrave, 1965). However, the protests and allegations helped the DMK win a landslide majority in the 1967 assembly elections, bringing Annadurai to the position of Chief Minister of Madras, which he later renamed Tamil Nadu.

This story demonstrates that Annadurai's characteristics, values, vision, and gumption were much appreciated by the people of Tamil Nadu. He left behind a huge legacy and a large following in the state, evidenced by the fact that the Congress Party continues to perform poorly in Tamil Nadu even today. *India Today* magazine listed him as one of the "top 100 people who shaped India by thought, action, culture, and spirit". That India's knowledge-based services has competitive advantage in global markets because of English language proficiency is in large measure due to his leadership, without which Indians would be proficient in another language. When asked why India has an edge over other nations like China in this sector, Azim Premji, CEO of the third largest software company in India, noted that the only thing holding the Chinese back is the English language proficiency of Indians (Ramamurti, 2001). Although competitive advantage was not directly one of Annadurai's motivations in the struggle, this effect of his influence should not be ignored. After all, his struggle was truly representative of the people in the state and instrumental in changing Central Government policy on the language issue. His struggle and emergence as a successful leader are further evidence of the unity-in-diversity principle in India. Whereas the Nehru–Gandhi dynasty of leaders wanted unity and homogeneity (in language), Annadurai reaffirmed his commitment to unity (the Republic) in diversity (in language), symbolized by his protest slogan. More importantly, he stood for the broader issue of the right to self-determination and the upliftment of the downtrodden, both of which were so clearly conveyed through his policies.

The behavior of people is predominantly driven by religious/superstitious beliefs. The upper castes used this fact to assert their domination over the lower castes. It is perhaps for this reason that Annadurai allowed himself to be strongly influenced by his staunchly atheist mentor in the *Dravidar Kazhagam*. As Chief Minister, Annadurai ordered the removal of pictures of gods and religious symbols from public offices and buildings. Not only was this consistent with India's secular stance, but it also served to induce, albeit slowly, rational thought and action in lieu of behavior sometimes driven by religious and superstitious beliefs. More importantly, it marked the start of the decline of caste domination and got the state moving faster than others in this regard. As noted earlier, even before he took office, he strongly opposed an education scheme that reinforced caste-based occupations, albeit indirectly. He would later revise his party's stance on religion to "one race, one god", something much closer to his own personal beliefs. He also described himself as, "a Hindu without the sacred ash, a Christian minus the Holy Cross, and a Muslim without the prayer cap," to convey his belief in secularism. All of these initiatives only served to increase his popularity with the people. Annadurai was perhaps the first of many Indian leaders to use the literary and media route to reach people far and wide. Understanding that a majority of the people were illiterate, he chose the medium of film to convert many of his literary works thereby facilitating communication with the masses. Filmgoing has always been very popular in India and this ensured that the people heard his party's messages loud and clear.

Annadurai was best known for his rhetorical and oratorical skills; his public speaking was very well received replete as it was of metaphors and alliterations, some of which can also be found in his written works. He published several novels, short stories, plays, and hundreds of newspaper articles. He served as a journalist and newspaper editor for a significant period of his adult life. Some of his books were provocative at the time and used a social reform approach. *Arya Mayai* (*Aryan Illusion*), for instance, highlighted the dream of bringing about an equal society without any caste dominance, clearly targeting the upper castes, while awakening the lower castes. His novel *Velaikari* (*Servant Maid*), which was later made into a movie, made direct references to suppressive landlords, who were mostly allied with Nehru and the Congress Party. His real stroke of genius was to convert his books into movies and to write screenplays for movies directly, as part of an overall attempt to use the medium of film as a tool for Dravidian political propaganda. His first movie *Nallathambi* (*Good Brother*, 1948) promoted cooperative farming and abolition of the *Zamindari* system (system of feudal landlords). After a huge struggle, the *Zamindari* system was eventually abolished by the Indian government, paving the way for a green revolution in the country. A known promoter of women's rights, Annadurai legalized self-respect marriages, devoid of Brahmin priests who traditionally presided over such ceremonies, as a mechanism to fight against caste domination and the system of arranged marriages. He envisioned a higher number of inter-caste marriages and "love marriages", as they are popularly known in India, where individuals choose their own life partners. These self-respect marriages were also designed to eliminate the social evil of dowry payments, involving huge sums of money, typically paid by the bride's family to the new couple. The dowry system resulted in the accumulation of huge debt by parents of female children, and also resulted in the highly offensive practice of female infanticide in the country. The country would eventually outlaw the practice of dowry as a result of similar movements in many other parts of the country. Annadurai's brilliance rested on his understanding that the elimination of social evils needed social change – not simply legal change. Thus, overall, he stood for a host of desirable values from the perspective of both the state and the whole nation. His efforts were recognized by the Indian government when it issued a INR5 commemorative coin in his honor to mark his centenary celebrations in 2009. A noted analyst of South Asian politics commented, "There is no doubt that this powerful orator is the single-most popular mass figure in the region."[5] He won further international acclaim when he became the first non-American to receive Yale University's Chubb Fellowship, and was a guest of the U.S. State Department in April/May 1968 when he traveled there to receive the honor.[6]

Like Rajiv Gandhi in the previous story, Annadurai also epitomized many traits of knowledge leadership. One of the first requirements of knowledge leadership is the leader's own personal knowledge of the major problems in his or her domain and a clear personal recognition of the means by which these problems can be tackled (Lakshman, 2008b). Addressing the topic of lack of leadership in India, one of India's greatest military leaders, Field Marshall Sam Manekshaw, said:

"The first, the primary, indeed the cardinal attribute of leadership is professional knowledge and professional competence. Now you will agree with me that you cannot be born with professional knowledge and professional competence even if you are a child of Prime Minister, or the son of an industrialist, or the progeny of a Field Marshal. Professional knowledge and professional competence have to be acquired by hard work and by constant study. In this fast-moving technologically developing world, you can never acquire sufficient professional knowledge. You have to keep at it, and at it, and at it. Can those of our political masters who are responsible for the security and defence of this country cross their hearts and say they have ever read a book on military history, on strategy, on weapons developments. Can they distinguish a mortar from a motor, a gun from a howitzer, a guerrilla from a gorilla, though a vast majority of them resemble the latter."[7]

Annadurai had answered Manekshaw's rhetorical question years ago by clearly demonstrating competence and knowledge of what people valued and desired, and what it took to address many of the evils ailing society. He is popularly addressed by his nickname *Anna* (elder brother) and solemnly recognized as *Arignar Anna* (wise brother). He was the first of a long line of leaders in India who used the medium of film to get a range of political messages over to the masses, which they eagerly accepted. Urging the illiterate masses to move away from dogmatic and superstitious religious beliefs to more rational and scientific reasoning and increasing access to education for lower castes were among his critical contributions in the domain of knowledge leadership. That all his messages were eagerly supported and appreciated by the masses is testimony to his effectiveness, and his legacy still continues to dominate in Tamil Nadu today.[8] A noted historian and Tamil writer argued, "The Indian nation state owes much to him for safely accommodating Tamil nationalism within it."[9]

Leadership for total revolution

"I believe firmly that for Hindu society, revival is essential if it is to put forth its best and reach its height of achievement. But the revivalism now taking place will push Hindu society further backward, and may incidentally destroy even what we have of the unity of our nation. The Hindu religion is a strange mixture of good and bad, sublime and low, the most emancipated thought and bigoted obscurantism. What happens to the future of Hindu society depends upon which of these strains are to be selected, nourished and propagated."

(J.P. Narayan in a Convocation Address to Delhi University, 1966)

If Annadurai and his Dravidian movement represent the success of a political movement that resulted in the first non-Congress party being successful at the state level in India, Jayaprakash Narayan's story here represents the successful efforts of a movement that led to the first non-Congress government at the center. Additionally, this story of the man popularly known as J.P. or *Lok Nayak* (People's Leader) is related to the possible revival of the BJP, the right-wing Hindu party, contesting this year's (2014) elections. The leader of the BJP and the man in our fourth story was widely expected to become India's next Prime Minister at the time of the initial writing of this chapter, despite the party's losses in the two previous general elections. The very fact that a non-Congress party could come to power in India would not have been possible but for J.P.'s efforts in the 1970s. Yet, his views on religion and its role in modern India are quite complex and reflect the country-of-contrasts theme projected throughout this book. Needless to say, his views on religion are very different from the populist themes propagated by the BJP today.

J.P., the independence movement activist who obtained fame for his role in the 1942 Quit India Movement,[10] is especially remembered for his leadership of the opposition in the 1970s against Prime Minister Indira Gandhi and for calling for a total revolution to overthrow her. His call for such a revolution came during a massive rally at the Gandhi Maidan in Patna. On that day in June 1974, following a period of war with Pakistan, high inflation and unemployment, growing cases of corruption and nepotism, and increasing shortages of commodities and supplies, he said to the crowd that had gathered, "This is a revolution, friends! We are not here merely to see the *Vidhan Sabha* (State Assembly) dissolved. That is only one milestone on our journey. But we have a long way to go ... After 27 years of freedom, people of this country are wracked by hunger, rising prices, corruption ... oppressed by every kind of injustice ... it is a Total Revolution we want, nothing less!" This rally was preceded by a silent march in April of about 10,000 people in Patna, who were attacked by the police with batons. J.P. had also led a similar protest rally in the state of Gujarat for similar reasons. He had been traveling across states to gather support among non-Congress parties to provide an alternative to the Congress Party at the Center. His efforts in Bihar followed a series of protests by student organizations for related issues. Being a true Gandhian, he agreed to spearhead their efforts as long as they abstained from violence.

The economic problems of rising prices, high inflation, and high unemployment were particularly common to Gujarat and Bihar, two Congress Party–ruled states. In contrast with the reality in 1974, the Congress government at the center had come to power in 1971 on the strength of a *Garibi Hatao* (Eliminate Poverty) campaign. Concerned by millions of refugees entering India from neighboring East Pakistan (now Bangladesh), Indira Gandhi had led the country into war with Pakistan in support of the Bangladesh call for liberation. The U.S. government had stopped all aid to India in the wake of the war and oil prices continued to rise, causing even more economic trouble for India. In contrast with the low industrial growth, inflation was at a peak ranging from 23 to 30 percent in the years preceding these protests. Poor monsoons caused declines in agricultural productivity by as much as 8 percent. The freezing of government worker salaries to reduce expenditure led to massive strikes in such organizations as the Indian Railways, which extended and worsened the economic crisis. Worsening economic conditions and corruption in high places in Gujarat led to protests resulting in the dissolution of the Gujarat Assembly. The ensuing elections led to the victory of Morarji Desai, who would soon also become the next Prime Minister of the country. Having led the Gujarat protests, J.P. was in the forefront of the Bihar protests, which were also gaining support nationally. Corruption and nepotism again showed their ugly faces in the form of Prime Minister Indira Gandhi's nomination of the Chief Justice of India, setting aside the seniority of three other judges just because their prior rulings were against her government's decisions. Additionally, her own election to parliament was ruled invalid by the appropriate high court in June 1975, following a petition brought against her for unfair and illegal tactics. She could no longer remain an MP and therefore not serve as Prime Minister, unless reelected within six months. A few days later J.P. led a huge rally in the capital with the support of several non-Congress parties. During this rally he urged the army, police, and government employees to join the civil disobedience movement and not follow any illegal or immoral orders. This event proved to be the proverbial straw that broke the camel's back. Prime Minister Indira Gandhi, in an unprecedented move, declared a national emergency, provided for in the constitution only in response to a serious external threat. Under the Indian constitution, once an emergency is declared, the federal distribution of powers is suspended and all powers are concentrated in the hands of the federal government. During an emergency none of the fundamental rights enshrined in the constitution are guaranteed and can be curtailed including the freedom of the press. This brought all disquiet to an abrupt stop and all the protest leaders were arrested. When the emergency, one of the most controversial political episodes in Indian history, was released after 18 months of severe national distress, the ruling Congress Party lost and had to give way to the first non-Congress Party Indian government since independence.[11] J.P. had founded the Janata Party, an electoral fusion of a number of parties including today's BJP, which had succeeded in toppling the dominant Congress Party. J.P. himself could not contest or participate in the government because of ill health. This very same reason was likely responsible for the early demise of the Janata Party when it took the helm, which resulted in new elections being held before completion of the five-year term in 1979. J.P.'s death signaled the end of the unifying force in the electoral fusion of parties. However, his efforts had sown the seeds for future alternatives to the Congress Party to take power, thereby making the Indian democracy a viable institution. More importantly, the vision, values, and practices he stood for were widely appreciated by the majority of Indians.

His knowledge of Indian society, Hindu religion, and Indian democracy were unparalleled. Born into a humble family in eastern India (Bihar), young J.P. obtained an education in sociology and politics from Bihar Vidyapeeth, a college run by the Congress Party, before going to the U.S.A. and getting a master's degree.[12] He took a number of jobs to support himself in the U.S. but had to return home without obtaining his desired doctorate in sociology because of his mother's ill health. He joined the Congress Party on his return to India and became a part of the independence movement. He is known for his writings on several topics: the award-winning essay on the state of Hindi in Bihar,[13] religious revivalism,[14] democracy, and his vision of total revolution. His writings reveal his excellent knowledge of Indian society and his comparative knowledge of society and democratic institutions across countries. He used these knowledge sources to full measure in developing his vision for total revolution, which was shared with his followers in the form of a letter.[15] J.P. was jailed and tortured several times by the British during the war for independence. Being a true Gandhian and inspired by Gandhi's philosophies, he believed in the values of service to the nation and utilitarian (*Sarvodaya*) practices. In a letter to Prime Minister Indira Gandhi asking her to revoke the emergency, J.P. wrote that corruption was the central point of the revolutionary movement he led.[16] That he was able to rally forces against this central issue of corruption is clear evidence of the fact that Indians deplore corrupt governments. As noted in the first story, there have been several instances of the country's people removing parties from power for corruption-related scandals. Corruption and Indian values on this issue were central to the recent 2014 parliamentary elections, to be discussed in the next story. J.P.'s views on Hinduism reflected the contrasts within the religion and were in stark contrast with the typically fundamentalist views held by the BJP and its leaders, as will be seen in the next story. Thus, although the founding members of the BJP were part of J.P.'s total revolution, their views on the role of religion in government and society were in stark contrast with each other. While J.P.'s movement helped bring about the first non-Congress Party government in India, the BJP's religious crusades succeeded in bringing about a more stable version of non-Congress Party government.

Indians are typically religious, regardless of the religion they believe in, with very few exceptions. Annadurai and his party in the previous story are exceptions to this norm of religiosity. Thus, the way in which politicians use religion and its values in political campaigns is critical to the country's development and tests the collective values of Indians at large. Although J.P. believed that the all-pervasive problem with Indian society was the decline of religion, and that a revival of Hinduism was essential for Indian society, his views on how this should be brought about were very different from the current brand of Hinduism on which today's leaders are waging their political campaigns. That some of them have succeeded in the last two decades with such a brand of Hinduism, despite violence and controversies, is evidence of the complexity religion brings. J.P.'s initial quote in this story notes that the Hindu religion is a bundle of contrasts, blending the good and the bad, the sublime and the low, and the most emancipated thought along with bigoted obscurantism. This statement suggests that, although he believed in the need for a revival of religion, the current attempt at Hindu revivalism could push the country backward.[17] Whether or not the man in the next story can lead the nation through a more positive revival remains to be seen. But it is interesting to note here that J.P. and the movement he founded, which were critical in bringing a string of non-Congress Party governments to power, possessed values very different from those bandied about today. If the main asset of the Congress Party was a host of independence era leaders, J.P. began a movement that provided the country with an equally strong number of independence era thinkers and fighters.

J.P. held strong views about the poor and downtrodden in society and was seriously concerned about the role and status of women in India.[18] This set of values is common to many of India's popular leaders, as they are core issues in India even today. In his letter to his followers on total revolution, J.P. outlined a number of issues ranging from caste discrimination, education, the dowry system, communalism, and social and cultural integration. He outlined his vision as well as action plans to bring it about. He was a strong orator and had the ability to use the evocative poetry of national poets in his speeches to communicate his vision. Thus, not only did he have excellent knowledge of society's problems, but he also came up with remarkably better ways these problems could be addressed by newer governments than ever before. Like Annadurai in the previous story, he believed that it would take vigorous social movements rather than simple legal changes to bring about changes in social evils such as dowry, untouchability, and zamindari[19] practices. Whereas Annadurai had been successful with these messages in the late 1960s and early 1970s in Tamil Nadu, these efforts were only starting to take root in states like Bihar in the late 1970s. J.P.'s essential criticism of preceding Congress Party governments was precisely the extraordinary length of time since independence it had taken the government to address these issues. Perhaps India had been moving just as slowly on the social front as on the economic front. Jayaprakash Narayan received India's highest civilian honor, the Bharat Ratna award, and gained international recognition by being an awardee of the Magsaysay Award[20] for public service.[21]

Leadership for business and economic development

> "O kite,
> It is the celebration of aiming for the skies,
> It is my flight to the sun.
> O kite,
> It's my glory in this life and beyond
> I hold my own strings . . .
> With my footprints on ground
> And skies,
> I have the bird's eye view.
> My kite,
> It does not get entangled
> With a host of other kites. . .
> Nor does it get caught in boughs of trees."
>
> (the first part of a poem by Narendra Modi[22]
> posted on Twitter on the occasion of Sankranti)

The protagonist in this final leadership story, Narendra Modi, was heavily involved in Gujarat in J.P.'s protests against corruption and the revolution against preceding Congress Party governments. When the emergency was declared in 1975, the founding members of the BJP were arrested under preventive detention measures, but Modi escaped the massive manhunt that was launched for him by disguising himself as a Sikh.[23] His audacious political activism during his participation in the movement against oppression under J.P. was the main reason for the manhunt. In his twenties at the time, Modi was a member of the Rashtriya Swayamsevak Sangh

(RSS), one of the family of organizations (Sangh Parivar) that included the BJP.[24] He successfully demonstrated his professional competence and knowledge of governance during his more than 12-year reign as Chief Minister of the state of Gujarat. Exit polls of the early phases of the 2014 general election in India indicated that Modi could very well be India's next Prime Minister, which turned out in fact to be the case.[25]

After first taking the position of Chief Minister in October 2001, as a result of the incumbent departing due to ill health, Modi led the BJP party to victory in three successive elections and remained Chief Minister up to 21 May 2014. His brand of leadership, based on actions more than words, continues to be what the people of his state, as well as many others around the country, want. In addition to being an able administrator, Modi's impeccable organizational skills, strong developmental focus, progressive vision, views of governance concerning privatization and "small government", track record of reducing corruption levels, tough anti-terrorist stance, diplomacy, and statesmanship have been critical virtues in his political career thus far. He is a self-declared Hindu nationalist, a position which is sometimes criticized as being anti-Muslim; some label him as a Hindu fundamentalist, a perception that has led to numerous controversies both within and outside the country. Despite allegations of his government's passiveness and inaction following the Godhra[26] incident which stoked Hindu–Muslim riots and violence, he was absolved of all blame in this regard by the highest court in the country. The U.S.A., the EU, and the U.K. all lifted diplomatic bans on Modi after numerous investigations failed to produce any evidence to support the allegations against him. The U.S. also reaffirmed its intent to work with any democratically elected Indian leader, including Modi. However, he continues to remain a controversial figure in the eyes of many.

Within six months of his first period as Chief Minister, Gujarat witnessed a major Hindu–Muslim riot in 2002, in which hundreds of people of both religions died or were reported missing, and hundreds of places of worship were destroyed. These riots caused serious destruction in the state and led to Modi's eventual resignation and dissolution of the state assembly. The riots were triggered by rumors that Muslim arsonists were responsible for setting fire to a train carrying many Hindu pilgrims near Godhra. The order to bring the bodies of the dead to Ahmedabad (the state capital) was widely considered to be a contributory if not the main factor behind the ensuing violence. However, the BJP under Modi's leadership won a significant majority in the next set of elections returning him as Chief Minister. His subsequent record as Chief Minister was exemplary and the BJP's campaign in the 2014 elections was based on expanding the Gujarat Model across the whole nation. When he took over as Chief Minister in 2001, the state was struggling with a shrinking economy following the massive earthquake of 2001. His efforts to turn the state economy around bore fruit with the economy growing 10 percent during his first term, the highest in the nation. Modi was reported to have ruled with an iron fist, especially when it came to taking anti-corruption action, making the state an attractive destination for investment by MNCs. His government's rhetoric against terrorism continued to grow ever more vociferous in light of incidents such as the Mumbai blasts of 2006 and the 2008 Mumbai attacks. His efforts in protecting the 1600-km-long Gujarat coastline resulted in increased speedboat surveillance by the Central Government. Wide-ranging measures put in place during his administration led to a record 10.97 percent agricultural growth between 2001 and 2010 period, the highest in the nation. Using ideas from the International Water Management Institute (an NGO), he put in place an innovative electricity distribution system for farmers, which not only reduced the cost of agricultural subsidies for the state government, but increased the efficiency of farmers. Although successful in making Gujarat one of the fastest growing states in the country on the economic front over the entire period, his achievements on the social front, including the Human Development Index, were widely criticized, despite remarkable improvement from starting levels that were very low. Critics noted the poor performance of the state vis-à-vis poverty alleviation, nutrition, and education. Gujarat ranks 13th in the country for poverty, 21st for education, and is on the India State Hunger Index for poor nutrition.[27] However, state officials point to success in the improvement rates of multiple indicators including female education, decline in school dropout rates, and decline in maternal mortality. Some experts point to the need for rural areas to be included as part of state overall growth, while others point to the need for the state government to shed the communal image to succeed in the future.[28]

Modi had a very humble beginning; he was born into a family of grocers and helped his father sell tea at the local railway station. He ran a tea stall with his brother near a bus terminus when he was in his teens. Modi obtained a bachelor's degree in political science from Delhi University and a master's degree in the same discipline from Gujarat University, while serving as a RSS volunteer.[29] His exemplary work in this role and subsequent demonstrations of the capability to organize rapidly led him from local-level to state-level leadership roles in the BJP, and launched him on a career path that would lead to national leadership within the party. Having written three books and many poems, Modi is recognized today as a passionate author, poet, and lover of culture. He has always been a powerful orator, and during the most recent elections impressed many with his ability to use poetry to attract audiences.[30] He is an active Twitter user, technologically adept, and is the first Indian leader to have engaged in live chats with the public at large through the Internet, which were broadcast live on YouTube. He is also media savvy and a crowd puller in such contexts. He leads a frugal life style, wears suits to business meetings but homespun tunics for political/administrative meetings. He is a straight shooter and carries a no nonsense image. He surrounds himself with knowledgeable and competent officials (career bureaucrats) rather than politicians to run the administration.[31] His preferred way of working demonstrates a reliance on personal knowledge as well as that of a trusted group of professionals as well as a propensity to share and leverage information and knowledge useful for decision making. His long stint as Chief Minister in the state of Gujarat, the longest by anyone, suggests he possesses the values needed to do the job. According to a recent research report, backed up by widely held views by experts in India's stock markets, if other states boosted manufacturing employment levels to those achieved by Modi in Gujarat, India would create 40 million industrial jobs in the next decade.[32] Thus, Modi's brand of leadership augurs well for business and economic development in India.

Desirable leadership qualities in India

The above four stories of political leaders from the four corners of India point up many of the values and characteristics that the people of India require of their leaders. Culturally, people value and prefer leaders who possess knowledge leadership; furthermore, they respect their leaders' personal knowledge and competence in the professional domain. MNCs and their managers will find that such preferences supersede most other characteristics and traits that leaders could or should possess. Analysis of the leader traits of these four, but also of others in India, suggests that Indians value leaders who are strong orators and can use sophisticated language deftly. In fact, looking at leadership candidates within political parties and comparing those who achieve leadership positions with those who do not, what stands out is a significant difference in language proficiency, which provides the leader with an aura of credibility. The ability to write or recite poetry when addressing audiences is also something that is highly appreciated by many Indians. What stands out from simply looking at the attributes of past prime ministers is their level of education, wisdom, knowledge of languages, oratorical skills, and strong administrative capability – although not all within the same individual.

Many Indians value technology and technological development, especially as it pertains to their own or family member careers. Thus, leaders with a natural inclination to focus on these issues are more likely to be preferred than others. Indians do appreciate visionary leadership, especially that which strikes a balance between the idealistic and the pragmatic. Self-respect, self-rule, self-determination, and an individual's own ability to accomplish things are high among the list of values Indians hold dear to their hearts. Thus, leaders who can enhance such values in their subordinates are more likely to be successful than others. Self-determination also implies valuing diversity. Many Indians take pride in the unity-in-diversity doctrine and expect leaders to value diversity in all its complexity. India is a high-context culture and people prefer leaders to use stories that metaphorically address key issues to provide answers. High-context cultures are those where communications are rich but not always direct, where non-verbal communication is as important as verbal communication, and where what is not explicitly stated could sometimes be more important than what is. This is perhaps why people in India prefer leaders who are more proficient when it comes to language, prose, and poetry. Such leaders tend to be immensely more popular than others who lack these skills.

Indians value trust and loyalty in relationships, and subordinates depend on their managers to support them through tough times. Many experts have noted the practice of paternalistic leadership[33] in India. Indians also value integrity, straightforwardness, and administrations devoid of corruption. In valuing these latter traits of integrity and straightforwardness, they place priority on interpersonal manager–subordinate relationships more so than broader relationships with the collective. In essence, subordinates expect their managers to include them in high-trust relationships and expect to be nurtured and developed over time. Thus, the levels of trust, integrity, and relationship quality are likely to be higher in interpersonal relationships than in broader group relationships in organizational contexts. Indians take pride in their indigenous ingenuity and seek to enhance their professional competence in this domain. This is possible only within high-trust relationships; hence, managers wanting to enhance innovation outcomes need to take this on board. This author's own research suggests that knowledge leadership is likely to be highly effective in India for such important outcomes as business performance and innovation. The four stories related above also underline the importance of leaders' knowledge and of knowledge management in Indian organizations.

Knowledge leadership for MNC managers in India

Indians revere their seniors, especially those with high levels of knowledge and wisdom. The preference for metaphorical stories and the proficient use of language, rich in alliterations and analogies, highlights the value of tacit knowledge in effective management. Managers can become effective knowledge leaders by engaging in: (a) orientation towards knowledge sharing, (b) creating a climate that supports knowledge sharing, (c) supporting individual and group learning, and (d) acting as role models regarding learning and knowledge sharing.

Orientation

Managers should first and foremost provide overall directions based on their vision and goals to facilitate a broad understanding of the overall direction in which knowledge sharing and learning is to take place in a specific context. In providing such orientation, managers should promote common planning and ideation at work, in addition to organizing discussion forums for the purpose of searching for and acquiring critical information and knowledge needed to make decisions. It is to be noted that Indians speak of "taking decisions" rather than the American notion of decision making. This difference highlights the separate processes of ideation and planning, as distinct from the leader making up his or her mind in choosing a particular solution. In other words, despite Indians actively participating in planning, ideation, and related processes, they look to the leader to finalize and bring closure to the process. Overall, however, managers should provide this orientation and generally encourage information acquisition and knowledge sharing in the groups they lead.

Creating a climate that supports knowledge sharing

As noted earlier in this chapter, it is important for companies establishing businesses in India to have leaders capable of setting up relationships based on trust and loyalty. These are critical to fostering a climate that supports learning and knowledge sharing. MNC managers should foster a climate of trust and comfort – one that is conducive to learning, emphasizes a constructive approach to dealing with problems, is open to feedback, and listens to and appreciates the ideas of subordinates. This is likely to be highly critical to creating a climate conducive to knowledge leadership.

Supporting individual and group learning

Having provided the orientation for knowledge utilization and sharing as well as a conducive climate in which to work, the MNC manager can look to support individuals and groups to create, share, and leverage knowledge autonomously. It is here that managers should support the actual learning processes by identifying and developing key subordinate proficiencies, while also planning for and ensuring that the unit as a whole has the required set of knowledge capabilities. Knowledge flows only when the sources of knowledge are perceived to be credible and there is a sufficient level of trust. Managerial actions in this area are critical to establishing a system made up of competent individuals with adequate professional knowledge of the work domain. Managers should also remember that the process of generating and sustaining knowledge flows is ongoing and requires constant attention.

Acting as role models

It is not difficult to see that much of leadership involves leading by example. This is true of knowledge leadership as well. MNC managers need to act as role models by making appropriate use of information and knowledge in task domains. Further, it is important for managers to model the attitudes and behaviors appropriate for learning, thereby motivating subordinates to follow.

Knowledge leadership along these four dimensions, if properly displayed by managers, is likely to lead to positive outcomes in innovation and eventual performance. More importantly, they are likely to be seen as acceptable and desirable by employees and managers at all levels in India. The various stories and cases provided in this chapter serve to highlight the importance of this type of leadership in India.

This chapter started with the basic idea that as soon as MNCs have determined the business strategy to use to enter India, it is critical for them to implement it effectively. To do so requires the establishment of strong leadership systems. Using the examples and stories in this chapter, MNCs and their managers can easily identify the types of leaders they require at different levels in their organization. This chapter provides the reader with an understanding of culturally endorsed patterns of values and behaviors that are desirable of leaders in India. One broad type of leadership that is likely to work well in India is knowledge leadership, details of which have been provided here. Strong cultural preferences and entrenched values favor knowledge and professional competence and leadership that institutionalizes knowledge flows and knowledge sharing. Chapters 10 and 11 focus on organizational control systems and human resource management practices that are likely to be important for effective implementation of business strategies in India.

Notes

1. http://www.iloveindia.com/indian-heroes/rajiv-gandhi.html.
2. http://en.wikipedia.org/wiki/Rajiv_Gandhi.

3. *Dravida Munnetra Kazhagam* (DMK) means "Dravidian Progress Federation".
4. In a country of numerous languages, this majority was fairly thin at about 30 percent.
5. http://indiatoday.intoday.in/story/Letter+and+spirit/1/6878.html.
6. http://en.wikipedia.org/wiki/C._N._Annadurai.
7. Field Marshall Sam Manekshaw's lecture to the 1998 graduating class of the Defence Services College.
8. http://www.iloveindia.com/indian-heroes/c-n-annadurai-biography.html.
9. http://indiatoday.intoday.in/story/Letter+and+spirit/1/6878.html.
10. The movement often credited with triggering British intentions to leave India.
11. Today, after subsequent amendments to the constitution, an emergency can only be declared for internal disturbances resulting from an armed rebellion.
12. http://www.iloveindia.com/indian-heroes/jayaprakash-narayan.html.
13. http://en.wikipedia.org/wiki/Jayaprakash_Narayan.
14. http://www.mkgandhi.org/jpnarayan/hindu_revival.htm.
15. http://www.mkgandhi.org/jpnarayan/total_revolution.htm.
16. http://www.liberalsindia.com/freedomfirst/ff452-04.html.
17. http://www.mkgandhi.org/jpnarayan/hindu_revival.htm.
18. http://www.mkgandhi.org/jpnarayan/total_revolution.htm.
19. Zamindars were hereditary aristocrats holding vast swathes of land and exercising control over peasants, who were obliged to pay taxes.
20. Considered as Asia's Nobel Prize.
21. http://en.wikipedia.org/wiki/Magsaysay_award.
22. http://indiatoday.intoday.in/story/narendra-modi-uploads-poem-on-twitter-shows-literary-side-of-makar-sankranti/1/336104.html.
23. http://daily.bhaskar.com/article/GUJ-AHD-when-indira-gandhi-fear-turned-gujarat-chief-minister-narendra-modi-a-sardar-4208886-NOR.html.
24. http://en.wikipedia.org/wiki/Sangh_Parivar.
25. Since the time of this writing, Narendra Modi has been elected as the Prime Minister of the country with his party winning a significant majority in parliament.
26. In February 2002 a fire broke out on the Sabarmati Express killing 59 people. The victims were mainly Hindu. While a court convicted 31 Muslims of arson, the actual cause of the fire remains to be proven conclusively.
27. http://en.wikipedia.org/wiki/Narendra_Modi.
28. http://www.thehindu.com/news/national/shedding-communal-image-a-challenge-to-bjp/article5960600.ece?homepage=true.
29. http://www.iloveindia.com/indian-heroes/narendra-modi.html.
30. http://www.narendramodi.in/author-poet-and-lot-morelife-beyond-politics/.
31. http://www.thehindu.com/news/national/other-states/the-men-who-rule-modis-gujarat/article5983309.ece?homepage=true.
32. http://www.hindustantimes.com/elections2014/election-beat/business-bets-on-narendra-modi-to-defuse-country-s-jobs-time-bomb/article1-1215567.aspx.
33. A fatherly managerial style used to control and protect subordinate staff who are expected to be loyal and obedient.

Organization and control systems for India

10

"The difference between success and failure is people: it is they who make the difference. Whatever your plan, whatever your strategy, and whatever your vision, you can achieve it only when everybody shares it."
C.P. Jain, Chairman and Managing Director, NTPC

Chapter 9 highlighted the need to set up appropriate leadership systems in the India-based organizations of multinational corporations (MNCs) for them to do well in the country. Factors such as leadership, organizational structure and control systems, and effective human resource management are critical components of strategy execution. Without effective execution of strategies, even the best of strategies are likely to flounder. This chapter focuses on organizational structure and control systems that can make it easy for business leaders to effectively execute strategies specially chosen for India. In Chapter 11 the focus shifts to effective strategies to manage India's human resources so that overall business strategies can be carried out. Once a company has chosen a business strategy for operating in India, how does it go about deciding the best organizational structure and set of control systems to ensure successful execution of its strategies? Having entered the market and gained a strong foothold, what can a company do when things take a turn for the worse? How does a company arrest its slide in market share in the face of increasingly intense competition from a growing number of newcomers?

Consider the case of South African Breweries (SAB), which entered India soon after its investment was cleared by the Foreign Investment Promotion Board (FIPB) in 2000. SAB has been pursuing a global strategy of growth through acquisitions, evidenced by its acquisition of Miller Breweries in the U.S.A., to become the second largest brewer in the world. SAB Miller India had a strong run in India after its entry as a result of forming a joint venture (JV) holding company with local company Narang Breweries Ltd. SAB Miller India continued its aggressive strategy of growth through acquisitions in India by acquiring Mysore Breweries Ltd. in 2001, after having bought out its JV partner. In 2002 the company acquired Rochees Breweries and entered into a JV with Shaw Wallace Breweries Ltd., only to eventually buy out this JV partner as well. These initiatives helped the company gain 37 percent by volume of the beer market in India behind market leader UB Ltd.'s 45 percent in 2006. However, since then the company has been losing market share to an increasingly aggressive UB and to growing competition from newcomers such as Danish giant Carlsberg.[1] In 2009 SAB Miller India brought in Paolo Lanzarotti as Managing Director to arrest the slide in market share, which had by then dropped to 30 percent from its previous level. Whether or not this change in top-level leadership was accompanied by suitable changes in leadership at the middle and lower levels is an important question from the perspective of strategy execution. In 2012 its market share stood at 27 percent compared with the leader's 52.5 percent.

These results suggest that changes to the leadership system made by this company have not arrested its continuous slide in market share. More importantly, it is not clear whether this company has suitably refined its organizational structure and control systems to be able to forecast such events before they happen and then to take preventive action. The focus in this chapter is precisely on these organizational systems. Arguably, such systems are more difficult to establish when a company is growing through a phase of rapid acquisitions. In addition to the companies named above, SAB Miller India has also acquired the Indian operations of Australia's Foster's Brewing, in addition to a few other small operators. The difficulties of such a growth strategy make it all the more important to have strong control systems and reliable chains of command in the organizational structure to be able to retain strong leadership positions in the marketplace. That the domestic leader in the beer market, UB, has been following its own strategy of growth through acquisitions and gaining market share at the same time is illustrative in this context. Moreover, Danish giant Carlsberg, which has been present in India for only about three years, now commands a market share of 6 percent.

The beer market in India is a high-growth industry with a current value of about $4.5 billion, which is expected to grow to about $9 billion by 2016.[2] The market is so large that it has attracted all of the top beer manufacturers in the world. Needless to say, the intensity of the competition is at unbelievably high levels. That a domestic player is at the top of the leader board in this market just shows how difficult it is to succeed in this market. However, there is plenty of room for all players, but only those strategies that are well thought through and well executed are likely to succeed.[3] Anheuser-Busch, the largest brewer in the world, obtained 1.3 percent of the market after its recent entry.[4] Heineken now owns about 40 percent of the domestic company that leads this market, which previously was part of South Asia Brewers from Singapore. The question raised at the very outset of this book about why McDonald's wanted to be present in a country where people do not eat beef is equally applicable in this case. The annual per capita consumption of beer in India is a meager 1.7 liters, although growing. Traditional Indian society generally perceives beer and alcohol consumption negatively and Indian laws include beer in the same group as alcoholic products for taxation purposes. Taxation on all alcoholic products is the highest in the world, with about 49 percent of the retail price of beer made up of taxes compared with a global average of 34 percent. This means brewers in India can only get about 35 percent of the retail price after distribution and retail costs, whereas the global average is 55 percent. These heavy taxes make beer very expensive for the Indian consumer, relative to other items in the consumer basket. The high growth of the beer market in India – in contrast with home markets that are saturated and endure stiff competition from craft beer – is what motivates MNCs to establish larger bases in India, despite the challenges noted above. To complicate things, TV advertising for alcohol is banned in India and companies have to resort to surrogate advertising, in which companies use other products to carry the brand names they want to sell. SAB Miller advertises its High Life beer[5] by manufacturing clocks with the brand name on the clock face, while other companies put their names on bottled water or soda.

In a market where its share has slipped from more than one third a few years ago to less than one fourth in 2013, SAB Miller continues to pour money into increasing production capacity; its latest investment was about Rs. 440 crore.[6] The company is likely optimistic about the market doubling in just a few years and intends to entrench itself firmly in this attractive market. However, it needs more than optimism to make the company engage in further investment in a market where it has already invested upward of Rs. 3800 crore over the past 12 years. Laying out their longer term strategy, SAB Miller India's Managing Director Richard Ruston said in 2001, "The investment approach focuses on building a national presence. Acquisition of production capacity in key markets, upgrading and modernizing breweries, and also building indigenous brands will be the cornerstones of SAB Miller India's growth strategy" (Thadamalla, 2011). One solution to declining market share in a country where different states have different regulations on the sales and distribution of beer[7] is to establish local production capacity in states where the market is already big or growing fast.

Chapter 6 identified product differentiation, product proliferation, and cost leadership as the best strategies to use in India's high-growth markets. Although the company has a multi-brand approach, several brands have failed to take off in India. The company's brands are top heavy in the premium segment and need to use the positive benefits of higher volumes in the mass segment. Additionally, the company does have innovative features in its premium brands, such as a thermochromatic label that indicates optimum consumption temperature. More importantly, the company's operating margins are too low resulting in losses being reported in recent years, despite more than a 20 percent growth in sales in the most recent year.[8] Thus, the problem clearly lies in strategy execution and in creating an organization system that focuses on efficiency in production, distribution, and sales operations.

Although the leader in the beer market has more brands available at different price points than SAB Miller India, the problem of low margins in the face of sales growth points to SAB having serious internal problems, notwithstanding the continued flow of investment. The Indian market for beer, in particular, is unique in that the company requires approval from the Central Government and the State Governments concerned to establish manufacturing plants, but distribution and sales are under the control of State Governments alone.[9] This indicates that SAB needs to have an organizational structure consisting of a division for each state, with the division head responsible for overall profits in that state. In the absence of such a structure, it would become difficult for any organization with a national presence to manage its operations efficiently and ensure sales growth is achieved. Incentive compensation for progressive and gradual reductions in operating costs could be applied to state-level units to motivate them to achieve targets and thereby boost overall company performance.

The federalist nature of the country, where states have different legal drinking age limits and some completely prohibit the consumption of alcohol, makes it necessary for organizations to rethink their organizational structure and control system to fit the local environment. A senior official of Carlsberg, based in Copenhagen, says, "The major challenge in India is the presence of different labor necessities and taxation rules in the various states of India." This points up the need for an organizational hierarchy in which divisions are set up to handle multiple regimes across states.

Considering the fact that the market leader has 28 different breweries across the country, whereas SAB Miller India has 13,[10] it is clear that Indian companies navigate through these complex issues much more easily than MNCs, which are not used to these circumstances. By dispersing breweries across states it makes it easier to handle unique state-level regulations. Although the overall solution may lie both in the strategy used and in its execution, this chapter focuses solely on strategy execution. The case of Reliance Retail in Chapter 6 illustrates how organizational structure can be utilized to handle such complexities. In that instance Reliance used a combination of vertical profit centers for different retail formats and a geographical structure with state-level CEOs as owners of that geography. The purpose of such a complex matrix structure was to ensure that the heads of business verticals could be entrepreneurial and responsible for driving profits within the vertical. Additionally, geographical owners would be responsible for geographical performance, given local constraints and particularities. All companies facing such atomized local regulations perhaps need a variant of such a complex matrix structure to ensure their operations are profitable.

Organizational structure to match India strategy

Chapter 4 provided the reader with a description of the federalist system prevailing in India and a breakdown of domains subject to the jurisdiction of State Governments and Central Government. Nowhere is this more useful, especially in the planning stages, than in the domain of liquor. The MNC manager's first task is to look at the list and identify whether jurisdictional power rests with the Central Government or the State Governments for his or her focal industry. If the industry is predominantly subject to the jurisdiction of states, there is no alternative but for the company to have a complex organizational structure to handle the different environments across states. If the core business can be grouped into a focused vertical, then all that is required is a divisional structure organized around different regions further subdivided into different states, as appropriate. The case of Reliance Retail was a bit more complex with many different verticals, subject to different state-level regulations across the country, thereby necessitating a complex matrix-like structure. Although these structural issues seemingly involve simple decisions, they may end up having a huge impact on the organization's ability to execute the chosen strategy effectively. They are likely to be complicated further by a strategy of growth through acquisitions of domestic companies. Although a holding company structure, with different state-level operations managed independently, may work well in some cases, it did not work well for SAB Miller India. This was mainly the result of lack of integration across different companies that were gradually brought into the fold via acquisitions, a critical factor in obtaining coordination efficiency.

At a more fundamental level, a differentiation strategy with more than a dozen brands, as is the case of SAB Miller India, requires a structure that has geographical divisions with profit responsibilities. A look at the Indian market will reveal that there are differences in preferences across states in addition to different regulations. Although SAB Miller is present in all the states (mostly in the west and the south) where beer consumption is the highest, it has a relatively lower presence in states where growth in per capita consumption is the highest (mostly in the north and the east). In addition to market size and growth, there are other unique local preferences that need to be identified, with products being tailor-made to meet such needs. A divisional structure is the best way to achieve this. The marketing and R&D units in such a divisional structure could very easily focus on the needs within the divisional unit and take suitable actions, improving responsiveness to market needs. However, there are also cost concerns, as indicated by low profit margins and continuing losses at SAB Miller, which suggest the need to integrate and coordinate an ideal cost structure across state units. One outcome of SAB Miller's acquisitions of small regional players was to convert regional brands into national ones with varying degrees of success. Creating a national market and concerns for efficiencies are intricately intertwined in India's beer market. Thus, a strategy that aims to use a blend of differentiation and cost leadership necessarily requires a more complex structure. MNCs have to weigh these domestic structural requirements in India against the overall organizational culture prevailing in the company, both at headquarters and in other countries, to choose the most appropriate option.

Many multinationals enter India through joint venture agreements with domestic companies, which they eventually convert to wholly owned subsidiaries. Examples of companies using such an approach include Honda, Suzuki, McDonald's, Levi Strauss, SAB Miller, and the French multinational Legrand. Under such circumstances the legacy systems and structure left behind by the Indian-owned parts make a huge impact on MNC operations. The shift in the economic environment after the liberalization and privatization programs begun in the 1990s resulted in many Indian businesses changing character in terms of such systems and structure. Chapter 8 looked at the growth of the entrepreneurial spirit and the birth of hundreds of companies in the knowledge-based services sector, spawning a new breed of organizations with radically different organizational structures and control systems from those prevailing in pre-liberalization periods. Some factors of traditional Indian companies need to be considered before MNCs can respond appropriately in the post-acquisition scenario. These factors can be broken down into a number of dimensions: (a) top management characteristics, (b) formalization, (c) centralization, (d) organizational culture, and (e) reward systems. Any one of these dimensions is likely to make the focal Indian business organization different from the parent MNC and thus may require different approaches to integration in the post-acquisition scenario. Traditional structural and cultural factors may also leave a lasting impact on the employees of the specific company and in the broader labor market. Therefore, suitable human resource management (HRM) practices may also be required to ensure strategy execution does not deviate from the planned course of action arising from unanticipated factors thrown up by these dimensions. Chapter 11 focuses more specifically on the contrast between traditional and modern HRM practices in India.

Top management

Chapter 2 considered the prevalence of business groups in countries like India, where institutional voids (the absence of institutional intermediaries) are high. Conventional wisdom in management points out that business groups in emerging economies like India enable individual firms in the group, and therefore the whole group, to enjoy superior performance, mainly by virtue of their ability to fill institutional voids by mimicking institutions. Such business groups are typically family run: the Tatas, Ambanis (Reliance), Birlas, Modis, Godrejs, Goenkas, and Hindujas, to name just a few. Despite variance in the characteristics of top managers across the individual firms in these larger groups by virtue of different practices vis-à-vis career (professional) managers, there are some common tendencies. Top managers of individual firms in these larger groups, which occupy much of India's economic space, are typically risk averse and wield lower levels of power than companies not affiliated to business groups. Thus, top managers in India are typically less powerful and more risk averse than elsewhere. This top management tendency in business groups manifests itself in higher levels of debt financing, higher levels of firm diversification, and higher levels of local orientation (Carney et al., 2011). This characteristic becomes all the more true when the once powerful public sector is considered, especially in pre-liberalization times. High levels of risk aversion combined with a high level of centralization breed a managerial workforce with high levels of such characteristics. MNCs need to suitably accommodate these managerial characteristics across all levels in their business practices. However, Indian firms in recent years have become less risk averse and more global in orientation, signaling widespread changes in these characteristics and serving as a caveat to the conclusion just arrived at.

Formalization

India's economic space in pre-liberalization times was dominated by the public sector, with business groups forming the bulk of the private sector. In an effort to attract managerial talent away from the dominant public sector, family-run business groups wanting to shake off their non-professional images increased their levels of formalization to public sector levels in the pre-liberalization period. Thus, traditional Indian firms in the pre-liberalization period were characterized by high levels of formalization. Formalization is the degree to which rules define managerial and employee roles, authority, relations, communications, norms and sanctions, and procedures in organizational activities. Higher levels of formalization in the organizational structure indicate higher levels of predictability and stability, on the one hand, and higher levels of rigidity, on the other. Higher levels of formalization also indicate the degree to which work is standardized in organizations. Although pre-liberalization firms were high on formalization, a host of firms across sectors in the post-liberalization era are moving away from this trend. However, there still are remnants of such practices scattered across the economic spectrum. More importantly, there are a number of senior managers who have come of age in this system and may still carry those beliefs and attitudes as part of their implicit theories of organizational success. Hence, MNCs either need to change those parts of organizations acquired from domestic firms to facilitate smooth integration or consider these factors in recruitment and selection decisions when hiring in the Indian labor market.

Centralization

Indian firms typically used to be highly centralized, regardless of whether they were in the public sector or in the private sector dominated by business groups. Centralization refers to the concentration of decision making at higher hierarchical levels in organizations and to the absence of delegation of authority and decision making. Business groups in the pre-liberalization era tended to focus more on stability and survival than on performance, thereby seeking to retain control at higher levels in business organizations. High levels of centralization and formalization make for a bureaucratic organization. Whereas public sector firms pre-liberalization were high on centralization (limited delegation of decision making), the private sector post-liberalization is increasingly decentralized. The post-liberalization period has seen the growth of career managers (not part of the family running the group) and their ascent to top management positions of individual businesses in the larger group. This phenomenon has been common across business groups in India and is the result of a variety of internal and external factors ranging from competitiveness to attracting managerial talent. These practices have also seen increased levels of decentralization in the private sector, mirrored by higher levels of decentralization in privatized versions of former public sector organizations. However, remnants of the traditional system in the form of entire organizations or the critical mass of senior managerial talent in the labor market with traditional attitudes to management may still persist. Thus, MNCs need to properly account for these factors in either their own post-acquisition integration attempts or in the recruitment of talent from the labor market. Succeeding in the increasingly competitive Indian marketplace may require higher levels of decentralization, as exemplified by the SAB Miller India experience.

Organizational culture

Organizational culture can be defined as the shared beliefs and values that help individuals understand an organization and provide them with norms for behavior. Experts have classified organizational culture into four types based on variations in two dimensions: focus (internal v. external) and emphasis (stability v. flexibility) (Quinn, 1988). First, competitive cultures are characterized by their emphasis on competitive advantage and market superiority. Second, entrepreneurial cultures emphasize innovation and risk-taking, while focusing on external reality. Third, bureaucratic cultures are characterized by internal regulations and formal structures, with an explicit internal focus. Fourth, consensual cultures (or clan cultures) emphasize loyalty, tradition, and an internal focus. Employees typically point to there being a mix of all four types of cultures in their organizations, although one or two may be given higher emphasis in a specific case. Traditional Indian business organizations and firms in the pre-liberalization economic era were largely characterized by bureaucratic and consensual-type cultures, both characterized by high levels of internal focus and relatively high levels of emphasis on formal structure and loyalty. This has changed dramatically in the post-liberalization era, with organizations typically scoring higher on entrepreneurial cultural dimensions, while still remaining somewhat bureaucratic in culture. In fact, one study noted that the entrepreneurial culture is the most prevalent organizational culture type in Indian businesses today (Deshpande et al., 1993), consistent with the analysis in Chapter 8. The economic regime prevailing in the country after independence from the British evidently had a strong influence on business organizations and their behavior. These shared belief patterns in organizations have changed, and in many cases are continuing to change toward increasingly competitive cultures oriented toward global markets. The biggest factor in post-acquisition integration is the nature of the organizational culture prevailing in the two organizations involved in the process (Lakshman, 2011). Although the variation in culture from one organization to the next across India may be wide, it is illustrative to examine typical patterns in this regard. MNCs engaging in joint ventures with the intent to later buy out the JV partner (the most typical practice to date in India) would do well to gauge the culture of the partner organization before attempting to create a unifying culture.

Reward systems

As a result of the internal focus of Indian organizations the traditional focus of reward systems was the internal organizational hierarchy rather than the external market-place. Although conventional compensation systems are designed by considering the internal hierarchy and prevailing market wages, the focus in Indian organizations before liberalization was excessively on the internal hierarchy. Under such a system, salaries and overall compensation would consist almost entirely of *fixed* amounts of money (as opposed to *variable*) and would be exclusively focused on internal systems. Measurement and reward systems influence the overall organizational culture and the behavior norms within the broader cultural system. For organizations to have stronger emphasis on entrepreneurial and competitive cultures, it is essential to move to variable compensation tied to an external orientation. This is precisely what happened in India with the entry of MNCs in the post-liberalization era. Market-based reward systems are increasingly becoming prevalent in the Indian scenario more so than ever before, thereby favoring the increased presence of firms oriented toward markets. Hence, some of the characteristics of traditional managers that contribute to prevalent attitudes should be correctly attributed to prevailing reward systems, and thus subject to change when MNCs introduce new systems. As Western managers, in general, and American managers, in particular, realize all too well as a result of experience, managerial behavior can easily be shaped by reward systems. The most common problem in post-acquisition integration is the disparity in compensation between the two partners, in addition to the lack of clarity in the reward system of the joint entity (Lakshman, 2011). Thus, one cannot emphasize enough the importance of reward systems in shaping desired managerial behavior anywhere in the world including India.

Control systems

To get as close as possible to perfect execution of business strategies requires not only the most appropriate organizational structure but also a highly adapted control system. The organizational culture and reward systems discussed above could be considered critical components of an overall control system as they orient managerial behavior toward desired directions and distance them from undesired domains. Organizational control systems are designed to ensure that overall organizational goals and objectives are achieved, while providing a process-oriented approach to ensure that deviations from the norm are minimized and corrected. Figure 10.1 shows the different steps typically involved in an overall organizational control system.

The feedback model of organizational control presented in Figure 10.1 shows a logical process typically used by managers to ensure the achievement of strategic goals and objectives. It is important for managers of MNCs in India to set up the different elements of an overall control system to facilitate functions associated with the different steps in the control cycle. The first step in this rational process is to strategize and set goals and objectives in different performance domains (e.g., financial, internal processes, market and customers, learning and growth of employees) according to the firm's aspirations. The next step shows that it is equally important to set up control elements that help establish measures of performance based on desired performance standards. It is worth noting that what cannot be measured cannot be managed. With this in mind it is important to identify how best to measure performance in each of the domains and how precisely these measures indicate the level of performance achieved at any point in time. The next step in this cyclical process is to compare current performance against the standards and to identify the gap in performance achievement. Positive gaps in performance achievement may indicate that initial goal setting may have been improperly estimated or that the organization's potential to achieve higher

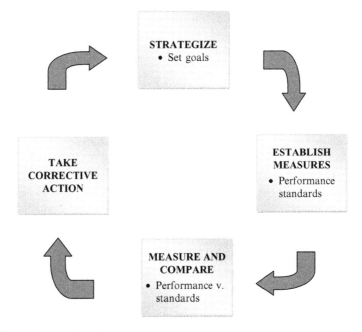

Figure 10.1 The control cycle

targets has been underestimated. Negative gaps in performance achievement indicate the need for appropriate corrective action to bring performance up to scratch. In any event, the assessments of gaps and the underlying reasons for such gaps form a critical component of this feedback model. The final step involves taking corrective action to ensure achievement of desired performance and to aid in the next strategic planning cycle. Such a cyclical process of feedback and analysis helps managers to learn the internal and external realities of business in specific contexts on an ongoing basis. Organizations typically use a wide range of information systems as part of an overall management information system (MIS), consisting of IT elements as well as non-IT elements. Many MNCs use enterprise resource planning (ERP) systems to help move from one step of the control cycle to another, especially in today's context where value chain activities are globally dispersed to a great degree. However, IT systems for a MIS range from fairly low-level operational decision-making aids such as transaction-processing systems (e.g., bar code and scan systems used at checkout counters) to highly strategic ERP systems. Thus, IT systems have a highly critical role to play in ensuring the smooth functioning of an organization by providing the desired level of control.

Control systems are typically defined as the set of formal routines, reports, and procedures that use information to maintain or alter patterns in organizational activity. The four elements typically considered the core of any control system are budgets, financial reports and periodic non-financial statistics reports, reward systems, and quality control systems. The use of each of these elements involves one or more steps in the control cycle. Although organizations worldwide have been traditionally focused on financial performance measures, they have increasingly begun to use tools such as the balanced scorecard (BSC) to ensure all-round performance. Noting the importance of all-round performance for a long-term presence in India, Graham Mackay, Chief Executive of London-based SAB Miller said,

> "We are in India for the long term and will balance the immediate demands of the market with our long-term duties to stakeholders – to investors, a fair return; to employees, a safe and rewarding job; to suppliers, a fair dealing; to governments which tax and regulate us, open and honest relations; to local communities and wider society, a commitment to enhance and work for the common good."
>
> (Thadamalla, 2011)

While highlighting the need for broader measures to be included as indicators of long-term performance, Mackay's statement also reinforces the notion of the BSC. For SAB Miller to accomplish the different duties identified in the statement, the company would have to identify measures of performance in each area that can stand comparison with the specific goals set during the planning process. How would the company measure "fair dealing with suppliers", for instance? Developing consensus in the organization across the different states in India on what would adequately measure performance in this dimension on a recurring basis would be critical to the accomplishment of long-term objectives. This would be true for all the other dimensions of performance highlighted by Mackay's strategic statement. Similarly, measuring "a safe and rewarding job to employees" would require adequate measures, developing consensus around the measures and their use in the organization, and continuous improvement in this performance dimension. To be able to accomplish objectives in all these dimensions of performance, companies have begun to use strategic tools, sometimes accompanied by IT enhancements which executives can easily access using dashboards.[11] One such tool is the BSC. It was developed as a comprehensive management control system with the ability to track traditional financial measures using operational measures related to what are identified as critical success factors. The typical balanced scorecard, as originally conceived, contains four major focal areas: financial performance, customer service, internal business processes, and the organization's capacity for learning and growth. The BSC was designed to address common concerns about the lack of integration between strategy formulation and strategy execution (Kaplan and Norton, 2000).

The BSC has been used by many organizations globally and notably by pharmaceutical companies and public sector firms in India. The following illustration focuses on the efforts of ITC, the Indian company featured in Chapter 7. ITC successfully implemented the BSC as a performance management device to aid strategy execution as part of its initiative to holistically rebrand its chain of luxury hotels such as the ITC Maurya Sheraton, a 27-year-old luxury hotel in Delhi employing 1300 people. Following the onset of reforms and economic liberalization in India, many companies in the hotel business began to feel the heat of competition from old and new players. It became increasingly apparent to large hotel chains such as the ITC group that the organizational structures and control and reward systems of the past were no longer effective in providing them with the required competitive edge. ITC Hotels Ltd. realized that financial measures alone were not enough to achieve key targets in other dimensions of performance that were critical to longer term survival and competitiveness in the hotel business.

Although the market was growing, increased competition from world-class hotel chains was making it difficult to attract customers, similar to what SAB Miller is currently experiencing. ITC realized that holistic measures to track and improve performance needed to be combined with performance appraisal and management systems to ensure that strategic objectives were achieved at all levels of the organization, a factor highly critical in the services sector. Human resources and their efficacy in providing high levels of service quality are much more important in the service sector than in manufacturing. ITC had been using traditional reward systems with a strong emphasis on fixed compensation, with variations in compensation levels matched only by variation in hierarchical levels. The proportion of variable compensation was very low and thus there was little motivation to improve performance. This meant there was very little in the system to differentiate outstanding performers from average ones. These factors were taking a toll on the brand image of the hotel chain, in general, but at the premium end of the spectrum, in particular. These challenges led to the overall strategy of rebranding all the hotels in the chain and to utilization of the BSC for strategy execution.

The company went one step further than most other implementers of the BSC by coming up with a performance management system that could be used in conjunction with the BSC and ensure that strategic goals would increasingly be achieved at all levels. Although most BSC implementers around the world use the BSC for organizational performance evaluation, ITC's efforts reflect the attempt to link individual evaluation of managers at multiple levels to overall organizational evaluation. ITC also expanded the scope of the BSC from four to five dimensions, adding one for social performance. Use of the BSC at the ITC Maurya Sheraton is shown in Figure 10.2.

Following BSC recommendations, the company engaged in a wide-ranging discussion with managers at multiple levels and achieved consensus on five broad areas (Figure 10.2). These discussions involved debates on whether or not something could be measured, how could it be measured and then managed, and what aspects of the dimensions should be measured at different hierarchical levels. Dovetailing individual performance assessment at managerial levels with organizational evaluation by means of the BSC was innovative. Control systems usually focus on outputs or individual behaviors leading to these outputs, with each type being applicable in different contexts. The managers at ITC decided to use objective measures of outputs in the new BSC-based performance management system. A number of subjective measures (appraisals) were introduced in varying degrees at different levels to ensure that the overall results would be fit for purpose and ensure the evaluation was balanced. For example, evaluating salespeople purely on objective measures would lead to overly aggressive sales efforts and cut-throat competition – the behavior of salespeople from the perspective of teamwork and cooperation is typically measured by successful organizations. Thus, ITC's approach involved the use of an appraisal evaluation form developed along the five dimensions of the BSC on which they were

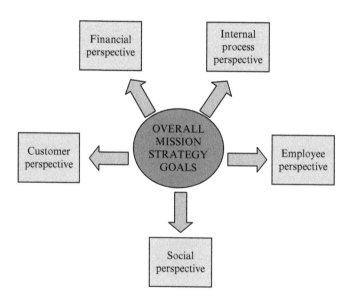

Figure 10.2 The big-five dimensions of the BSC at the ITC Maurya Sheraton

able to achieve consensus. Each position in the organization was to be evaluated for performance using a customized appraisal form. The extent to which each of the dimensions would be weighted in evaluating any one person's contribution to BSC-evaluated performance varied by functional characteristics and hierarchical level, with the focus being more strategic at higher levels and increasingly operational at lower levels.[12] Getting consensus on the exact weights to be used for different dimensions across positions in different functional and hierarchical levels was critical to successful implementation of the BSC, a subject not delved into here to preserve our focus on the nature of the system.

Let us focus on the BSC evaluation of the chief engineer at this hotel to get a better understanding of the system. The position of chief engineer is one where all five perspectives of the overall organizational BSC are used to evaluate the individual's performance on an ongoing basis.

Customer perspective

The chief engineer is first evaluated from the customer perspective, which is based on feedback from clients (constituting the Welcome Index) about things like overall service quality, room lighting, and reliability of equipment. Other measures within this perspective relate to areas of service quality such as responsiveness to customer complaints and number of repeat complaints. Critical to ITC's BSC implementation is availability of the previous year's performance on the same form as the current evaluation and provision of a blank space for next year's target setting. Thus, a rolling period of three years is used for each of the five dimensions of the BSC for each individual evaluated.

Financial perspective

The chief engineer's performance from the financial perspective is measured by indicators such as efficiency at asset utilization, inventory maintenance, and relationship with suppliers, cost vis-à-vis competition, and cost v. revenue ratios, all of which are readily captured by periodic audits and company records.

Internal process perspective

The chief engineer's performance on internal processes is assessed using measures that comply with standards on such subdimensions as hotel environment, safety, health, technology, and energy. Subjective (performance) appraisals of creativity, innovation, and proficiency in networking with regulators are made based on observations made by the chief engineer's immediate superior in addition to other means. It is noteworthy that all appraisal scores at ITC on specific aspects are finalized after discussions between the two parties taking part in the appraisal interview.

Employee perspective

The chief engineer is evaluated on his performance in this domain by considering employee turnover,[13] employee productivity and man-hours lost, employee learning and growth measured by hours of training and other indicators, and critical incidents in the leadership of the team.

Social perspective

The chief engineer's social performance is assessed by examining his or her contribution to welfare by means of talks, seminars, and awareness camps attended or conducted by the chief engineer. The company sees this as critical to its rankings on the Corporate Social Responsibility (CSR) Index.

Subjective evaluations made by this system are simply transferred onto the form from the output of a previous process. This previous process involves a career review, including self-assessment on the five dimensions by the appraisee and evaluations by the appraisee's immediate superior. The focus during the appraisal interview using this career review form is on identifying developmental needs to enhance future performance. Individual evaluations based on the five BSC dimensions are then used to calculate the amount of performance-based pay for each individual. Any individual's emoluments from such performance-based pay are dependent not only on his or her individual performance but also that of the overall organization. Thus, it is clear how ITC has innovatively blended the five dimensions of the BSC-based organizational evaluation to encompass every individual across all functions and hierarchical levels in the organization. Just as the company achieved triple bottom line performance in overall terms, as described in Chapter 7, the ITC group of hotels was able to achieve excellent performance in all the dimensions of the BSC in relatively quick time. It is little wonder they are among the leaders on various counts in this business in India.

If companies and their chief executives really mean what they say when making statements to the press, such as the one by Mackay of SAB Miller, they need to make comprehensive efforts at strategy execution. Leadership systems, appropriate organizational structures to suit local environmental needs, holistic control systems, and matching human resource management practices are all necessary components of good strategy execution. The performance consequences of poor strategy execution, despite great strategy content, are likely to be a major drag on a company's efforts in tough markets like India. It could be argued that strategy execution is perhaps more important than strategy formulation in this second most competitive market in the world.

This chapter used the case example of SAB Miller India to illustrate the common problem in India of lack of integration between strategy formulation and strategy execution. Different strategies need different types of organizational structure for proper execution. This is further complicated by the federalist nature of the system in India, amply illustrated by the unique difficulties experienced by manufacturers and marketers of beer in India. Any business subject to state-level regulation is likely to experience similar difficulties in strategy execution. Even when the business is subject only to federal regulations, the presence of unique regional preferences across different states in the country may necessitate more decentralized structural options. The most typical way of entering India is through joint ventures with local partners and then, with the consequent relaxation of restrictions, for the parent company to buy out the JV partner. All of which highlights the need for successful post-acquisition integration when there are two or more organizational units with different cultures. MNCs should focus their efforts on such post-acquisition integration and overhaul the control systems in the combined entity. Managers of such businesses should also be conscious of the need to design and implement comprehensive control systems to ensure strategy execution that is as close to perfection as possible.

Notes

1. http://timesofindia.indiatimes.com/business/india-business/Carlsberg-stirs-beer-story-with-No-2-spot-in-five-markets/articleshow/25028094.cms.
2. http://business.mapsofindia.com/top-brands-india/top-beer-brands-in-india.html.
3. http://timesofindia.indiatimes.com/business/india-business/Tuborg-breaks-into-list-of-Indias-top-5-beers/articleshow/20712220.cms.
4. http://articles.economictimes.indiatimes.com/2013-10-08/news/42829422_1_sabmiller-india-premium-beer-beer-market.
5. http://business.mapsofindia.com/top-brands-india/top-beer-brands-in-india.html.
6. http://articles.economictimes.indiatimes.com/2013-05-20/news/39392745_1_beer-market-beer-consumption-sabmiller-india.
7. http://adage.com/article/news/global-beer-brands-growth-india/236231/.
8. http://articles.economictimes.indiatimes.com/2013-10-08/news/42829422_1_sabmiller-india-premium-beer-beer-market.
9. http://www.euromonitor.com/beer-in-india/report.
10. http://business.mapsofindia.com/top-brands-india/top-beer-brands-in-india.html.
11. Dashboards provide at-a-glance views of key performance indicators relating to particular objectives or a business process.
12. This section draws extensively on the case description provided by Bhatnagar et al. (2004).
13. ITC traditionally has a culture of valuing life-time employment and loyalty.

Successful HRM for India

"Culturally, in India if you give an overview of what needs to be done, we deal with fuzzy logic very well, we take help, we collaborate and we get there. In other cultures like Japan the path has to be well defined and instructions have to be clear, step-by-step. Anything beyond that they start asking questions. Also, for instance, in the US, it may be cool to say things upfront while it's not so in India because of the way we have been brought up."

Ajoyendra Mukherjee, VP and Global Head of HR,
Tata Consultancy Services[1]

Despite the fact that human resource management (HRM) practices need to be more culturally contingent than any other business function, five MNCs figure in the most recent list of the best places to work in India.[2] The Indian arms of Google, Intel, American Express, Forbes Marshall, and Marriott Hotels figure in the 2013 version of the annual ranking produced by the Great Places to Work Institute. All these companies have HR practices that are very different from traditional Indian HR practices. Most of the top 10 companies are in the rapidly growing services sector (many of them in knowledge-based services), and therefore very different from more conventional manufacturing sector companies. Additionally, the average size of these top 10 companies is 5800 employees, much smaller than India's largest IT exporter, TCS, at 226,000 employees. Clearly, there are huge differences between large and small companies in terms of how they look and feel from the employee's perspective. However, TCS has been in the list of best place to work many times before; it achieved top position in 2011 in another ranking published by India's *Business Today*.[3] All companies in the Tata group are known for the quality of their HRM practices including TCS. The perspective of TCS' Global Head of HR, given in the quote at the start of the chapter, is illustrative in this respect. Ajoyendra Mukherjee mainly conveys the idea that Indians are different from say the Japanese or the Americans in their ability to handle fuzzy issues and lack of upfront direction by management. Despite differences with other cultures, the sheer number of MNCs in the broader list of top 100 employers in India suggests that engaging the typical Indian employee in sound HR practices is not likely to be difficult for MNCs. That does not mean, however, that HRM in India is likely to be a cakewalk. Many MNCs face occasional challenges in dealing with their employees, especially in terms of labor unrest in the manufacturing sector.

Consider the case of Nokia, which has been forced to offer a voluntary retirement scheme (VRS) to as many takers as possible at its 7500-strong handset-manufacturing plant near Chennai. As of the deadline established by the company, 5000 people had opted for the VRS proposed by the company, with some wanting an extension of the deadline.[4] Nokia faced tough times globally in the mobile phone market and sold its phone business to Microsoft, after a series of layoffs involving thousands of people elsewhere in the world. Originally established in 2006, the Chennai plant had grown rapidly achieving revenues of Rs. 150,000 crore in its first seven years by exporting to around 75 countries.[5] As a result of growing troubles and a changed strategy, the devices business of the company ended up in the hands of Microsoft. However, Microsoft does not want anything to do with the Chennai plant. This is mainly because of the tax troubles Nokia is facing with the Central Government and the State Government of Tamil Nadu. The federal government and Tamil Nadu government are in a multimillion dollar (more than Rs. 20,000 crore) dispute with the company for not having paid tax on royalties and for having sold more domestically than in the export market to qualify for tax breaks, respectively. As soon as Microsoft hesitated to pay these amounts the transfer of this plant to the company's control was blocked by the Indian government. Hence, the responsibility to settle the dispute fell to Nokia who had to decide what to do with the plant. After having faced severe criticism in Germany for closing down a plant and moving their operations to Romania a few years earlier, the company is now engaged in a series of HR practices that will likely ensure that the bitter pill of redundancy goes down more easily. First, the VRS provides the people opting for it with a golden handshake in the form of a sizable financial severance package. Next, the company is also engaging in what it terms a "bridge initiative", consisting of job training and outplacement assistance for all those accepting the VRS. Given the critical situation of the company, most observers appreciate the company's efforts to care for its employees, as opposed to making it a target of serious protests and criticism.

Although all may end well in this continuing situation, the lead-up to this crisis situation has been stormy. About a year ago, the Nokia India Employees Union at the plant called a strike and petitioned the Delhi High Court to have the Chennai plant included in the Nokia–Microsoft deal. With the tax dispute not allowing the Chennai plant to be included in the deal, the workers were getting increasingly concerned about their future. Looking to draw attention to their plight, the employees staged a one-day hunger strike in the weeks leading up to the offer of VRS. One of the remaining issues concerns whether the VRS is really voluntary and therefore optional. Union sources claimed that production at the Chennai plant, one of Nokia's biggest facilities in the world, had declined from 13 million handsets a month to about 4 million and that key machinery had already been shifted to Vietnam. In the process the plant had reduced the number of shifts from three to two. As a result of ongoing problems, the plant, which is not part of the Microsoft deal, is now operating as a contract manufacturer, precisely what the trade union feared.[6] Against this backdrop, the Nokia India Employees Union alleged the company was forcing people to take the VRS. A source alleged, "The management is asking to take VRS. For those employees who have rejected VRS, the company has already stopped transportation services."[7] The company insists that the VRS is optional and agreed not to force the employees through any means when the matter was taken to the Ministry of Labour and Employment.[8] Additionally, as part of the bridge initiative, the company is not only providing banking consultancy services to its employees but also bridge grants to support the entrepreneurial/academic ambitions of employees who have worked with the company for more than six years. The company also intends to seek an amicable resolution of the tax dispute with the new Indian government. In a press statement, a company spokesperson said, "Nokia is keen to work with authorities in India to resolve the tax disputes. As one of our actions Nokia has sent a letter under Finland India Bilateral Investment Treaty (BIT) to the Hon'ble

Prime Minister of India. The letter seeks for amicable resolution of the current tax disputes".[9] Such a backdrop of experiences has led to Indian labor laws being perceived as overly restrictive. The experience of Nokia in Germany in the midst of plant closures and the move to Romania should give the lie to such a perception. The German experience was much more difficult for Nokia than its experience in India. Most European nations provide a level of employee security that is much higher than in the U.S.A., for instance – and the situation in India is little different.

Labor disputes are not uncommon in India, nor are they a recent phenomenon. The leader of one of the largest business groups in India, Ratan Tata, shot to fame as a leader of strong caliber by handling one of the bloodiest strikes at Tata Motors Ltd. (previously called TELCO[10]) in 1989. Sensing that workers feared the consequences of breaking an "unjust" strike called by a militant, Ratan Tata took up residence at the plant for three days and workers slowly started filtering back. He launched a public relations campaign advertising how work was progressing inside the plant; this finally broke the strike and led to the arrest of the militant. Ratan Tata says that this was a turning point for labor relations for the company.[11] An expert on labor relations said, "the ability to handle and resolve conflict is a business requirement."[12] Given the trend toward violent labor disputes in India in recent years, MNCs entering the manufacturing sector in India will need strong business leaders.

While many point the finger at both management and unions, there are many who call for changes to archaic labor laws in India that restrict the business flexibility of companies. Looking at the history of labor disputes in the last ten years or so in Indian manufacturing, the scene is littered with disputes. In addition to the Nokia crisis, several other companies, most notably in the automobile sector, have experienced tough times in their labor relations. Few automobile manufacturers have avoided labor trouble in India in recent years. The list of companies that have dealt with fractious employees includes local companies like Tata and Mahindra & Mahindra, and MNCs like Maruti Suzuki, Honda India, Toyota Kirloskar Motors (TKM), Hyundai, BMW, GM, and Ford.[13] Strikes and protests have ranged from being entirely peaceful and Gandhian, on the one hand, to extremely violent, on the other. In 2012 a Maruti Suzuki plant was shut down for a month as a result of a strike in which a manager was burned to death and more than 100 supervisors were injured. A more typical event occurred at TKM, when worker demands for pay increases led to working to rule and sit-in protests resulting in a management lockout – one of a series of such events since the plant was established in 2000.[14] In stark contrast to these two cases, workers at the Ford plant near Chennai are engaging in peaceful protests, by refusing to accept free lunches at the plant and free transportation services, against the company's policy of reducing performance-based bonuses from 26 percent in 2012 to 15.8 percent last year, despite a production increase of 15 percent in 2013.

Flexibility for businesses v. problems of contract labor

There are a number of common elements in typical labor disputes in India, none of which apply to the dispute at the Ford plant. Businesses have limited flexibility in hiring and firing workers; government permission is needed for layoffs and plant closures at times of crisis. Thus, they employ significant numbers of contract laborers (often called casual labor in India), who neither have the same rights nor are subject to the same laws as regular employees. Different estimates put the number of contract laborers employed in India anywhere between 45 and 55 percent of the total labor force in the private sector.[15] This predominant shift to contract laborers is seen as the underlying reason for the nature of disputes in India, and especially the one at Maruti Suzuki. According to the International Commission for Labor Rights (ICLR), 75 percent of Maruti Suzuki's employees are contract laborers.[16] The series of violent incidents leading to the death of an HR executive at the Suzuki subsidiary were triggered by arguments and disputes between contract workers and factory officials.[17] The wages, working conditions, and rights of contract workers are often at the heart of other Indian disputes both directly and indirectly. Some experts suggest that the issue of contract labor is indicative of larger problems in the economy, labor market, and political environment. It is worth noting that many of India's labor and trade unions are the arms of various political parties – indicative of the fact that labor disputes are often where political games are played out.

Wages, workers' rights, and union recognition

Almost all labor disputes in India are triggered by demands for wage increases; sometimes they are associated with the right to be represented by the union of their choice. Asian multinationals prefer there to be no union or at best a company union and work aggressively in this direction, refusing to recognize other unions that employees may want. Many people wonder how minor disputes in the areas of wage increases can get out of control and lead to riots and violence, as in the case of Honda Motorcycle & Scooter India (HMSI Ltd.).[18] Many experts argue the answer lies in a more mature approach to managing labor–management disputes including proactive management, collaborative spirit, and open communication. India does allow its workers the right to unionize and unions have been instrumental in obtaining key victories in a civil and peaceful manner, with very few exceptions. One trade union leader, A.K. Padmanabhan of the Center of Indian Trade Unions (CITU), notes, "These companies respect trade union laws in their own countries but ignore them in India." In this particular context, the focal company Hyundai recognized an apolitical union over one that was affiliated to the Communist Party.[19] In terms of wage disputes, workers making between 47 and 92 cents (USD) an hour at a GM plant, for instance, complained that they were being shortchanged on overtime pay and that unsafe working conditions had led to more than 269 spinal cord injuries.[20] In the dispute at TKM, the difference in the workers' demand for a pay raise of INR8000 ($140) per month and the company's rejected offer of INR3005 ($50) per month did not seem to merit the management lockout at the plant, especially when there are indications that the union would gladly accept a pay increase of $70 per month.[21] Although India and its markets currently play a very minor role for Toyota, the company is losing production of up to 570 cars per day.[22] These incidents and the insignificant amounts of money involved in the disputes go to show how attitudes on both sides harden as conflicts escalate over time. In the dispute at Honda India, when workers and their families were beaten by the police outside their factory gates, the company issued a press release stating that it was none of their concern since the incident took place outside the factory. The company was widely criticized for its lack of sensitivity.[23] According to the ICLR, workers rights are not as well protected in India as business rights. Nevertheless, the solution lies in sound HRM practices and collaborative labor–management relations. Things at Ford India are indicative of greater trust and a tradition of creative teamwork, sensitivity, and mutual respect between management and workers, making management's cutback of performance bonuses without any dialogue very surprising.[24] Another positive example of how to deal with unions involves the efforts made by O.P. Bhatt, chairman of SBI (the largest public sector bank), to bring about change. In an interview following his success, he said,[25]

> *"These are important stake-holders, and I brought senior representatives from the unions and officers' associations together in a meeting similar to the management conclaves. I spent four days with 30 leaders from across the country. Some of my best advisers at the bank warned that the leaders weren't trustworthy and could be disruptive, but by being different and asking them to a conclave – like monks in a cave – I built up huge curiosity. They wanted to know what I was doing. I told them I'd sit with them, but only if they came as friends of the bank ... The results were fantastic. They had the good of the bank as much at heart as anybody else ..."[26]*

The manufacturing sector highlights the many problems in HRM across both public and private companies as well as domestic and multinational companies, and would do well to take on board the best practices in this regard that typically come from the knowledge-based services sector.

Key HRM challenges in India

With the overall objective of bridging the often large gap between strategy formulation and strategy execution touched on earlier in this chapter, let us look at the key challenges facing HRM practices in India. In addition to the challenge of managing labor–management relations in appropriate sectors, the Indian environment throws up a number of other significant challenges. As noted in Chapter 10, successfully integrating two entities in a post-acquisition environment is likely to be a critical challenge for most MNCs who enter the market via joint ventures and then buy out the venture partner. Such post-acquisition integration is likely to be challenging, to say the least, and require the HRM function of organizations to constantly keep an eye on the ball. Moreover, although most top managers are aware of integration challenges in cross-border acquisitions, more often than not they put this issue on the back burner. This only serves to aggravate the integration challenge in the Indian context where HRM typically lags eight to ten years behind cutting edge HRM in the West (Som, 2006). This might pose a huge barrier for MNCs wanting to implement their own conventional HRM practices in the merged entity. The Indian environment also poses a number of other challenges to MNCs. First, despite the availability of world-class talent in India, the capabilities of the large labor pool vary so much that it takes special competence in recruitment and selection to acquire the best talent. In keeping with the country-of-contrasts theme, it is often the case that the best candidates are sitting side by side with the worst in your selection pool. Next, as a result of increased foreign direct investment (FDI) and growing competition from a host of MNCs across sectors spilling into new growth areas in rural India, the labor market is highly dynamic. This presents a unique problem in terms of employee turnover and attrition rates. Some reports suggest that firms need to brace themselves for an average attrition rate of 15–20 percent, with the corresponding rate in the knowledge-based services sector going well beyond 30 percent in some cases (Holtbrugge et al., 2010). Finally, in the context of the new economy where skills become obsolete much faster than before, employees are constantly looking to upgrade their skills. In the absence of opportunities to upgrade skills within focal firms, the new generation of Indians increasingly value job hopping over traditional life-long loyalty to firms. Thus, successful firms will be those that provide skill-building opportunities in the form of training and development or interesting job assignments that lead to high retention of talent.

Best HRM practices in India

Although there is a general perception and consensus among experts that the HRM practices of MNCs operating in India are more professional than and superior to those of domestic firms (Budhwar and Varma, 2010), there are several indications to the contrary. First, a closer look at the lists of best places to work over the last decade reveals home-grown firms in the top ranks alongside foreign MNCs. For instance, the latest list includes the National Thermal Power Corporation (NTPC), a recently (partially) privatized Indian firm; it occupies sixth place in the top 10 list of companies with the best HR practices. Additionally, as noted earlier in the chapter, there are five domestic firms (four from the knowledge-based services sector and NTPC) and five MNCs on that list. Second, one of the most comprehensive survey studies to date on the effectiveness of HR practices in India reports that such practices as performance management, professional development, and relative performance are more effective in Indian firms than in international firms (Stumpf et al., 2010). One of the reasons for this contrasting evidence is the cultural shift in India from collectivism to individualism and from high power distance to low power distance (Ramaswami and Dreher, 2010). This shift in cultural values is happening rapidly among the younger generation of Indians who are much more exposed to MNCs and information and communication technologies than the older generation. Thus, the country-of-contrasts theme can be seen once again in HRM with the presence of the best in class alongside the stereotypical "informal and less professional" HR systems of domestic firms.

Recruitment and selection

NTPC employs more than 25,000 people and great care is taken to recruit the best employees. Following a policy of lifetime employment, NTPC predominantly recruits at the entry level, with the selection process comprising written tests, group discussions, and interviews. Moreover, it avoids the premier institutes of technology and targets the second and third-tier engineering schools for the annual recruitment intake of around 400 executive trainees. This provides the company with the flexibility to mold these engineers to fit its unique culture of committed world-class professionals. These and other policies have put NTPC in the top rankings list many times in the past decade. It is common among Indian public sector organizations to conduct written aptitude tests, followed by group discussions and interviews to narrow down the relatively large applicant pool to manageable numbers among other objectives. Thus, the typical selection process in India is more of a *deselection* process than a selection process. The large number of applicants for all positions is common in India and MNCs need to have the ability to handle such large numbers. Many other companies in the list of the top 10 best places to work that recruit entry-level people in large numbers (e.g., Infosys, TCS) use rigorous selection mechanisms including group discussion and interviews, with testing added to the mix in many cases (e.g., HCL). Many successful Indian firms cooperate closely with the prestigious Indian institutions of management and technology to attract talented future managers through campus recruitment (Som, 2006). These institutions have ridiculously low selection ratios (1 in 10,000 in many cases) and, thus, represent the cream of the crop. This also makes for serious talent shortages in the immediately lower levels, and hence many companies rely more on in-house training and development to build capabilities.

Training and development

The HR function in India is more often referred to as HRD (human resource development) than HRM. As a result of historical factors and pioneering institutions and leaders, the Indian HR system has become more development oriented than perhaps other systems. At L&T Ltd., ranked tenth in the most recent list of best places to work,[27] this is very important. The company employs 50,000 people and hires thousands of new recruits every year. L&T is in the heavy engineering and construction business and has to develop leaders in-house to fill increasingly higher managerial level positions, as a result of there being very few other companies in the business from which to attract staff. Thus, L&T uses its well-established Management Development Center to train many of its employees and managers in business and leadership skills; it does so in close cooperation with the management schools.[28] Another top-ranked company, NTPC (the subject of the last two sections), has the highest training budget in the industry and provides its executives with an average 56 hours of training and development at its designated center (Chaturvedi and Dutta, 2005). It is common across sectors in India for companies to dedicate budget resources to training and managerial development, as well as to sponsor employees showing high potential for graduate education.

Professional development

One thing that is common to all top 10 ranked companies on the 2013 list of best employers is the strong emphasis on professional development. This is the key ingredient to reducing attrition rates to manageable levels in this increasingly challenging environment. Although professional development takes many different forms, the focus remains on helping people both collectively and individually develop their professional competency and at the same time keep a focus on pursuing their passions. Many of these companies focus on rotating people through different jobs and assignments to enhance their overall expertise. For instance, at Google India employees have the possibility of reflecting on their careers in a breakout room and then sharing their aspirations for company roles from product engineering to human resources. These aspirations are usually fulfilled by the company – something that has helped the company retain key talent. At TCS and L&T employees are regularly moved through different jobs and sent abroad on assignments to broaden their experience. At Infosys, faced with the increasing challenge of shaking off its paternalistic image, the company has engaged in adult–adult communication strategies, replacing their traditional parent–child nature of communications. Infosys has also introduced its own social networking platform, Infy Bubble, to engage employees collectively with one another and top executives of the company. To develop well-rounded personalities in employees where such opportunities are lacking, other companies use practices that help employees focus on their passions and search for meaning in their lives. Although the Indian education system produces highly competent professionals, its focus on extracurricular activities leaves much to be desired. IBM provides opportunities for its employees to participate in the company's involvement in schools in remote villages – something that enhances pride in working for the company. HCL Technologies allows its managers to set up groups that help employees pursue their passion in areas such as art or sport. While wanting to recruit people who are passionate about technology, HCL also wants its people to pursue their other passions.

Other companies use more conventional means such as work flexibility and the in-house development of ideas. For instance, RCOM rewards employees who come up with ideas to bring products to market faster than competitors; it also encourages employees to move across functions. Microsoft gives its employees the benefit of flexible hours. Accenture allows its employees to donate hours of work to other employees who are suffering personal emergencies.[29] L&T allows its employees to participate in simulated strategy discussions covering such topics as the movement of the dollar on the currency markets, the possibility of a bad acquisition, and project delays – with the objective of getting them to think strategically. In short, a strong professional and personal developmental focus is essential to winning in India.

Performance management

One of the most comprehensive surveys into the effectiveness of HR practices in India reports that performance management and relative performance are highly effective in both domestic and multinational firms in India (Stumpf et al., 2010).

Performance management through goal setting, standards, evaluation, and feedback is critical to an overall HR strategy that reduces the gap between strategy formulation and strategy execution in India. The balanced scorecard – a tool for performance management used at ITC Hotels, discussed in Chapter 10 – is an excellent example of such a practice. With a new CEO in place at Wipro, the third largest software company in India, the change initiative that followed focused heavily not only on bringing role clarity but also on clarity regarding goals, objectives, and accountability. This helped Wipro reduce attrition from 23.2 to around 14 percent in 2011–12 and helped the company retain valued employees. Practices at TCS mirror those in the larger Tata group in using 360-degree feedback systems to manage performance through a developmental focus. TCS ensures that employees are recognized through promotions – something that is key in India because designations are significant and a recognition of performance.[30] Intel, American Express, and Philips figure high in the list of companies whose performance management systems are considered the best in class.[31] Although important across sectors, best-in-class performance management systems are somewhat more important in the growing service sector than in manufacturing in India.

Compensation and reward systems

Performance management and reward systems are intricately related to each other in terms of their effectiveness in India. Studies have found that reward systems are much more effective when they are performance oriented (Holtbrugge et al., 2010). There is evidence that performance-oriented reward systems and performance-oriented career management are negatively related to employee attrition. Thus, reward systems can be an effective tool to manage the above-normal attrition rates found in India. For instance, Wipro increasingly ties its reward systems to performance at all hierarchical levels in the organization, a message constantly conveyed by its founding chairman Azim Premji.[32] The balanced scorecard used by ITC hotels was closely linked to reward systems based on individual as well as organizational goal accomplishment, which helped the company successfully rebrand the hotel chain. NTPC made use of the balanced scorecard when designing its reward systems, which, combined with a 360-degree performance feedback system, resulted in greater transparency in its high-performance culture (Chaturvedi and Dutta, 2005). In many Indian firms promotions are linked and oriented to performance and thus both directly and indirectly tied to rewards. Traditional seniority-based systems are increasingly giving way to performance-based systems of rewards, in line with the aspirations of the country's increasingly young workforce. The traditional paternalistic system of management is giving way to those whose power distance is smaller as seen by the shift in communication style at Infosys in the "Professional development" section. A combination of these factors results in Indian employees valuing not only the absolute value of compensation but also their ability to enhance it by reward systems linked to performance.

As a result of the rapid influx of FDI and growth in demand for labor, overall compensation levels are not only highly fluid but increasing rapidly from year to year. Traditional compensation systems focused more on variations in the internal hierarchy of organizations and paid little attention to market factors. This is rapidly being replaced by market-based compensation systems, with internal consistency in the hierarchy playing a secondary role. This is essentially dependent on industry or economic sector, with sectors that are more dynamic changing more rapidly than those that are less. These changes are usually in the upward direction in terms of absolute compensation level. However, as discussed above, an increasing proportion of pay packages is taken up by the variable component thereby reducing the importance of the fixed component of pay. Companies in less dynamic economic sectors are increasingly faced with the proposition of having to pay higher levels of absolute compensation to attract the flow of talent away from the more dynamic sectors which pay better. For instance, L&T deliberately pays its initial recruits more in the knowledge that the rate at which pay increases with tenure is higher in the more dynamic sectors. Conventional pay systems in India, such as those at NTPC, also focus on benefits that cover children's educational expenses, scholarships, pension scheme, superannuation, and complete reimbursement of medical expenses for the employee and his or her immediate family.

Integrating an Indian JV partner post acquisition

As has already been pointed out, the most typical way MNCs enter India is via joint ventures with local partners that are later acquired by the MNC. For instance, in India's nascent e-commerce industry online auction platform eBay is increasing its level of investment in Snapdeal.com, a growing domestic e-tailer. After initially investing $50 million in Snapdeal in 2013, eBay followed this up by investing $133.7 million in the second round sparking rumors of an eventual buyout.[33] This comes against the backdrop of a rapidly growing industry where two highly successful online fashion retailers, Flipkart and Myntra, recently announced a merger valued at around $300 million.[34] Flipkart's acquisition of Myntra is seen by many as a response to the largest online retailer Amazon ramping up its operations and the fast-narrowing gap in sales with Snapdeal. These events are simply the tip of the iceberg and are a harbinger of times to come in India. Thus, although the growth in merger and acquisition activity, especially of Indian firms by MNCs, is rapidly increasing, very few of these companies pay enough attention to successful post-acquisition integration. As noted in the case of SAB Miller India in Chapter 10, a significant proportion of failures in merger and acquisition activity is the result of failure to successfully integrate the two entities post acquisition. Additionally, although most top managers realize the importance of post-acquisition integration, very few have the time and wherewithal to cope with the challenges of post-acquisition integration. There now follows a comprehensive look at the human resource practices necessary to make this possible and put the merged entity on track to achieving high performance in an increasingly uncertain marketplace (Lakshman, 2011).

The failure of top managers to address the problem is due to the inherent multidisciplinary nature (e.g., strategy, finance, HR) of mergers and post-acquisition integration. Integration attempts are usually associated with the HR function of organizations, which is typically thought of as being critical to the success of integration in post-buyout scenarios. However, few if any HR managers are involved in making buyout deals involving one MNC and one domestic JV partner, such as eBay's rumored buyout of Snapdeal.

Leadership is very important to organizational change initiatives, such as integration in a post-buyout scenario. An overall climate of high uncertainty among managers and employees at all levels in the acquired entity typically follows the acquisition of any organization. A range of highly emotional issues from job security to new roles and performance management expectations cloud the thinking of people within both the acquired entity and the acquirer. It is therefore imperative for the integration leader to address causal ambiguity before anything else. Causal ambiguity relates to organizational learning and dynamic capabilities and represents the heightened levels of uncertainty felt by employees and managers including loss of power and loss of control. Most buyouts by MNCs in India, as elsewhere, have the objective of transferring local knowledge to the merged entity. Reciprocally, the MNC transfers its domain knowledge to help the merged entity be successful in the Indian marketplace. SAB Miller's difficulties and rapid loss of market share (Chapter 4) were the result of lack of integration with local entities, especially within the federalist system that prevails in India.

Although cultural transfer and learning are critical to integration, very few managers are equipped to focus on this issue. Although technological knowledge transfer and learning are overriding objectives in acquisitions, very few companies have focused on transferring knowledge about cultural and organizational capabilities. The author's research suggests that viewing the transfer of cultural and organizational knowledge as an additional base of knowledge to be transferred and integrated into the merged entity could provide valuable insights into the integration process and thereby enhance business performance. Such a knowledge-based perspective has the potential to provide managers with the necessary focus on HR practices within the confines of an overall HR system.

Reducing causal ambiguity

Managers of MNCs should realize the importance of reducing causal ambiguity among managers and employees, an issue that is central to all post-buyout scenarios. Causal ambiguity can be seen as the degree of ambiguity or uncertainty in understanding the relationship between individual inputs and results. This uncertainty among employees and managers can be so great in a post-buyout scenario that it can bring about inaction. Causal ambiguity is a direct function of cultural distance between the merger partners and is especially evident in cross-national buyouts, such as those involving SAB Miller or eBay in India. Thus, such a context is fraught with causal ambiguity between integration decisions and outcomes. The resulting effect is that management and employee behavior resembles that of rats in a maze, increasingly lost and dumbfounded.

Integration leader

The first and most important task for the MNC is to assign a leader or a team to take on responsibility for integrating the two entities organizationally and culturally. This is a full-time job and leaving it to the HR manager is not an option because it is too much for one person to handle alone. The integration role requires knowledge of both organizational entities and intimate knowledge of the people within. The role requires patience and special competency in relationship building on the part of the person managing the integration process. The best person for this role is someone who is bicultural, someone who has had experience in both entities involved in the buyout. If no one fitting this profile can be found, a team of people made up of representatives from both sides is required to lead and carry out this task. Even if someone fitting this role can be found, it makes sense to back him or her up with a team of assistants made up of representatives from both entities to bring about integration as smoothly and quickly as possible. The first task for this integration leader is to reduce the causal ambiguity inherent in the situation by bringing clarity to various aspects of the merger in the post-buyout scenario.

Cause–effect belief knowledge of integration leaders

The extent to which integration leaders possess knowledge in the form of clear cause–effect beliefs pertaining to knowledge transfer in integration contexts is positively related to a reduction in causal ambiguity among participants of both organizations. Knowledge transfer in the previous statement refers to technological knowledge as well as organizational/cultural knowledge of the two entities. Leadership and strategy theorists have emphasized the importance of cause–effect beliefs on the part of executive leaders in effective decision making leading to improved organizational performance. Studies have found empirical evidence to support the argument that confidence and clarity or firmness in the beliefs held by executive leaders is strongly related to organizational effectiveness. This research has also found that clarity in cause–effect beliefs on the part of executives is strongly related to uncertainty reduction among strategy implementers. By espousing their knowledge of integration in post-buyout scenarios and using their influence through other means, integration leaders can put their subordinates and team members at ease and reduce causal ambiguity both in their minds and in the context setting, thereby making the process of integration smoother.

The extent to which integration leaders possess knowledge in the form of clear cause-effect beliefs pertaining to knowledge transfer in integration contexts is positively related to their establishment of sociocognitive mechanisms of knowledge transfer in post-acquisition integration contexts. Specifically, integration leaders will use sociocognitive mechanisms to get target personnel involved in the design of the integration process as early as possible. Integration leaders who are familiar with the process of integration through their experience in such settings will realize that the organizational and cultural knowledge to be transferred is largely tacit and thus sociocognitive mechanisms such as learning communities, cross-entity teams (members from both organizations), taskforces, and other such groups are more important than technological mechanisms and codification efforts. Accordingly, integration leaders are likely to make early use of the social interaction mechanisms noted above, between the two formerly independent entities. Thus, in addition to facilitating the establishment of the right climate for smooth knowledge transfer by reducing causal ambiguity, cause–effect beliefs are also critical in terms of their relationship to the actual mechanisms of knowledge transfer established.

Motivation for cultural integration

Behavioral variables like motivation and trust are critical to countering the political and organizational uncertainties involved in post-acquisition integration. Some studies highlight the huge cultural gap in many cross-national acquisitions; hence, the importance of motivation mechanisms like stock options in influencing, shaping, and managing the culture of the merged entity. It is also critical to align the two cultures in cross-national acquisitions.

Reward systems

The integration leader's first tasks are to align the two disparate reward systems and to clarify how the system will work in the combined entity. The extent to which integration leaders establish appropriate reward systems (both carrot and stick) is positively related to reducing causal ambiguity, especially that emanating from potential lack of clarity or fluidity on the part of the HR system. Moreover, alignment of the reward systems needs the participation of those involved in the integration process. Appropriate reward systems are also positively related to the active involvement of target personnel in the knowledge integration process.

Resolution of conflicts by the integration leader

The prototypical integration process involves three stages: contact, conflict, and adaptation. Attempts by one culture to dominate the other or one organizational group to wield more power over corresponding groups in the other entity are common in these stages. Engaging in such activities under the guise of culture is also common in such contexts. Proposals for new practices may be questioned or shot down by individuals who complain it is against their culture to engage in such practices. Therefore, leader conflict resolution is critical to reducing conflict and increasing the involvement of integration participants. There are two reasons for this. First, causal ambiguity and mistrust are key features of post-acquisition integration and need to be addressed. Second, accurate and unbiased ways of reducing complexity, uncertainty, and conflict and converting them to cooperation are imperative.

Impartial conflict resolution

The ability of integration leaders to make accurate and unbiased assessments of the behavior of participants in conflict situations has the positive effects of reducing causal ambiguity and increasing the participation of target personnel in post-acquisition integration. Conflict resolution can only be effective when the cause of the conflict is identified. It is important here not to take sides and remain as objective as possible. Leaders who are capable of doing this are more likely to succeed in integrating the two sides.

Causal ambiguity reduction

Knowledge transfer cannot take place in the presence of heightened levels of uncertainty (i.e., causal ambiguity). This is precisely why the integration leader's actions in aligning reward systems and resolving conflicts are critical to the subsequent core process of knowledge flows in both directions. The reduction of causal ambiguity in the minds of those involved in post-acquisition integration leads not only to successful establishment of the sociocognitive mechanisms of cultural knowledge sharing identified above but, more importantly, to the involvement and participation of target personnel in the post-acquisition integration process. Needless to say, the participation of target personnel in the integration process is just as important as establishing the right process to integrate organizational and cultural knowledge.

Cultural knowledge-sharing mechanisms

There are two broad approaches to transferring and sharing knowledge between two organizations. The first is the technological route to sharing knowledge through databases and information technology based on codifying the knowledge. This is excellent for technological knowledge but not so good at transferring cultural knowledge on how each entity in the post-buyout scenario carries out its day-to-day work. It is important to use sociocognitive mechanisms based on face-to-face communication of teams of people from both sides to transfer and share such organizational and cultural knowledge.

Sociocognitive means of cultural knowledge sharing

Post-acquisition integration that involves higher levels of knowledge sharing through face-to-face and other personal approaches is likely to be much more effective.

Target involvement in integration process

It is important to develop relational HR systems that give employee cohorts opportunities to interact with each other and at the same time build up motivation and trust with the objective of getting them to share knowledge. Post-acquisition integration is much more likely to be successful when target personnel are involved in the integration process.

Early target involvement in integration process design

If the differences between acquirer and acquired in terms of organizational structure and culture are substantial, it is critical to grant the acquired companies as much autonomy as possible as well as day-to-day freedom to manage their businesses. The granting of autonomy needs of course to be tempered by the degree of control sought in the acquisition. For this to be effectively managed, it is important not only for target personnel to be actively involved but to have a major say in designing the integration process to be used. Post-acquisition integration efforts in which target personnel are involved at early stages in the design of the integration process are much more likely to be effective.

Reducing the gap between strategy formulation and strategy execution requires an understanding of the most appropriate HRM strategies to use in a given context. This is even more critical because HRM is perhaps the most culturally contingent of all business functions. The Indian environment has more than its fair share of labor disputes for a number of reasons related to labor laws, ineffective management, and aggressive labor attitudes. In a broader sense the Indian environment poses a number of unique challenges to MNCs when it comes to managing human resources. Very high attrition levels in the rapidly changing situation for the demand and supply of high-quality labor is arguably the most critical challenge faced by MNCs. MNCs have been able to adapt their practices to the Indian context as is evident from getting ranked in the best-places-to-work surveys conducted annually. However, domestic firms also have very capable HRM systems in their own right, again evidenced by occupying prominent positions in the same ranking lists. The author has identified what he deems to be the best HRM practices in India; hopefully this will provide the reader with an idea of what is likely to work best. Finally, in keeping with the typical trend of entering India by means of a joint venture and then buying out the domestic venture partner, this chapter has highlighted the need for effective post-buyout integration through appropriate HR practices.

Notes

1. http://businesstoday.intoday.in/story/tcs-hr-head-interview/1/22420.html.
2. http://www.greatplacetowork.in/best-companies/indias-best-companies-to-work-for.
3. http://businesstoday.intoday.in/coverage/139/1/best-employers.html.
4. http://www.thehindu.com/business/Industry/golden-handshake-for-5000-employees-of-nokias-chennai-plant/article6009004.ece.
5. http://www.thehindu.com/business/Industry/labour-pains-at-nokia/article5951454.ece?ref=relatedNews.
6. http://www.thehindu.com/business/Industry/nokias-chennai-factory-head-resigns/article5916186.ece?ref=relatedNews.
7. http://www.thehindu.com/business/nokia-workers-say-vrs-forced-on-them/article5915566.ece?ref.
8. http://www.thehindu.com/business/Industry/vrs-is-optional-to-employees-says-nokia/article5916035.ece?ref=relatedNews.

9. http://www.thehindu.com/business/Industry/nokia-takes-to-bilateral-treaty-route-to-end-tax-dispute/article6009373.ece?ref=relatedNews.
10. TELCO is short for Tata Engineering and Locomotive Company.
11. http://www8.gsb.columbia.edu/chazen/globalinsights/node/229.
12. http://www.irii.co.in/sep-oct-nov/fourir_insights_from_the_maruti_suzuki_strike_by_vivek_patwardhan.pdf.
13. http://wardsauto.com/plants-production/ford-india-workers-emulate-gandhi-pay-protest?page=1.
14. http://www.icmrindia.org/casestudies/catalogue/Human%20Resource%20and%20Organization%20Behavior/IR%20Problems%20at%20Toyota%20Kirloskar%20Motor%20Private%20Limited.htm.
15. http://businesstoday.intoday.in/story/bt-500-india-inc-grapples-with-growing-labour-unrest/1/189143.html.
16. http://www.tehelka.com/first-on-tehelka-what-really-happened-at-maruti/.
17. http://blogs.wsj.com/drivers-seat/2012/07/20/workers-riot-at-indias-maruti-suzuki/.
18. http://www.csr-asia.com/weekly_news_detail.php?id=4373.
19. http://automotivehorizon.sulekha.com/hyundai-india-plagued-by-labour-problem_newsitem_230.
20. http://www.thedetroitbureau.com/2011/04/gm-facing-labor-crisis-in-india/.
21. http://wardsauto.com/plants-production/ford-india-workers-emulate-gandhi-pay-protest?page=1.
22. http://timesofindia.indiatimes.com/business/india-business/Labour-department-to-take-up-Toyota-lockout-today/articleshow/32269408.cms.
23. http://www.csr-asia.com/weekly_news_detail.php?id=4373.
24. http://wardsauto.com/plants-production/ford-india-workers-emulate-gandhi-pay-protest?page=2.
25. http://www.irii.co.in/sep-oct-nov/fourir_insights_from_the_maruti_suzuki_strike_by_vivek_patwardhan.pdf.
26. The banking sector in India is unionized with both clerical workers and officers represented by separate unions.
27. http://businesstoday.intoday.in/story/best-to-10-companies-to-work-india-survey-business-today/1/22286.html.
28. http://businesstoday.intoday.in/story/larsen-and-tourbro-hr-challenges/1/22421.html.
29. http://businesstoday.intoday.in/story/manoj-biswas-india-hr-head-accenture-interview/1/22410.html.
30. http://businesstoday.intoday.in/story/tcs-hr-head-interview/1/22420.html.
31. http://www.greatplacetowork.in/best-companies/indias-best-companies-to-work-for/special-category-winners.
32. http://www.thehindu.com/business/Industry/premji-benefits-most-from-wipro-pay-hike/article6034066.ece?homepage=true.
33. http://www.thehindu.com/business/Industry/ebay-leads-133m-snapdeal-investment/article5730955.ece?ref=relatedNews.
34. http://www.thehindu.com/business/Industry/flipkart-buys-out-myntra-for-300-m/article6037600.ece?homepage=true.

References

Aguilera, R. V., Rupp, D. E., Williams, C. A., & Ganapathi, J. (2007). Putting the S back in corporate social responsibility: A multilevel theory of social change in organisations. *Academy of Management Review, 32*(3), 836–863.

Akshobh (2009). *ICl: A rebel with or without a cause.* Available from: http://www.isport.in [Accessed 16.07.09].

Annamalai, K., & Rao, S. (2003). *ITC's e-choupal and profitable rural transformation (What Works Case Study Series).* Ann Arbor, MI: University of Michigan.

Aulakh, P. S. (2009). Revisiting the internationalization–performance relationship: Implications for emerging economy firms. *Decision, 36,* 25–39.

Aulakh, P. S., Kotabe, M., & Teegen, H. (2000). Export strategies and performance of firms from emerging economies: Evidence from Brazil, Chile, and Mexico. *Academy of Management Journal, 43,* 342–361.

Basu, K., & Palazzo, G. (2008). Corporate social responsibility: A process model of sensemaking. *Academy of Management Review, 33*(1), 122–136.

Bhaskar, R. N. (2011). Retail business is growing not only because people are buying, they are buying more. *Daily News & Analysis,* 3 January.

Bhatnagar, J., Puri, R., & Jha, H. M. (2004). Managing innovative strategic HRM: The balanced scorecard performance management system at ITC hotels. *South Asian Journal of Management, 11*(4), 92–110.

Bhattacharya, S. (2006). 40 Aircraft for Mukesh Ambani's retail supply chain. *Daily News & Analysis,* 23 April.

Bhattacharya, S. (2006). Reliance retail in acquiring mode. *Daily News & Analysis,* 5 May.

Bhattacharya, S. (2007). Reliance retail may face protest in state as well. *Daily News & Analysis,* 3 October.

Bies, R. J., Bartunek, J. M., Fort, T. L., & Zald, M. N. (2007). Corporations as social change agents: Individual, interpersonal, institutional and environmental dynamics. *Academy of Management Review, 32*(3), 788–793.

Birkinshaw, J., Hamel, G., & Mol, M. J. (2008). Management innovation. *Academy of Management Review, 33,* 824–845.

Bruton, G. D., & Lau, C. (2008). Asian management research: Status today and future outlook. *Journal of Management Studies, 45*(3), 636–659.

Budhwar, P., & Varma, A. (2010). Guest Editors' introduction: Emerging patterns of HRM in the new Indian economic environment. *Human Resource Management, 49*(3), 345–351.

Cadieux, D., & Conklin, D. (n.d.). India's failure to attract FDI (ecch Case for Learning, Reference No. 9B06M082). Available from: www.ecch.com.

Carlson, D. S., & Perrewe, P. L. (1995). Institutionalisation of organisational ethics through transformational leadership. *Journal of Business Ethics, 14,* 829–838.

Carney, M., Gedajlovic, E. R., Heugens, P. P. M. A. R., Van Essen, M., & Van Oosterhout, J. (2011). Business group affiliation, performance, context, and strategy: A meta analysis. *Academy of Management Journal, 54*(3), 437–460.

Carroll, A. B. (1979). A three-dimensional conceptual model of corporate social performance. *Academy of Management Review, 4*, 497–505.

Carvalho, B. (2008). Hyperactive. *Business Today*,15 June.

Chakraborty, A. (2009). Bloc U-turn on agri retail. *Times News Network*, 8 October.

Chaturvedi, N. R., & Dutta, S. (2005). *Human resource management practices at the National Thermal Power Corporation (NTPC) in India.* Available from: www.icmrindia.org.

Chittoor, R., Sarkar, M. B., Ray, S., & Aulakh, P. S. (2009). Third-world copycats to emerging multinationals: Institutional changes and organizational transformation in the Indian pharmaceutical industry. *Organization Science, 20*, 187–205.

Credit Suisse (2013). *India: The silent transformation, Asia Pacific/India Equity Research Investment Strategy.* Available from: https://doc.research-andanalytics.csfb.com/docV iew?language=ENG&format=PDF&document_id=1012167501&source_id=emrna& serialid=erLQ%2fRnWpQDitseUzFl0a2fE0aE6pvdDtKzprncyifI%3d.

Cricinfo (2007a). *Business mogul announces new cricket league.* London: ESPN Cricinfo. Available from: http://www.espncricinfo.com/india/content/story/288641.html, Accessed 25.09.11.

Cricinfo (2007b). *ICL hopes to bring innovations in cricket.* London: ESPN Cricinfo. Available from: http://www.espncricinfo.com/india/content/story/300972.html, Accessed 25.09.11.

Cricinfo (2007c). *Zee sports denies signing of stars.* London: ESPN Cricinfo. Available from: http://www.espncricinfo.com/india/content/story/294055.html, Accessed 25.09.11.

Dash, K. (n.d.). McDonald's in India (*ecch* Case for Learning, Reference No. A07–05–0015). Available from: www.ecch.com.

Datta, D. K., Guthrie, J. P., & Wright, P. M. (2005). Human resource management and labor productivity: Does industry matter? *Academy of Management Journal, 49*(1), 135–145.

Della Penna, P. (2012). *T20 is a product that fits the American market.* London: ESPN Cricinfo. Available from: http://www.espncricinfo.com/ci/content/page/156066.html, Accessed 25.07.12.

Deshpande, R., Farley, J. U., & Webster, F. E. (1993). Corporate culture, customer orientation, and innovativeness in Japanese firms: A quadrad analysis. *Journal of Marketing, 57*(1), 23–27.

Deveshwar, Y. C. (2007). Chairman Y.C. Deveshwar's address at *ITC's 96th Annual General Meeting. 27 July.* Available from: www.itcportal.com Accessed 25.08.08.

Deveshwar, Y. C. (2013). Chairman Y.C. Deveshwar's address at *ITC's 102nd Annual General Meeting, July 26.*

DiMaggio, P. J., & Powell, W. W. (1983). The iron cage revisited: Institutional isomorphism and collective rationality in organizational fields. *American Sociological Review, 48*, 147–160.

Dyer, J. H., & Nobeoka, K. (2000). Creating and managing a high-performance knowledge-sharing network: The Toyota case. *Strategic Management Journal, 21*, 345.

Enderwick, P., & Nagar, S. (2010). The Indian premier league and Indian cricket: Innovation in the face of tradition. *Journal of Sponsorship, 3*, 130–143.

Gardner. (2012). Cairns wins libel case against Modi. http://www.espncricinfo.com/ci/content/story/558806.html.

Goldman Sachs (2003). *Dreaming with BRICs: The path to 2050.* (Global Economics Paper No. 99). Available from: http://www.gs.com/insight/research/reports/report6.html.

Goldman Sachs (2007). *India's rising growth potential.* Available from: www.goldmansachs. com/our-thinking/archive/archive-pdfs/brics-book/brics-chap-1.pdf.

Goldman Sachs (2008). *Ten things for India to achieve its 2050 potential.* (Global Economics Paper No. 169). Available from: https://portal.gs.com.

Gopalan, K. (2008). Radical shift: Reliance strikes two joint ventures – and stays a minority partner. *Business Today*,18 May.

Griffeth, R. W., Hom, P. W., & Gaertner, S. (2000). A meta-analysis of antecedents and correlates of employee turnover: Update, moderator tests, and research implications for the new millennium. *Journal of Management*, *26*(3), 463–488.

Gupta, J. (2007). *A league of their own*. Available from: http://www.espncricinfo.com/magazine/content/story/288693.html, Accessed 25.09.12.

Gupta, S. (2008). Match fixing cloud over ICL, probe begins. *The Indian Express*, (online), http://archive.indianexpress.com/news/matchfixing-cloud-over-icl-probe-begins/379390/, Accessed 15.09.14.

Hannan, M. T., & Carroll, G. R. (1992). *Dynamics of organizational populations*. New York: Oxford University Press.

Hardgrave, R. (1965). The riots in Tamilnadu: Problems and prospects of India's language crisis. *Asian Survey*, *5*(8), 399–407.

Hegde, J. S. (2005). Zee Telefilms Ltd. & Anr vs Union of India & Ors. In: S. C. O. I. Judgment (Ed.), Case no: writ petition (civil) 541 of 2004.

Holtbrugge, D., Friedmann, C. B., & Puck, J. F. (2010). Recruitment and retention in foreign firms in India: A resource-based view. *Human Resource Management*, *49*(3), 439–455.

Iverson, R. D., & Zatzick, C. D. (2011). The effects of downsizing on labor productivity: The value of showing consideration for employees' morale and welfare in high performance work systems. *Human Resource Management*, *50*(1), 29–44.

John, S. (2006). *Biyani will take on Reliance, not Wal-Mart*. Available from: http://www.dnaindia.com/money/report_biyani-will-take-on-reliance-not-wal-mart_1052207.

John, S. (2006). Reliance retail will straddle 1,500 towns. *Daily News & Analysis*,27 June.

Kamath, R. (20 May 2010). *Reliance retail scripts ambitious growth plans*. http://www.business-standard.com/article/companies/reliance-retail-scripts-ambitious-growth-plans-110052000058_1.html, Accessed 15.05.14.

Kaplan, R. S., & Norton, D. P. (2000). *The strategy focused organization: How balanced scorecard companies thrive in the new business environment*. Boston, MA: Harvard Business School Press.

Kapur, D., & Ramamurti, R. (2001). India's emerging competitive advantage in services. *Academy of Management Executive*, *15*(2), 20–32.

Katju, M. (2005). Board of Control for Cricket in India vs. Zee Telefilms Ltd. In: M. H. C. Judgement (Ed.), W.a.no.636, w.a.no.638, w.a.no.676, w.a.m.p.no.1246, w.a.m.p.no.1292.

Khanna, T., & Palepu, K. (2010). *Winning in emerging markets: A roadmap for strategy and execution*. Boston, MA: Harvard Business School Publishing.

Khanna, T., Palepu, K. G., & Sinha, J. (2005). Strategies that fit emerging markets. *Harvard Business Review*, 63–76, June.

Kumar, A., & Bhattacharya, S. (2006). *War for dominance: Wal-Mart takes retail war to back-end*. Available from: http://www.dnaindia.com/money/report_war-for-dominance-wal-mart-takes-retail-war-to-back-end_1066526.

Kumar, A., & Bhattacharya, S. (2006). War for dominance: Wal-Mart takes retail war to back end. *Daily News & Analysis*,27 November.

Lakshman, N. (2006). AV Birla begins retail headhunt. *Daily News & Analysis*, 25 August.

Lakshman, C. (2007). Organisational knowledge leadership: A grounded theory approach. *Leadership & Organisation Development Journal*, *28*(1), 51–75.

Lakshman, C. (2008a). Conditions for hosting mega-sporting events in Asia: Comparing Japan and India. *Asian Business & Management*, *7*, 181–200.

Lakshman, C. (2008b). *Knowledge leadership: Tools for top executives.* New Delhi, India: Sage Response Books.

Lakshman, C. (2011). Effective post-acquisition integration: A knowledge-based approach. *Human Resource Management, 50*(5), 605–623.

Lakshman, C. (2012). Attributional assumptions of organizational schools of thought: Classification, evaluation, and managerially relevant knowledge. *European Management Review, 9,* 153–167.

Layak, S. (2009). Timeout? *Business Today,* 22 March.

Lepak, D. P., & Snell, S. A. (1999). The human resource architecture: Toward a theory of human capital allocation and development. *Academy of Management Review, 24*(1), 31–48.

Matten, D., & Moon, J. (2008). "Implicit" and "explicit" CSR: A conceptual framework for a comparative understanding of corporate social responsibility. *Academy of Management Review, 33*(2), 404–424.

Nambisan, R., & Lakshman, N. (2006). Mukesh Ambani's Reliance Retail gets "A" team in place. *Daily News & Analysis,* 26 March.

Neuman, S. (2013). Available from: http://www.npr.org/blogs/thetwo-way/2013/11/04/243082266/why-indias-mars-mission-is-so-much-cheaper-than-nasas [accessed 5 November 2013].

Palrecha, R., Spangler, W. D., & Yammarino, F. J. (2012). A comparative study of three leadership approaches in India. *The Leadership Quarterly, 23,* 146–162.

Panagiotou, R., & Story, J. (2004). *India: the world's largest democracy, Hindu elephant or Asian tiger? INSEAD CASE Study.* (Reference number 204–181–1 ecch) .

Prahalad, C. K. (2004). *The fortune at the bottom of the pyramid: Eradicating poverty through profits.* Upper Saddle River, NJ: Wharton School Publishing.

Quinn, R. E. (1988). *Beyond rational management.* San Francisco, CA: Jossey-Bass.

Ramamurti, R. (2001). Wipro's Chairman Azim Premji on building a world class company. *Academy of Management Executive, 15*(2), 13–19.

Ramaswami, A., & Dreher, G. F. (2010). Dynamics of mentoring relationships in India: A qualitative exploratory study. *Human Resource Management, 49*(3), 501–530.

Reuters (2007). *BCCI may lure back unofficial league players.* New York: Thomson Reuters. Available from: http://in.reuters.com/article/idINIndia-30702020071126, Accessed 13.03.12.

Samiuddin, O. (2009). *ICL recruits begin fight against bans with letter to PCB.* London: ESPN Cricinfo. Available from: http://www.espncricinfo.com/iclarchive/content/story/387988.html, Accessed 27.08.12.

Saraf, R. (2013). *The myth of the great Indian middle class: Roughly 30% of India's population still lives below the poverty line.* http://www.dailymail.co.uk/indiahome/indianews/article-2327182/The-myth-great-Indian-Middle-class-Roughly-30-Indias-population-lives-poverty-line.html, Accessed 15.09.14.

Schwab, K. (Ed.). *Global competitiveness report 2013–21042014, Full data edition.* World Economic Forum. Available from: www.weforum.org/gcr.

Seelos, C., & Mair, J. (2007). Profitable business models and market creation in the context of deep poverty: A strategic view. *Academy of Management Perspectives, 21*(November), 49–63.

Singh, G. (2012). Is greed killing cricket? The nimbus fiasco points to the greed, fatigue in indian Indian cricket. *Business World,* 20 Jan, 2012. www.businessworld.in.

Sinha, P. (2007). Reliance retail eyes Rs. 1 lakh crore revenue. *Times News Network,*30 January.

Som, A. (2006). Bracing for MNC competition through innovative HRM practices: The way ahead for Indian firms. *Thunderbird International Business Review, 48*(2), 207–237.

Srivastava, P. (2007a). Shutters down, for now: Reliance retail stops its fresh business in the state. *Business Today*,16 December.

Srivastava, P. (2007b). Bizarre punishment: Why Reliance retail will be back in Uttar Pradesh. *Business Today*,21 October.

Stumpf, S. A., Doh, J. P., & Tymon, W. G. (2010). The strength of HR practices in India and their effects on employee career success, performance, and potential. *Human Resource Management, 49*(3), 353–375.

Subramanian, A. (2008). *Gwyn Sundhugal: Bettering Indian lives.* Business Today.

Suchman, M. S. (1995). Managing legitimacy: Strategic and institutional approaches. *Academy of Management Review, 20*, 571–610.

Thadamalla, J. S. (2011). *SAB Miller India marketing strategies: Navigating in Indian beer market.* (*ecch* Case for Learning, Reference No. 311-150-1). Available from: www.ecch.com.

Thakkar, J. (2013). *Levis Strauss in India: Creating a youth brand.* (*ecch* Case for Learning, Reference No. 513-009-1). Available from: www.ecch.com.

Viitala, R. (2004). Towards knowledge leadership. *Leadership & Organisation Development Journal, 25*(5/6), 528–544.

Vilaga, J. (2012). *Indian premier league.* New York: FastCompany. Available from: http://www.fastcompany.com/mic/2010/profile/indian-premier-league, Accessed 25.09.12.

Further reading

Brokaw, S. C., & Lakshman, C. (1995). Cross-cultural consumer research in India: A review and analysis. *Journal of International Consumer Marketing, 7*(3), 53–80.

Lakshman, C. (1998). *Compulsory Groupthink: The Case of a New System Implementation.* New Delhi: Association of Indian Management Schools, This case study won the best case study award.

Lakshman, C. (2007). Knowledge-based performance management strategies: tools for the new economy. In G. Singh, R. G. Nandagopal, & R. G. Priyaadarshini (Eds.), *Strategic Human Resource Management in a Global Economy.* New Delhi: Excel Books.

Lakshman, C. (2007). The role of attributions and attributional accuracy in managing subordinate performance: The Indian context. *International Journal of Indian Culture and Business Management, 1*(1/2), 83–103.

Lakshman, C. (2008). Conditions for hosting mega-sporting events in Asia: Comparing Japan and India. *Asian Business & Management, 7,* 181–200.

Lakshman, C. (2008). Grounded theory of the emergence of leadership: Gandhi in South Africa. Paper presented at *Academy of International Business 2008 Conference in Milan, Italy.*

Lakshman, C. (2008). *Knowledge Leadership: Tools for Top Executives.* New Delhi: Sage Response Books.

Lakshman, C. (2009). Corporate social responsibility through *knowledge leadership* in India: ITC Ltd. and Y.C. Deveshwar. *Asian Business & Management, 8*(2), 185–203.

Lakshman, C. (2010). The importance of SHRM for services in emerging markets: The case of Reliance Retail. Paper presented at the *EAMSA 2010 Meeting, New Delhi, India.*

Lakshman, C. (2011). Effective post-acquisition integration: A knowledge-based approach. *Human Resource Management, 50*(5), 605–623.

Lakshman, C. (2013). Biculturalism and attributional complexity: Cross-cultural leadership effectiveness. *Journal of International Business Studies, AOP.* http://dx.doi.org/10.1057/jibs.2013.36, 15 August 2013.

Lakshman, C., and Akhter, M. (forthcoming). Corporate governance scandals in the Indian premier league: Implications for Labour. *Labour & Industry, 23*(1), 1—18. Available from: http://dx.doi.org/10.1080/10301763.2013.769859.

Lakshman, C., Ramaswami, A., Alas, R., Kabongo, J., and Pandian, J.R. (in press). Ethics trumps culture? A cross-national study of CSR perceptions regarding employee downsizing. *Journal of Business Ethics.*

Schwab, K. (Ed.). *Global Competitiveness Report 2013–2014, Full data edition.* World Economic Forum, Geneva, Switzerland. Available from: www.weforum.org/gcr.

Index

Note: Page numbers followed by *f* indicate figures and *t* indicate tables.

A

Acquisitions, 44–45, 78, 80–81, 84, 98, 138–139, 165–166, 168–169, 185–186, 191, 193
Advertising, 6, 10, 24–25, 31–32, 71, 73, 82–83, 114–115, 166, 183
AirAsia, 49–50, 83–84
Auto(mobiles), 3, 4, 6, 42, 44–45, 46–47, 66–67, 69–70, 73–74, 77–78, 81, 83, 183
Autonomy, 53–54, 147–148, 149–150, 195

B

Balanced Scorecard, 174–175, 189
Bottom-of-the-pyramid, 6–7, 9, 109–129, 130, 133
BPO, KPO, 11
Business ecosystem, 2–3, 4–5, 7–8, 9–10, 13, 16–17, 77, 134

C

Caste, 68, 111–112, 150–153, 154, 157–158
Centralization, 50–51, 147–148, 149–150, 169–170, 171
Compensation, 11, 104, 167, 172, 175, 189–190
Competitive advantage, 10, 45, 47–48, 68–69, 78, 103, 104, 133, 135, 138–140, 141, 146–147, 148–149, 152, 154
Competitiveness, 4, 5, 16, 45–46, 171, 175
Connectivity, 46–47, 62*t*, 63–64, 70, 71–72, 109–110, 113–115, 117–128
Constitution (of India), 9, 10, 15–16, 50–52, 53–54, 55–58, 77, 151–152, 155–156
Control Systems, 8*f*, 11, 163, 165–166, 167–179
Corporate social responsibility (CSR), 117–119, 120–129, 178
Cost advantage, 4, 17–18

Cost leadership, 83–84, 109, 167, 168–169
Country of contrasts, 10, 39–40, 59, 62*t*, 68–69, 155, 185–186
Cultural, 2–3, 6, 9, 11, 15, 18–19, 28–29, 53, 56, 61, 72–73, 78–80, 82, 85, 91–92, 109–112, 114–115, 133, 136–137, 141, 146, 148–149, 157–158, 161, 163, 169, 171–172, 181, 186, 191, 192–193, 194–195

D

Democracy, 9, 10, 52–54, 77, 146–147, 155–156
Differentiation, 10, 82, 83–84, 109, 167, 168–169
Dispersion, 109–110, 114–115, 119–120
Diversity, 4–5, 7, 10, 16–17, 26, 53–54, 55–56, 58–59, 64–65, 68–69, 91–92, 109–110, 111, 114–115, 145, 146–147, 149–150, 152, 161

E

Economic reforms, 5, 18–19, 37, 42, 43, 62–63, 77, 79, 110, 136–137, 147
Economic stability, 9, 43–44, 46, 47–48
Emerging market, 1–2, 3, 7–8, 9, 13, 18–19, 29–30, 33, 37, 43–44, 46, 71, 77–78, 84–85, 93, 104, 106, 141, 147

F

Federal(ist), 4–5, 9, 10, 15–17, 37, 49–51, 53–59, 77, 113, 146, 147–148, 149–150, 155–156, 168, 178–179, 181–182, 191
Formalization, 46–47, 169, 170, 171

G

Global brands, 2

H

Human capital, 6–7, 87, 99–103, 136–138, 139–141

I

Informal economy, 5–6, 9, 10, 46–48, 69, 77, 78, 79–80
Infrastructure, 1, 5, 9, 14–15, 20–21, 24, 26–27, 37, 38–40, 42, 43–44, 56–58, 68, 77, 90, 91–92, 94–95, 114–115, 116–129, 134–135, 137
Intellectual, 6–7, 8*f*, 11, 39–40, 46–48, 133, 139, 145, 146–160, 161–163
ITC, 10–11, 91, 109–110, 113–114, 115, 116–129, 130, 175–177, 178, 188–189

J

Joint venture, 3, 34, 37, 42, 49–50, 83–84, 91, 96–97, 97*t*, 98–99, 100, 101, 165–166, 169, 171–172, 178–179, 185–186, 190, 195

K

Knowledge-based services, 133, 134, 135–141, 148–149, 152, 169, 181, 185, 186
Knowledge leadership, 11, 118–119, 120–121, 122, 124–125, 126–129, 148–149, 154, 161–163

L

Labor management, 184–186
Leadership, 8*f*, 11, 26, 95, 96–97, 99–100, 104, 118–119, 120–121, 122, 124–125, 126–129, 134, 145, 146, 147–160, 161–163, 165, 166, 167, 168–169, 178, 187, 191, 192
Life-cycle, 79–85, 104*f*

M

Macroeconomic, 7, 8*f*, 9, 10, 34, 37, 43–44, 77
Material(ism), 2, 6, 61, 62–63, 62*t*, 65–66, 72–73
McDonald's, 1, 13, 15, 16–17, 78–79, 81–83, 101, 102*t*, 166, 169
M-commerce, 6, 71–72, 73–74

Media, 6, 18–19, 20, 21, 22, 25, 28, 31, 33–34, 42, 61, 68, 73–74, 81–82, 124–125, 133, 134, 152–153, 160
Medical tourism, 11, 45, 134–135, 136–137, 139
Metro AG, 16–17, 50–51, 58–59, 87, 90
Middle class, 5–7, 9, 46–47, 81–82, 91, 93

O

Openness, 2, 3, 34, 38–39
Organizational culture, 168–169, 171–172
Organizational structure, 165, 166, 167, 168–179, 195

P

Parliament, 5, 16–17, 37, 42, 43, 50–51, 52–53, 69, 147, 148–150, 151–152, 155–157
Performance management, 11, 175–177, 186, 188–189
Post-acquisition Integration, 171–172, 185–186, 190, 191, 192–193, 194, 195
Professional development, 186, 187, 188

R

Recruitment, 100, 101, 102*t*, 103, 106, 115, 170, 171, 185–186, 187
Research and development (R&D), 6–7, 17–18, 82, 84–85, 133, 134, 140–141, 168–169
Resources, 10–11, 15, 18–19, 26, 33, 55–56, 61, 83–84, 87, 99–100, 102–103, 116, 118–120, 121, 122, 130, 165, 175, 187, 188, 195
Retail, 4–5, 6, 9, 10, 15, 16–17, 18–19, 33–34, 41–42, 45–47, 50–52, 65, 77, 78–105, 88*f*, 89*f*, 92*t*, 93*t*, 97*t*, 106, 113–114, 116–117, 126–127, 134, 166, 167–168, 190
Reward system, 169, 172–173, 174, 175, 189–190, 193, 194

S

SAB Miller, 58–59, 165, 166, 167, 168–179, 190, 191
Selection, 11, 20, 23–24, 26, 28, 93*t*, 100–101, 103, 170, 185–186, 187

Software, 22, 133, 134, 135–136, 137–139,
    140–141, 148–149, 152, 154
Spiritual(ism), 2, 6, 61, 62–63
Strategic framework, 2–3, 7–11, 8*f*
Strategy, 1–2, 7, 8*f*, 9–10, 11, 15, 18–19, 21,
    24, 34, 51–52, 65, 77, 78–79, 82,
    83–85, 93, 94–99, 101, 103, 104, 105,
    106, 122, 145, 154, 163, 165, 166, 167,
    168–179, 181–182, 185–186,
    188–189, 191, 192, 195
Strategy execution, 165, 166, 167, 168–179,
    185–186, 188–189, 195

T

Talent, 2, 17–18, 21, 22, 24, 25–26, 30–32,
    46–47, 86, 87, 93, 100, 101, 102–103,
    104–105, 115, 116, 133, 134,
    136–137, 139–140, 141, 170, 171,
    185–186, 187, 188, 190

Technology, 1, 31–32, 33, 38–39, 42, 43,
    45, 62*t*, 63–64, 66–67, 69, 73–74,
    92*t*, 97*t*, 116, 133, 134, 136, 137,
    140–141, 147–149, 161, 177, 187,
    188, 194

V

Value(s), 2, 53–54, 61–74, 77, 114–115,
    120–121, 122, 145, 146–147,
    148–149, 152, 153, 155–156,
    157–158, 161, 163, 171–172, 186
Value chain, 83–84, 87, 90, 94, 115, 124,
    125, 126–129, 133, 139–140, 141,
    173–174

W

Women, 62–63, 62*t*, 68, 69–70, 72–73,
    98–99, 115, 120, 122, 130, 153,
    157–158

Printed in the United States
By Bookmasters